HAROLD GARFINKEL: STUDIES OF WORK IN THE SCIENCES

This volume includes an unpublished manuscript and selected portions of five seminars by Harold Garfinkel – the founder of ethnomethodology – on the topic of practices in the natural sciences and mathematics. The volume provides a coherent and sustained account of his program for the study of ordinary and specialized social actions. Presenting broader theoretical and methodological initiatives, as well as discussions and summaries of exemplary studies of social phenomena within and beyond the sciences, this work dates to the period in the 1980s during which the field of Science and Technology Studies was taking shape, with ethnomethodological studies of scientific practice forming a major part of its development at the time. Aside from their historical importance, the manuscript and seminars present a distinctive perspective on the natural and social sciences that remains highly original and pertinent to research on science, social science, and everyday life today. Offering critical insights and proposals relating to developments in Ethnomethodology and Conversation Analysis, this volume will appeal to scholars of Sociology and Science and Technology Studies with interests in the work of Garfinkel.

Harold Garfinkel (1917–2011) was a professor of sociology who spent most of his career at the University of California, Los Angeles, USA. He acquired an international reputation as the founder of ethnomethodology, the study of practical actions and reasoning in everyday life and specialized fields of action.

Michael Lynch is Professor Emeritus in the Department of Science and Technology Studies at Cornell University, USA, and Research Professor in the School of Media and Information, University of Siegen, Germany. He has authored and edited numerous books and has written more than a hundred peer-reviewed articles on practices in science, law, and other fields of action. From 2002 to 2012, he was editor of *Social Studies of Science*, a leading journal in the field of Science and Technology Studies.

Directions in Ethnomethodology and Conversation Analysis

Series Editors: Andrew Carlin, University of Macau, Macau SAR, China, and K. Neil Jenkings, Newcastle University, UK.

Ethnomethodology and Conversation Analysis are cognate approaches to the study of social action that together comprise a major perspective within the contemporary human sciences. Ethnomethodology focuses upon the production of situated and ordered social action of all kinds, whilst Conversation Analysis has a more specific focus on the production and organisation of talk-in-interaction. Of course, given that so much social action is conducted in and through talk, there are substantive as well as theoretical continuities between the two approaches. Focusing on social activities as situated human productions, these approaches seek to analyse the intelligibility and accountability of social activities 'from within' those activities themselves, using methods that can be analysed and described. Such methods amount to aptitudes, skills, knowledge and competencies that members of society use, rely upon and take for granted in conducting their affairs across the whole range of social life.

As a result of the methodological rewards consequent upon their unique analytic approach and attention to the detailed orderliness of social life, Ethnomethodology and Conversation Analysis have ramified across a wide range of human science disciplines throughout the world, including anthropology, social psychology, linguistics, communication studies and social studies of science and technology.

This series is dedicated to publishing the latest work in these two fields, including research monographs, edited collections and theoretical treatises. As such, its volumes are essential reading for those concerned with the study of human conduct and aptitudes, the (re)production of social orderliness and the methods and aspirations of the social sciences.

Harold Garfinkel: Studies of Work in the Sciences
Harold Garfinkel
Edited with an Introduction by Michael Lynch

For more information about this series, please visit: www.routledge.com/Directions-in-Ethnomethodology-and-Conversation-Analysis/book-series/ASHSER1190

HAROLD GARFINKEL: STUDIES OF WORK IN THE SCIENCES

Harold Garfinkel

Edited with an introduction by Michael Lynch

LONDON AND NEW YORK

First published 2022
by Routledge
2 Park Square, Milton Park, Abingdon, Oxon OX14 4RN

and by Routledge
605 Third Avenue, New York, NY 10158

Routledge is an imprint of the Taylor & Francis Group, an informa business

© 2022 Anne Rawls, on behalf of Harold Garfinkel, and Michael Lynch

The right of Anne Rawls, on behalf of the author, Harold Garfinkel, to be identified as copyright holder of this work has been asserted in accordance with sections 77 and 78 of the Copyright, Designs and Patents Act 1988.

All rights reserved. No part of this book may be reprinted or reproduced or utilised in any form or by any electronic, mechanical, or other means, now known or hereafter invented, including photocopying and recording, or in any information storage or retrieval system, without permission in writing from the publishers.

Trademark notice: Product or corporate names may be trademarks or registered trademarks, and are used only for identification and explanation without intent to infringe.

British Library Cataloguing-in-Publication Data
A catalogue record for this book is available from the British Library

Library of Congress Cataloging-in-Publication Data
Names: Garfinkel, Harold, author. | Lynch, Michael, 1948- editor.
Title: Harold Garfinkel : studies of work in the sciences /
   Harold Garfinkel ; edited by Michael Lynch.
Description: 1 Edition. | New York, NY : Routledge, 2022. |
   Series: Directions in ethnomethodology and conversation analysis |
   Includes bibliographical references and index.
Identifiers: LCCN 2021048451 (print) | LCCN 2021048452 (ebook) |
   ISBN 9781032000749 (hardback) | ISBN 9781032000756 (paperback) |
   ISBN 9781003172611 (ebook)
Subjects: LCSH: Garfinkel, Harold. | Sociology. | Ethnomethodology.
Classification: LCC HM481 .G374 2022 (print) | LCC HM481 (ebook) |
   DDC 301—dc23/eng/20211006
LC record available at https://lccn.loc.gov/2021048451
LC ebook record available at https://lccn.loc.gov/2021048452

ISBN: 978-1-032-00074-9 (hbk)
ISBN: 978-1-032-00075-6 (pbk)
ISBN: 978-1-003-17261-1 (ebk)

DOI: 10.4324/9781003172611

Typeset in Bembo
by Apex CoVantage, LLC

For Arlene Garfinkel

FIGURE 0.1 Harold Garfinkel

Image courtesy of the Harold Garfinkel archive, Newburyport, Massachusetts.

CONTENTS

Editor's acknowledgements   ix
Michael Lynch

Editor's introduction   1
Michael Lynch

PART I
Respecifying the natural sciences as discovering sciences of practical action, I & II: doing so ethnographically by administering a schedule of contingencies in discussions with laboratory scientists and by hanging around their laboratories   17
Harold Garfinkel

Editor's introduction to Part I   19
Michael Lynch

Respecifying the natural sciences as discovering sciences of practical action   21
Harold Garfinkel

Appendix 1: Postscript and preface   53
Harold Garfinkel

Appendix 2: Some notes on the play of basketball in its circumstantial detail   58
Douglas Macbeth

Appendix 3: Detail* 71
Harold Garfinkel

Appendix 4: Collections of studies I–VII respecifying the
natural sciences as discovering sciences of practical action 77
Harold Garfinkel

Acknowledgements, notes and references 81
Harold Garfinkel

PART II
**Discovering work of the sciences: five seminars on
the work of the discovering sciences, Department of
Sociology, UCLA (May–July 1980)** 99
Harold Garfinkel

Editor's introduction to Part II 101
Michael Lynch

Seminar 1: Discovering work of the sciences (May 22, 1980) 104
Harold Garfinkel

Seminar 2: Discovering work of the sciences (May 27, 1980) 125
Harold Garfinkel

Seminar 3: Discovering work of the sciences (June 3, 1980) 139
Harold Garfinkel

Seminar 4: Discovering work of the sciences (June 19, 1980) 154
Harold Garfinkel

Seminar 5: Discovering work of the sciences (July 1, 1980) 171
Harold Garfinkel

References to Part II 199

Index *203*

EDITOR'S ACKNOWLEDGEMENTS

(The author's acknowledgements are presented on pages 81-82 in Part I.)

I would like to thank Arlene Garfinkel, who encouraged me to edit and prepare for publication the previously unpublished manuscript in Part I of this book. When I met with Arlene during the year following Harold Garfinkel's death, she assured me that Harold had hoped that I would edit the manuscript. Arlene worked in the field of lipid chemistry and furnished Harold with stories and insights that informed his discussions of laboratory practice in this book. I also would like to thank Douglas Macbeth for permitting the republication of Appendix 2 ("Some Notes on the Play of Basketball in Its Circumstantial Detail"), and for updating the paper for inclusion in this book. I'm also very grateful to Anne Rawls, Harold Garfinkel's literary executor, for giving me access to archival materials currently housed at the Garfinkel archive in Newburyport, Massachusetts, and for permitting the publication and republication of the selection of those materials in this book. She and Jason Turowetz, Clemens Eisenmann, and Jakub Mlynář also provided invaluable help by locating the transcripts and other materials used in Parts I and II, and by sending scanned and digitized copies of transcripts and recordings to me. Tristan Thielmann and the staff at the School of Media and Information, University of Siegen, Germany, made it possible for digital recordings to be made of the seminars included in Part II, which were very helpful for reviewing the transcripts.

EDITOR'S INTRODUCTION

Michael Lynch

Introduction

This volume includes previously unpublished writings and lectures from the 1980s by Harold Garfinkel (1917–2011), the founder of Ethnomethodology. Ethnomethodology is the detailed study of the observable performance of ordinary and specialized practical actions that produce and sustain social order. The writings and lectures in this volume provide a coherent and sustained account of Garfinkel's program for the study of work in the natural sciences and mathematics. They also discuss broader theoretical and methodological initiatives, as well as giving summaries of exemplary studies of social activities within and beyond the sciences. Garfinkel's studies of work in the social and natural sciences not only were important for ethnomethodology, they also were one of the major influences on the development of the field of Science & Technology Studies (STS) in the 1970s and 1980s. Aside from their historical importance, the manuscript and seminars present a distinctive perspective on the natural and social sciences that remains highly original and pertinent to research on science, social science, and everyday life today. They also provide critical insights and proposals about developments in Ethnomethodology and Conversation Analysis which remain as pertinent today as they did at the time.

The core of this volume is a long article Garfinkel prepared in 1988 for publication in an edited volume (Boden and Zimmerman 1991). After a dispute with the editors, Garfinkel withdrew the manuscript before the volume was published. The manuscript has a long title: "Respecifying the Natural Sciences as Discovering Sciences of Practical Action, I & II: Doing So Ethnographically by Administering a Schedule of Contingencies in Discussions with Laboratory Scientists and by Hanging around Their Laboratories." The manuscript, which I shall call "Respecifying" for short, was expanded with some long footnotes and four appendices, including one (Appendix 2) made up of a paper written by Douglas Macbeth and later published as a stand-alone item (Macbeth 2012). In the late 1980s, Garfinkel circulated copies of "Respecifying," bound in a blue cover (some of us referred to it as Garfinkel's "Blue Book," in joking reference to Wittgenstein's [1958] *Blue Book*). In its fully expanded form, it constituted a short monograph, but was never published in his lifetime.

In 2012, while attending a memorial meeting commemorating Garfinkel's life and work at UCLA, I visited his wife Arlene at their home in Los Angeles, and during the visit she took me to Harold's study. By then, it had been largely emptied of books, papers, files, and tape recordings. Many of these materials had been moved to a temporary location in Newburyport, Massachusetts, where Anne Rawls, his literary executor, had begun the daunting task of organizing an archive. A smaller amount of his materials had been taken by the UCLA archivist for an archive at that university. One thing that remained in Garfinkel's study was a stack of bound copies of a book-length manuscript, entitled *Working Out Durkheim's Aphorism, Book Two: The Lebenswelt Origins of the Sciences*. A notation on the cover page said, "This Version is currently being worked on as of 2/21/'04". The title listed Garfinkel as author and Anne Rawls as editor. Rawls, who edited a collection of Garfinkel's papers that had *Working Out Durkheim's Aphorism* as its subtitle (Garfinkel 2002), later informed me that Garfinkel had hoped that I would edit the unpublished collection on the sciences. Garfinkel never asked me directly, though during my visit Arlene mentioned that he had hoped I would, in her words, "carry on with the work," by among other things bringing the volume to publication.

Following the visit, I examined the bound volume with the aim of editing it for publication. The "Respecifying" manuscript, together with its appendices, notes, and references, was the main chapter in it. It was supplemented by several other chapters, including an introduction and a chapter on the "*Lebenswelt* origins of the sciences," a chapter on queues co-authored by Garfinkel and Eric Livingston, and a chapter on "working artefacts" by Lucy Suchman, Randy Trigg, and Jeanette Blomberg. Most of the other chapters had already been published (Garfinkel 2007; Garfinkel and Liberman 2007; Garfinkel and Livingston 2003; Suchman et al. 2002), and the remaining material, with the exception of "Respecifying," was fragmentary and incomplete. "Respecifying," together with its appendices and notes, seemed complete and coherent enough to publish with light editing, and by itself it would make up a substantial part of a book. The full paper and its appendices make up Part I of the present volume.

In addition to preparing the "Respecifying" manuscript for publication, I had hopes of finding some companion pieces that would supplement it more effectively than those that Garfinkel originally had selected. Following several trips to the nascent Garfinkel archive in Newburyport, with help from Anne Rawls and Jason Turowetz, I found a series of five transcribed seminars that Garfinkel convened over a two-month period starting in May 1980. Although colloquial and at times dialogical, the seminars largely consisted of lectures by Garfinkel on the subject of "Discovering Work in the Sciences," in which he elaborated on many of the topics that later appeared in "Respecifying." While reading the transcripts of the seminars, I recognized that I had attended some of them myself while on a postdoctoral fellowship at UCLA, and like others who attended, I participated in dialogues with Garfinkel during portions of them. Several topics ran through the seminars, but the main agenda was to prepare for a plenary session at a forthcoming conference in Toronto, at which Garfinkel was scheduled to present a paper on the discovery of an optical pulsar at Kitt Peak Observatory in 1969 (later published as Garfinkel et al. 1981). In the course of the seminars, he also presented a number of related topics that preoccupied his research in the decades following his major work *Studies in Ethnomethodology* (1967). An edited and abridged version of the five seminars makes up Part II of the present volume.

Later in this introduction, I briefly discuss some of the topics and arguments in the seminars and manuscript, but first I want to address some of the peculiar challenges involved in editing those materials.

On the challenges of editing Garfinkel

During his lifetime, Harold Garfinkel cultivated a reputation for being an especially challenging writer. Some of the reviewers of his major work *Studies in Ethnomethodology* dismissed the text as unnecessarily obscure, complaining that it presented readers with a barrage of long multi-phrasal sentences laden with arcane and undefined jargon, including the neologism "ethnomethodology" itself. They also pointed out the irony that Garfinkel resorted to such obscure prose in order to characterize, of all things, ordinary actions and commonsense reasoning. As Garfinkel himself noted on a number of occasions, the question "What is ethnomethodology?" persisted for decades despite (or perhaps because of) his efforts to answer it.

> Ethnomethodology gets reintroduced to me in a recurrent episode at the annual meetings of the American Sociological Association. I'm waiting for the elevator. The doors open. I walk in. THE QUESTION is asked. "Garfinkel, what IS Ethnomethodology?" The elevator doors close. We're on our way to the ninth floor. I'm only able to say, "Ethnomethodology is working out some very preposterous problems." The doors open.
>
> *(Garfinkel 2002: 91)*

As usually posed, the question marked a mixture of puzzlement and curiosity about what the word, and field, could after all be about. Garfinkel seemed to delight in keeping his audiences baffled, and his long career was shadowed by a small cottage industry aiming to *explain* Ethnomethodology to the uninitiated and unconvinced.[1]

Garfinkel had little respect for the demand that academic writing should be transparent for an open-ended community of educated readers. Instead, he wrote for the

---

1 Garfinkel was more than capable of writing clear, intelligible prose for the "average intelligent reader." His first publication, "Color trouble" (Garfinkel 1940), was a short story about an interracial incident on a bus, written while he was pursuing an MA at the University of North Carolina, which was republished in an anthology of *Best Short Stories of 1941*. For an interesting analysis of that article based on a comparison with an account by one of the participants in the historical incident (Pauli Murray, who later became an attorney and important civil rights leader), see Rosenberg (2013). Garfinkel also wrote a prosaic and very interesting report for the Army Air Force during World War II (Garfinkel 2019a [1943]).

relatively few readers who were inclined to seriously engage with his writings and to undertake the studies he promoted in those writings. In a bibliography he assembled as part of his application for a promotion in the mid-1970s, he divided the ethnomethodology literature into two broad collections. One consisted in ethnomethodological studies *of* "naturally organized ordinary activities": studies that took up ethnomethodology in a substantive, empirically engaged way. The other collection was made up of studies *about* ethnomethodology: textbooks, review articles, theoretical interpretations, and comparisons between the ethnomethodological "perspective" and those associated with other approaches to sociology or philosophy. Even though a substantial number of his own writings were presented as introductions for novices – where "novices" included distinguished scholars with a passing interest in ethnomethodology – Garfinkel emphasized the practical mastery of *doing* studies as the key to understanding ethnomethodology, in contrast to an ability to talk in an erudite way about its theoretical and methodological underpinnings and implications.

In taking on the job of editing Garfinkel's writings, I am often tempted to go on at length to explain and interpret what he says. But then I am reminded of questions that Melvin Pollner raised about such an endeavor:

> Why does Garfinkel need interpretation? What is the warrant for editing? . . . Editing suggests an insufficiency in Garfinkel's writing. It does not quite say what the work is about or, perhaps more significantly, it does say what it is about but the meaning of the specific saying is not evident. But interpretation differs from what Garfinkel is saying. The reader is almost literally dizzied, not by the vertigo of the abyss of a radical constructionism, but by the ambiguous, cryptic, allusive, internally referring explication. The ambiguity, contradictions, heterogeneity of formulations, temporal development, trickster-like reflexive watchfulness of Garfinkel's writing assure that any formulation will necessarily exclude, revise or disattend what Garfinkel has actually said.
>
> (Pollner 2012: 41–42)

Pollner had his own criticisms of Garfinkel, but unlike critics who dismissed his writing as an exercise in obscuring the obvious, he suggested that a reader's difficulties are by design, and are part of a pedagogy. One indication of such design can be found at the start of Appendix 3 of "Respecifying," where Garfinkel proposes to use the word "detail" in a "tendentious" way. Although he gives advance warning about the peculiar way he speaks of "detail," he proposes to deliberately refrain from defining how he is doing so, for the reason that what he could possibly have been talking about all along will only dawn on the reader later in the text. He marks such tendentious usages, or "shibboleths" as he sometimes called them, with an asterisk.

"Tendentious" itself could have been marked with an asterisk, because Garfinkel's use of the term is not covered by the standard definition of the word as a biased, one-sided way of speaking. Consequently, to explain the meaning of such terms in an editor's introduction would be to spoil the pedagogy that Garfinkel proposes by giving away the lesson in advance of its delivery – where the delivery is an unavoidable feature of the lesson.

Those of us who worked with Garfinkel, and who have read his published and unpublished writings, know that he drafted and redrafted his texts with great care to challenge conventional understandings. During a decade (2002–2012) as editor of the journal *Social Studies of Science*, I did not hesitate to suggest extensive and detailed revisions to many authors for the sake of clarifying their prose. However, in this case, my policy has been to use the editorial pen (or, rather, modifications of digital text) in a highly conservative way. The reason for this is that Garfinkel deliberately aimed to challenge "easy" understandings of the phenomena he discussed, and his prose often requires multiple readings before yielding even a partial grasp of what he was saying. For an editor, even one with extensive acquaintance with Garfinkel's writings, to preemptively "clarify" his texts by repunctuating and rephrasing his laboriously constructed prose is to deprive readers of a challenge that the author deliberately set for them. The difficulty an editor faces is to know when to correct typos and grammatical errors or fill in incomplete references and passages, and when to leave as they are sentences, phrases, and larger aspects of textual organization that are strangely, if not ungrammatically, composed.

An editor's job is largely one of imposing organizational and literary standards on documents, but Pollner's question "What is the warrant for editing?" counsels restraint in the exercise of that job. Consequently, rather than *explaining* what Garfinkel might have meant with particular terms, phrases, or concepts, my editorial strategy is to allow Garfinkel to do that himself. The five seminars included in this volume provide elaborations, answers to participants' questions, and other expansions on some of the terms and themes that appear in "Respecifying." Readers may notice that, while he often speaks in a colloquial way during his seminars, he speaks in prose in a way that places strong demands on his audience to work out what he might be talking about. Nevertheless, the seminars provide suggestions, hints, and candid elaborations that supplement the manuscript in a way that may prove helpful for the task of working out what it says.

Garfinkel did most of the talking in the seminars, and for long stretches they take the form of lectures. Because the present volume is focused on Garfinkel's arguments and examples, for the sake of coherence and economy I have deleted student presentations, many of the interventions by participants in the seminars, and some of Garfinkel's digressions from the main line of his discussion. I deleted several of my own interventions, as well as those of others in attendance. The anonymous transcriber (who generally did a very precise job) often did not supply the full names of speakers other than Garfinkel, and many questions and comments (including some that I believe were my own) are assigned to "SPEAKER." The original transcripts have been scanned, along with many other documents in the archive, and efforts are being made at the University of Siegen, Germany, to place them on an archival website, so that readers interested in a more complete record of the seminars will be able to have access to them. Eventually, the audio recordings of the seminars should also be available online.

The peculiarities of Garfinkel's writing extend beyond his prose and make up an extended "breaching experiment" on the norms of academic publication. These breaches include unusual assignments of authorship. The title page of the 1988 draft used in this volume lists five authors: Harold Garfinkel, Eric Livingston, Michael Lynch, Douglas Macbeth, and Albert B. Robillard. Other drafts that overlap substantially with that version list other authors, including John Weiler, D. Lawrence Wieder, Christopher Pack, and Perry Taka. For example, an abridged draft dated April 1994 was titled "A Study of Discovering Work in the Natural Sciences" and was prepared for "the Stanford Meeting on Interviews in Writing the History of Recent Science." That draft listed as authors Garfinkel, Livingston, Lynch, Robillard, and Weiler. Yet another list of authors is cited in a footnote of Garfinkel (2007: 45, n. 41): Garfinkel, Livingston, Lynch, Pack, Robillard, and Wieder. Moreover, Garfinkel is sole author of other drafts preserved in the files at Newburyport, which substantially overlap with this one. When Garfinkel gave me a copy of the "Blue Book" in 1988, I was surprised to find that I was listed as a co-author. Others who were listed have told me that Garfinkel informed them in advance that he wanted to list them. However, with the exception of Macbeth's authorship of Appendix 2, it is my strong impression that Garfinkel wrote the entire text. This is not to discount that he was acknowledging those of us he listed as collaborators for what he learned from our writings and from conversations with us, and in some cases from material help with setting up and running exercises and demonstrations with inverting lenses, inclined planes, and so forth. Academic authorship is a tricky and contentious business. In this case, after much deliberation and discussion with listed co-authors of the 1988 draft (with the exception of Robillard, who died several years ago), I am treating the "Respecifying" manuscript, with the exception of Macbeth's paper in Appendix 2, as Garfinkel's work. I realize that doing so individualizes credit that he aimed to distribute, but the inconsistency of his lists of co-authors, and the fact that some authors he listed had not even seen the document until after it was drafted, convince me that assigning authorship to Garfinkel is both fair and correct.

Given the many versions of "Respecifying" drafted in the 1980s and 1990s and preserved in Garfinkel's file cabinets in the archive, there is a question about which one to select for purposes of publication.[2] The reason for selecting the 1988 version to make up Part I of this volume is that Garfinkel himself initially produced and distributed copies of it informally, and also prepared it for publication. The core arguments in that version also appear with very little modification in later drafts, some of which were abridged and retitled for delivery at academic meetings.

The five seminars in Part II also present challenges. For the most part, I have treated them as lectures by Garfinkel, but I also have tried to preserve Garfinkel's inimitable colloquialisms, and to selectively retain some of the exchanges with participants without detracting from the coherence of his presentations. I also supply footnotes and, when able to do so, full references to authors and sources that Garfinkel mentions. In some instances, names were transcribed with phonetic spelling with no further elaboration. Consequently, my editing of the seminars in Part

---

2 Anne Rawls informed me (personal communication, March 2020) that she also had difficulty when selecting one of many versions of Garfinkel's *Parsons' Primer* (Garfinkel 2019b), which he had drafted over a lengthy period of time starting in the 1950s.

II is more active than with the "Respecifying" manuscript in Part I. In both the manuscript and in the seminars, all footnotes are mine, whereas all of the endnotes to "Respecifying" were included in the original draft, including some very long forays, as well as two incomplete or blank endnotes which are retained as they stood in the manuscript in order to preserve cross-references between the notes, and between particular notes and the main body of the text.

Editors often, indeed typically, express a detached attitude toward the written works they edit; they pose as intermediaries who facilitate the publication of someone else's writing without unduly intruding upon the content. *This* editor faces the unusual difficulty of editing this particular text, as I was listed as a co-author of "Respecifying." In addition, a book (originally a dissertation) of mine is critically discussed in "Respecifying," Section [2], in comparison with a book/dissertation by Livingston. The comparison is asymmetric, as Lynch (1985) is used to exemplify what Garfinkel calls "analytic ethnography," and is the subject of a list of "dissatisfactions," while Livingston's (1986) treatment of the work of mathematical proving exemplifies the "unique adequacy requirement of methods." Garfinkel denies making an invidious comparison between the two projects. Among other things, he lists similar "dissatisfactions" with his own "analytic ethnography" presented in "Respecifying." Although I do not share some of his dissatisfactions, editing his text is enough of a challenge without trying to argue with it. Aside from what I might say on my own behalf, one of my reasons for undertaking the task of editing "Respecifying" is that it sets out what I regard as an innovative approach to organizing interview-based research: as Garfinkel describes it, he collected stories from practitioners, and used previous stories to elicit further stories from other informants. By itself, that is a fairly common way to build a base of interviews (sometimes called "snowball sampling"), but Garfinkel's account of it emphasizes how each next story does not simply fill in gaps in the "analytic ethnographer's" prior understandings, nor does it provide empirical grounding for a theory; instead, his account of the procedure provides an elaboration through the voices of the informants of what the ethnographer unknowingly was talking about all along. Garfinkel uses the expression *coat hangers* to describe a list of topics (or, as he calls them, "contingencies") on which he and his informants hang their stories, and while some of the topics used as coat hangers have been elaborated in other ethnographies of scientific work, he formulates and elaborates many of them in his own inimitable way. Despite the dissatisfactions he presents, in my view his account of the coat hangers is an original and substantive contribution in its own right.

A related difficulty is organizational: in Appendix 4 of "Respecifying," Garfinkel presents the manuscript as the first two parts of a seven-part series, and he repeatedly emphasizes that the remaining five parts are necessary, not only to supplement, but also to provide a more adequate understanding of what is provisionally developed in the first two. To my knowledge, from having gone through portions (though by no means all) of the relevant materials in the Newburyport archive, Garfinkel never completed the other parts, and many remained in the form of outlines and fragmentary texts. The published materials in Garfinkel (2007) are themselves fragmentary and incomplete.

8 Editor's introduction

Consequently, while the first two parts in the seven-part series he outlined are marked as provisional, incomplete, and inadequate, they are the most complete texts we have.

Science studies in the 1980s and afterwards

The "Respecifying" manuscript and the five seminars exhibit a limited engagement with contemporaneous developments in history, philosophy, and social studies of science. In the 1980 seminars, Garfinkel extensively and effusively discusses Gerald Holton's (1978) study of Millikan's oil drop experiment and Thomas Kuhn's "Postscript" to the second edition of *The Structure of Scientific Revolutions* (1970). He also discusses personal communications with Holton during a year they both spent at the Center for Advanced Studies in the Behavioral Sciences. In the 1980 seminars, Garfinkel discusses a study of an astronomical discovery he was preparing to describe later that year in a plenary session of a large meeting of historians, philosophers, and sociologists of science. During the meeting, Garfinkel was exposed to work by Michael Mulkay and David Bloor. Bloor (1976), with his proposals for a "Strong Programme" in the sociology of knowledge, aimed to "strengthen" the sociology of knowledge by targeting the technical contents of the natural sciences and mathematics. Superficially, Bloor's proposal may seem akin to Garfinkel's aim to investigate the technical work that constitutes the sciences and professions. Garfinkel also had discussions at that meeting (and also at an earlier meeting in 1979 at Wolfson College, Oxford) with Steve Woolgar, Harry Collins, Trevor Pinch, and other participants in the "British invasion" in the sociology of scientific knowledge. Although he does not mention them by name in the seminars, he likely knew of (and had possibly read) available work by Collins (1975), Mulkay (1979), Latour and Woolgar (1979), and contributors to the volume edited by Barnes and Shapin (1979), as well as relevant work on pulsar research by Edge and Mulkay (1976) and Woolgar (1976). By the time the "Respecifying" manuscript was drafted, the "new" constructionist social studies of science had greatly expanded and consolidated, and Garfinkel certainly knew about the key writings and had met, or knew of, Bruno Latour, Karin Knorr Cetina, and many others.

Readers who are familiar with developments in social studies of science starting in the 1970s are likely to notice that many of the themes Garfinkel discusses were covered by other studies, such as the highly influential ethnographies by Latour and Woolgar (1979) and Knorr-Cetina (1981). These studies also emphasized the difference between received versions of science and the picture of science that arises from on-site observations of laboratory practices. Some of the "contingencies" that Garfinkel lists in the "Respecifying" manuscript, such as *bricolage*, tacit knowledge, and "golden hands," were by that time also familiar to the philosophers, social historians, and sociologists who contributed to meetings of the Society for Social Studies of Science (founded in 1976) and the journal *Social Studies of Science* (initiated in 1971 under the title *Science Studies*).

Garfinkel's fascination in the 1980 seminars with gestalt theories of perception and how they illuminate scientific practice was anticipated by Hanson (1965) and Kuhn (1962, 1970), among others. Some of what Garfinkel says may strike readers as out of date, even at the time. For example, it is now rare in social studies of science to find discussions of "discovery," even as a scare-quoted term to be construed as the legacy of an uncritical, and even romantic, conception of modern science. Collins (1983) specifically critiqued what he took to be a presumption in Garfinkel et al. (1981) that a "discovery" could be located in a "night's work" at an observatory, as opposed to requiring a temporally extended, contingent, and (in principle) open-ended series of claims, counterclaims, and attributions, eventually resulting in "closure" among key participants in a technical community (a "core set"). Similarly, the distinctions Garfinkel draws between the social and natural (or "discovering") sciences – for example, that disputes can be "settled" in physics, but not in sociology – are likely to strike some readers as presuming an idealized demarcation between the natural sciences and social sciences. In fact, a version of such a distinction in earlier writings by Garfinkel drew critical commentary. Latour and Woolgar (1979: 153), for example, critically discuss Garfinkel's (1967: chap. 8) adoption of Schutz's distinction between the "rationalities" of scientific and commonsense reasoning, and argue that for the most part it rests on "tautological" assumptions about science resting on "scientific" and "logical" rationality, while "common sense" includes unquestioned and even irrational presumptions. In contrast, it became widely accepted in social studies of science to construe scientific practice as of a piece with ordinary practical action and practical reasoning, rather than to assign distinctive epistemic properties to it.

In the decades following the initial wave of arguments and ethnographies that sought to elucidate the "contents" of scientific practice, science studies followed the path of other academic fields in the humanities and social sciences, while retaining a distinctive edge by targeting the seemingly objective sciences as being subject to the ubiquitous epistemic inflections associated with Western, white, male, capitalistic, and colonial monocultures. Gerald Holton, who Garfinkel discusses at length, and who also commented on the pulsar paper in the plenary session in which Garfinkel presented it (Holton 1981), later reacted strongly against these trends (Holton 1993) and saw them to be naively abetting anti-science religious and political ideologies. However, Garfinkel's writings are not a particularly useful source for those who would either undermine scientific objectivity or undertake a restoration of it.

While it may seem that Garfinkel's treatment of the natural sciences largely recapitulates what was discussed and debated by contemporaries he does not mention, or worse maintains elements of older (currently deemed outmoded) conceptions of science, there are serious ways in which his program differed from the trends in science studies during the 1970s and 1980s. I have discussed and compared ethnomethodological and constructionist studies elsewhere (Lynch 1993), and aside from occasional footnotes, I do not delve into such comparisons with them here. However, a brief word is in order about why Garfinkel's manuscript and seminars in this volume continue to be relevant today. His manuscript and lectures on the natural sciences do not simply reiterate contemporary enthusiasms in 1980s-era science studies. Instead, they offer what still stands as highly original programmatic suggestions and exemplars. In the remainder of this introduction, I will focus very briefly on these original moves.

A brief gloss over topics and arguments in the manuscript and seminars

One original move that Garfinkel makes is announced in the long title of the "Respecifying" manuscript, which construes each natural science as a distinctively organized "discovering science of practical action." Garfinkel explicitly acknowledges that this proposal is "strange." Indeed, it is out of step with virtually all developments at the time (the late 1980s) in social and cultural studies of science, and it is increasingly out of step with developments in the decades since then. And yet, it remains a radical conception of science, social science, and practical action that has been rarely understood, let alone used, even within the narrow confines of Ethnomethodology and Conversation Analysis.

Note that Garfinkel is less interested in *discoveries*, in the sense of things of the world – entities, structures, principles, laws, and so forth – which are found, formulated, and/or credited for a first time. He is more interested in discovering *work*, though the object or objects of such work are far from irrelevant. Moreover, he is less interested in chronicling how such work finds new things or makes "nature" intelligible, than he is in elucidating how such work constitutes a "discovering science of practical action." A "discovering science of practical action" not only aims (sometimes successfully) to make empirical discoveries, develop novel proofs, or devise original theories and models. It also aims to *work out* how to do so, and *that* task (or bundle of tasks) is what preoccupies practitioners, often for very long periods of time. Making experiments work is not simply a matter of applying a protocol and working out the bugs. It is also a matter of "discovering" novel possibilities of *action*, and inventing and adapting instruments and procedures. Although we are, by now, familiar with the proposal that laboratory work is not simply a matter of following formal protocols, Garfinkel's argument is original in the way it implicates the relationship between the practices of a science and the social, historical, or philosophical description and analysis of scientific practice.

This is a truly original point, one that Garfinkel himself suggests verges on "lunacy." The point is that laboratory scientists (and this is easily extended to field sciences and theoretical sciences) are *investigating* as well as *using* practical actions, reflexively discovering a local organization of practical actions as well as *what* those practical actions disclose, stumble upon, negate, or prove. In the first seminar in the 1980 series, he likens such investigations to a reflexive "alchemical" investigation in and of laboratory practice. A plain way to put this is that scientists devise novel methods as a correlate and condition for discovering novel things. However, such a formulation is misleading in the way it implies a means-end relationship between methods and findings. The implications for a social science are not easy to grasp. Instead of distinguishing the social context from the technical work of a natural science, Garfinkel suggests that each natural science *is* a "discovering science of practical action" – that is, elucidating the practical context of innovation is *itself* a reflexive achievement of the selfsame innovation. And, because the "sociology" is *in* the work of a science, a requirement for an ethnomethodological study of such work is to master it technically as a condition for making it intelligible and describable.

As Garfinkel elaborates, the "discovery" that constitutes each natural science's burden and occasional achievement is of the "instructable reproducibility" of particular practices. "Instructable" is Garfinkel's preferred spelling; perhaps to be read as instruct-*able*. In a way, instructable reproducibility is a gloss for the local production of practical solutions to the well-known *problem* of replication in the philosophy of science. As Sir Karl Popper (1959: 99) described it: "An empirical scientific statement can be presented (by describing experimental arrangements, etc.) in such a way that anyone who has learned the relevant technique can test it." Popper (1970: 657) characterized it as a "social aspect of scientific method" that the sociology of knowledge had ignored. Harry Collins (1985) took up the theme of replication in a series of sociological investigations that pivoted from the philosophical problem to accounts of the practical contingencies, uncertainties, and disputes that attended particular historical attempts at replication. A different take on the problem was made by Harvey Sacks, who brilliantly observed that the very fact that replications are done provided a grounding for a science of social action (see Lynch and Bogen 1994). Sacks (1992: 804) observed that "adequate" (i.e., replicable by others) vernacular accounts of scientific methods were examples of instructions for reproducing practices. Rather than proposing that a social science should treat the natural sciences as a model for sociologists to emulate, Sacks proposed that natural sciences provide *instances* or *demonstrations* of adequate accounts of human activity (reproducible reports of the activity of performing an experiment successfully). Where Sacks treated the adequacy of such reports as a *grounding* for a natural science of human activity, Garfinkel (2002) treated it as a *phenomenon* for investigation, a phenomenon he dubbed "instructed actions" – which in the case of the natural sciences constitutes the "instructable reproducibility" of experimental practices.

A second original move is most elaborately developed in the five seminars. It has to do with what Garfinkel calls the "Gestalt themes." These "themes" are often conventionally treated as principles: figure-ground, temporal and spatial continuity, proximity, and closure of figures in fields of visual perception. Aron Gurwitsch's (1964) phenomenological treatment of Gestalt theory was Garfinkel's major source. Toward the end of the first of the five 1980 seminars, he goes into some of the well-known perceptual principles and the images that evoke them, such as the duck-rabbit and face-vase alternating figures. Although many other philosophers and social scientists have also drawn insight from gestalt theories of perception for analyzing scientific innovation, what he does with those themes is highly distinctive. Instead of delving into their salience to perceptual and/or cognitive aspects of observation, he uses them to illuminate embodied, praxiological work with instruments and materials. The gestalt themes become praxiological achievements rather than abstract perceptual processes.[3]

---

3 For an illuminating praxiological critique of Hanson's (1965) treatment of visual perception, see Coulter and Parsons (1991).

Garfinkel relies upon phenomenological treatments of embodied action and perception, but the field in which he locates the action is not a *perceptual* field – at least not as usually conceived. For example, in his seminars he invited students to wear headgear fitted with prisms that would act as inverting lenses that reverse the up-down orientation of the visual field. Merleau-Ponty (1958) also discussed inverting lens experiments devised by early 20th-century psychologists, but like the psychologists he was fascinated with a phenomenon experienced by subjects who wore the lenses without interruption for a few days. These subjects adapted to the upside-down visual world to the point that it would seem to flip back to a right-side-up orientation. The puzzle for the psychologists, and in a different way for Merleau-Ponty, was to explain how the adaptation occurred. Garfinkel was more interested in the immediate disruptions the inverting lenses occasioned: how wearing the lenses disordered the embodied performance of routine actions, such as walking to a destination, writing on a blackboard, playing chess, and so forth. The field in such instances was a field of *praxis* requiring the competent bodily engagement with its material constituents. Themes such as figure-ground became distinctively problematic to achieve as part of the relevant activities. This treatment of gestalt themes *thickens* the life-world in a way that notions of perceptual fields and cognitive processes abstract away from.

The five seminars, and also the text and appendices of "Respecifying," provide elaborations on a number of topics and case studies that preoccupied Garfinkel's work in the decades following the publication of *Studies in Ethnomethodology*. These include, in no particular order, the "phenomenal field properties" of queues, the use of wayfinding directions and "occasion maps," the myriad occasions and practices of "instructed action," and the "unique adequacy" requirement for ethnomethodological studies of practical actions. He also expresses views on the prospects of sociology. He characterizes sociology as a "talking science," whereas a discovering science in his view "can't be done without the talking, but it can't be done with the talking." He also sets out arguments about how ethnomethodology, as he envisions it, differs from conversation analytic studies that address distinctive organizations of practice as interactional structures of "talk"; this was an especially pertinent topic in the five seminars, because an audiotape was the most immediately available and detailed exhibit of "discovering work" that was at hand, and Garfinkel made clear that he aimed not to reduce the work of the discovery to the structured organization of talk.

The seminars also include some explications of how Garfinkel draws upon (including how he "misreads") phenomenological writings. He directly addresses Aron Gurwitsch and Maurice Merleau-Ponty on embodied perception, and less explicitly Husserl's (1970) conception of "Galilean science." In the case of the optical pulsar, he characterizes the Galilean object as an astrophysical entity with a precise location in outer space and measurable properties; he treats its presence and all of its properties as an achievement of the locally organized work of making them observable and reportable. In a 1993 seminar (recently published as an edited article [Garfinkel 2021; Eisenmann and Lynch 2021]) he mentions that, after the early 1960s, he no longer relied on Schutz's more explicit efforts to relate phenomenology to sociology, a reliance that was explicit and extensive in earlier work, especially Chapter 8 of *Studies in Ethnomethodology*. In the 1980 series of seminars presented in Part II of the present volume, it is abundantly clear that Garfinkel is not, like Schutz was, attempting to find a way to integrate phenomenology and classic sociology, but was *doing* phenomenology, not as a transcendental philosophy but as a distinctive form of empirical investigation. The lectures also include excursions into the difference between ethnomethodology and the praxeology of Tadeusz Kotarbinski (1955). In his writings and lectures, Garfinkel often was sparing in his discussions of scholarly matters, leaving it to readers and students to make out for themselves how ethnomethodology made use of scholarly sources; but in the lectures he occasionally reveals more about how he relates to prior philosophical and theoretical work – especially in phenomenology, where he is vigilant about resisting the voice of the transcendental analyst in favor of exposing the natural-analytic uses of a common language as an unavoidable constituent of scientific work.

As noted earlier, this volume is organized into two parts: Part I contains the "Respecifying" manuscript and its appendices; Part II consists of an abridged and edited text of the seminars on "Discovering Work in the Sciences." The reason that the manuscript in Part I (originally dated 1988) is presented before the 1980 seminars, rather than in chronological order, is that it represents a more comprehensive treatment of the conceptions of natural and social science that Garfinkel developed over several decades. The "Respecifying" manuscript also represents what, to my knowledge, is the most extensive and coherent of Garfinkel's writings in the final four decades of his life. As is evident in Appendix 4 of Part I, Garfinkel had the ambition to write and publish a lengthy series of volumes. For the most part, this ambition remained unrealized, although shorter pieces and fragmentary writings of his are included in the edited volume by Anne Rawls (Garfinkel 2002) and a special issue of *Human Studies* published in collaboration with Ken Liberman (Garfinkel 2007). Vast amounts of writings and recordings remain in the Garfinkel archive, and while it is possible that some relatively recent manuscripts of comparable length and coherence to the "Respecifying" manuscript may be lurking in a box or file drawer, I have yet to find such writings after having searched for them during several trips to Newburyport. For this reason, that manuscript is positioned front and center in this volume. The seminar transcripts in Part II should help to elucidate some of the points made in that manuscript, as well as to offer sundry reflections and extemporaneous commentaries that provide a vivid sense of Garfinkel's inimitable style and peculiar obsessions.

References

Barnes, Barry and Steven Shapin (1979) *Natural Order: Historical Studies of Scientific Culture.* Beverly Hills, CA: Sage.
Bloor, David (1976) *Knowledge and Social Imagery.* London: Routledge and Kegan Paul.
Boden, Deirdre and Don Zimmerman (eds.) (1991) *Talk & Social Structure: Studies in Ethnomethodology and Conversation Analysis.* Cambridge: Polity Press.
Collins, H.M. (1975) "The Seven Sexes: A Study in the Sociology of a Phenomenon, or the Replication of Experiments in Physics," *Sociology* 9: 205–224.
Collins, H.M. (1983) "An Empirical Relativist Programme in the Sociology of Scientific Knowledge," in K. Knorr-Cetina and M. Mulkay (eds.), *Science Observed: Perspectives on the Social Study of Science.* London: Sage, 83–113.

Collins, H.M. (1985) *Changing Order: Replication and Induction in Scientific Practice*. London: Sage.
Coulter, Jeff, and E.D. Parsons (1991) "The Praxiology of Perception: Visual Orientations and Practical Action," *Inquiry* 33: 251–272.
Edge, David, and Michael Mulkay (1976) *Astronomy Transformed: The Emergence of Radio Astronomy in Britain*. New York: Wiley.
Eisenmann, Clemens, and Michael Lynch (2021) "Introduction to Harold Garfinkel's Ethnomethodological "Misreading" of Aron Gurwitsch on the Phenomenal Field," *Human Studies* 44(1): 1–17.
Garfinkel, Harold (1940) "Color Trouble," *Opportunity*: 144–151.
Garfinkel, Harold (1967) *Studies in Ethnomethodology*. Englewood Cliffs, NJ: Prentice Hall.
Garfinkel, Harold (2002) *Ethnomethodology's Program: Working Out Durkheim's Aphorism*, edited with introduction by Anne Rawls. Lanham, MD: Rowman & Littlefield.
Garfinkel, Harold (2007) "Lebenswelt Origins of the Sciences: Working Out Durkheim's Aphorism," *Human Studies* 30(1): 9–56.
Garfinkel, Harold (2019a [1943]) *The History of Gulfport Field 1942, Part II*. Facsimile copy published by Media of Cooperation, University of Siegen, edited by Tristan Thielmann, with postscript by Anne Rawls & Michael Lynch. Originally Prepared for History Section of the US Army Air Forces.
Garfinkel, Harold (2019b) *Parsons' Primer*, edited by Anne Rawls, with Introduction by Anne Rawls and Jason Turowetz. Dordrecht: Springer.
Garfinkel, Harold (2021) "Ethnomethodological Misreading of Aron Gurwitsch on the Phenomenal Field," *Human Studies* 44(1): 19–42.
Garfinkel, Harold, and Kenneth Liberman (2007) "Introduction: The Lebenswelt Origins of the Sciences," *Human Studies* 30(1): 3–7.
Garfinkel, Harold, and Eric Livingston (2003) "Phenomenal Field Properties of Order in Formatted Queues and Their Neglected Standing in the Current Situation of Inquiry," *Visual Studies* 18(1): 21–28.
Garfinkel, Harold, Michael Lynch, and Eric Livingston (1981) "The Work of a Discovering Science Construed with Materials from the Optically Discovered Pulsar," *Philosophy of the Social Sciences* 11(2): 131–158.
Gurwitsch, Aron (1964) *The Field of Consciousness*. Pittsburgh, PA: Duquesne University Press.
Hanson, Norwood Russel (1965) *Patterns of Discovery: An Inquiry into the Conceptual Foundations of Science*. Cambridge: Cambridge University Press.
Holton, Gerald (1978) "Subelectrons, Presuppositions, and the Millikan-Ehrenhaft Dispute," *Historical Studies in the Physical Sciences* 9: 161–224.
Holton, Gerald (1981) "Comments on Professor Harold Garfinkel's Paper," *Philosophy of the Social Sciences* 11: 159–161.
Holton, Gerald (1993) *Science and Anti-Science*. Cambridge, MA: Harvard University Press.
Husserl, Edmund (1970) *The Crisis of European Sciences and Transcendental Phenomenology: An Introduction to Phenomenological Philosophy*, transl. David Carr. Evanston, IL: Northwestern University Press.
Knorr Cetina, Karin (1981) *The Manufacture of Knowledge*. Oxford: Pergamon.
Kotarbinski, Tadeusz (1955) *Praxeology: An Introduction to the Sciences of Efficient Action*. Oxford and New York: Pergamon Press.
Kuhn, Thomas S. (1962) *The Structure of Scientific Revolutions*, Second Edition. Chicago, IL: University of Chicago Press.
Kuhn, Thomas S. (1970) "Postscript – 1969," in T.S. Kuhn, *The Structure of Scientific Revolutions*, Second Edition. Chicago, IL: University of Chicago Press, 174–210.

Latour, Bruno, and Steve Woolgar (1979) *Laboratory Life: The Social Construction of Scientific Facts*. London: Sage.

Livingston, Eric (1986) *The Ethnomethodological Foundations of Mathematics*. London and New York: Routledge and Kegan Paul.

Lynch, Michael (1985) *Art and Artifact in Laboratory Science: A Study of Shop Work and Shop Talk in a Research Laboratory*. London: Routledge and Kegan Paul.

Lynch, Michael (1993) *Scientific Practice and Ordinary Action: Ethnomethodology and Social Studies of Science*. Cambridge and New York: Cambridge University Press.

Lynch, Michael and David Bogen (1994) "Harvey Sacks's Primitive Natural Science," *Theory, Culture & Society* 11: 65–104.

Macbeth, Douglas (2012) "Some Notes on the Play of Basketball in Its Circumstantial Detail, and an Introduction to Their Occasion," *Human Studies* 35(2): 193–208.

Merleau-Ponty, Maurice (1958) *Phenomenology of Perception*. London: Routledge and Kegan Paul.

Mulkay, Michael (1979) *Science and the Sociology of Knowledge*. London: George Allen and Unwin.

Pollner, Melvin (2012) "Reflections on Garfinkel and Ethnomethodology's Program," *The American Sociologist* 43: 36–54.

Popper, Karl (1959) *The Logic of Scientific Discovery*. New York: Harper and Row.

Popper, Karl (1970) "The Sociology of Knowledge," in J. Curtis and J. Petras (eds.), *The Sociology of Knowledge*. New York: Praeger, 649–660.

Rosenberg, Rosalind (2013) "'Rights Talk' Revisited: Incidents in the Life of Pauli Murray," *U.S. Intellectual History Blog*. Society for U.S. Intellectual History. Available at: https://s-usih.org/2013/03/rights-talk-revisited-by-rosalind-rosenberg/#_ftn16 (accessed March 24, 2021).

Sacks, Harvey (1992) "Appendix 1: '*Introduction*' 1965," in G. Jefferson (ed.), *Harvey Sacks: Lectures on Conversation, Vol. 1*. Oxford: Blackwell, 802–805.

Suchman, Lucy, Randall Trigg, and Jeanette Blomberg (2002) "Working Artefacts: Ethnomethods and the Prototype," *British Journal of Sociology* 53(2): 163–179.

Wittgenstein, Ludwig (1958) *The Blue and Brown Books: Preliminary Studies for the "Philosophical Investigations"*. New York: Harper and Row.

Woolgar, S.W. (1976) "Writing an Intellectual History of Scientific Development: The Use of Discovery Accounts," *Social Studies of Science* 6: 395–422.

PART I
Respecifying the natural sciences as discovering sciences of practical action, I & II

Doing so ethnographically by administering a schedule of contingencies in discussions with laboratory scientists and by hanging around their laboratories

Harold Garfinkel

EDITOR'S INTRODUCTION TO PART I

Michael Lynch

The draft of this manuscript was one of numerous versions that Garfinkel wrote in the late 1980s and early 1990s. The date December 12, 1988, was handwritten on the cover page of the manuscript. This version included a list of authors in the following order: Harold Garfinkel, Eric Livingston, Michael Lynch, Douglas Macbeth, and Albert B. Robillard. Other drafts included different lists of co-authors, and in some cases no co-authors (see editor's introduction to this volume), but this particular version was the one he chose to preserve for publication. In this section, and also in Part II of the present volume, all footnotes are the editor's footnotes. Those footnotes are denoted by superscripts, while Garfinkel's original notes are denoted with bracketed numbers and are listed as endnotes following the four appendices in Part I. Garfinkel organized the body of the manuscript into ten numbered sections, and also included many subsections. He was very fond of lists and sub-lists, and used various numbers and numerals to denote the listed items. I preserved his original ways of listing them, although they are not necessarily consistently used from subsection to subsection throughout the manuscript.

Garfinkel also included the following note in the draft copy he circulated in 1988. It addresses a volume edited by Boden and Zimmerman, for which he was invited to prepare a chapter:

> When this article was being written many topics that make up the ethnomethodological respecification of the natural sciences were discussed at appropriate length, but in endnotes and Appendices. The resulting argument was monographic in length. To make it possible to publish the article within the limits of the publisher's constraints a selection of materials was made. Further explanation will be found in Appendix 1, *Postscript and Preface*. To be published in *Talk and Social Structure*, Dierdre Boden and Don Zimmerman, editors, Polity Press, Cambridge (in press 1989 [published in 1991]).

As mentioned in the editor's introduction of the present volume, Garfinkel's chapter was not included in the Boden and Zimmerman volume and remained unpublished until now.

The above statement was followed by the table of contents. Note that the table of contents below refers to the layout of Garfinkel's manuscript, which now makes up Part I of the present volume. The editor's table of contents for the entire volume is listed above. Notes and references for Appendix 2 ("Basketball Notes" by Douglas Macbeth) are included at the end of that appendix. All other notes and references are listed at the end of Part I.

[1] Program and policies

- About the natural sciences as discovering sciences
- A provisional explanation of the natural sciences as discovering sciences of practical actions

[2] Contrasting ethnomethodological Studies by Michael Lynch and Eric Livingston furnish our studies a structure of inquiry and argument

[3] "Shop floor" contingencies of the day's work specify discovering work in the natural sciences

[4] Some points "about" the contingencies in the previous examples with which to follow their discussion

[5] Shop floor contingencies (cont'd). The schedule of "coat hangers"

[6] Administering★ the schedule of contingencies

- What are the contingencies for that saying so would ever specify?
- What did our incompetence consist of?

[7] A singularly cogent contingency: "what are the contingencies for?"

[8] Summary and dissatisfactions

[9] A second attempt to explain "sciences of practical actions" by detailing generalities

[10] A synopsis of the argument restated by calling ahead upon the finished seven collections of studies for a point of view

Appendix 1: Postscript and Preface, by Harold Garfinkel
Appendix 2: Basketball Notes: Finding the Sense and Relevance of Detail, by Douglas Macbeth
Appendix 3: Detail★, by Harold Garfinkel
Appendix 4: Collections of Studies I–VII Respecifying the Natural Sciences as Discovering Sciences of Practical Action, by Harold Garfinkel
Acknowledgements, Notes, and References, by Harold Garfinkel

RESPECIFYING THE NATURAL SCIENCES AS DISCOVERING SCIENCES OF PRACTICAL ACTION

Harold Garfinkel

[1] Program and policies

What is the work of a discovering science? This question is thematic throughout the bibliographies of science studies. It also shadows their number and obvious expertise with a curious absurdity. We can learn from them the relation between theory and practice in Hellenistic science, lists of Chinese medicines, the advent of experimental demonstrations in physics, the use of computable heuristics in scientific discovery, or the politics of Nobel prizes. But after these matters have been discussed an intractably questionable and material fact remains. Elusive and unexamined, it inhabits every page of this scholarly industry. Given that a physicist earns his living making discoveries in physics, and a mathematician must discover and prove mathematical structures, what does a physicist's or mathematician's discovering work consist of in its discipline-specific work-site details as the most ordinary organizational achievements of practical reasoning and practical action in the world? That questionable matter reaches with irremediable relevance into every line, acknowledged but tacit and unexamined, an unstated musical theme heard and understood in the midst of endless variations.

What is the work of a discovering science? With only rare exceptions, available studies, when they ask that question, understand it by devising representations of discovering work, and then so operate on these representations as to exhibit in them the analyzable specifics of discovering work as the details of an analytic consciousness. They seek to specify discovering-work-as-a-rule. The jobs of specifying discovering work in the natural sciences are addressed by attempts to recover, describe, teach, and reproduce scientists' practices by detailing generalities.

We seek the details of discovering work in and as a particular science. But we shall not look for them in invariants of formal analytic consciousness. We shall avoid all such attempts. We shall abandon, by remaining indifferent to such generics as Science, Scientific Research, Scientists' Practices, and Scientific Know How. The adequacy and universality of scientific methods, skills, findings, or knowledge generally speaking will be put aside as none of our concern.

Instead, we shall understand the question, "What is the work of a discovering science?" like this: Just what, in and as of only locally witnessable, technical, work-site details of a particular science, is discovering work in that science? Given that, and given because it is always and only the case that those details[1] of its discovering work are distinctive to the particular science as discoveries of practical action.

In carrying out this program we shall ignore the current and omniprevalent policies that argue the unity of the sciences, and, while adhering to this indifference we shall follow the policies instead (1) that the natural sciences are to be examined in their work-site practices, and therein they are to be discovered as sciences of practical action. (2) Each natural science is to be recovered in the entirety of its identifying, technical material contents as a distinctive science of practical action, (3) which is not interchangeable with any other discovering science, (4) and without bowdlerizing, reducing, neglecting, omitting, altering, or degrading its identifying, technical material contents, (5) yet without attenuating as its achievements the generality, universality, and transcendentality of its results, or in any way obscuring the growth of "hyphenated" sciences, and (6) without estranging the scientist from recognizing and carrying out the day's work, in his "shop," as a member of the local gang.

The heart of the program's tasks, and now with some results in hand, the heart of the program's claims, is twofold. First, the natural sciences are to be specified as discovering sciences. Each is to be uniquely specified as a discovering science. Second, in its technical, distinctive specifics, a particular science is to be discovered and is *only* discoverable as a distinctive discovering science of practical action.

Our first emphasis on discovering and only-discoverable is in irreconcilable contrast to *interpreted* as sciences of practical action, or represented, or exemplified, metaphorized, constructed, modeled, typified, or idealized – which is to say, in contrast to all attempts, no matter how thoughtful, to specify as examinable practice by detailing a generality.

In our second emphasis, each science is only to be discovered and is only discoverable as a *distinctive science of practical action*. This policy collects our aims, our tasks, our methods, and our results as a coherent program of studies.

These proposals are strange, and for readers who may not be acquainted with ethnomethodological studies, they can be strange in directions other and different than the reader can imagine. Their strange directions are unavoidable. In this article a few explanatory remarks, seriously inadequate remarks, are offered along with allusions to why they are inadequate. The tasks of explaining them make up the material arguments of collections III through VII.[2]

(1) About the natural sciences as discovering sciences

Speaking temporarily and misleadingly, but for the while unavoidably, in generalities, we shall say that in the natural sciences shop floor[1] contingencies of the day's work in the full quiddity of their real time, technical, performative details in a particular natural science specify the particular science in and as its phenomena as a distinctive discovering science.

The studies reported in this article focused on finding and specifying a "schedule" of contingencies. These "shop floor" contingencies occur and are oriented to as part of the day's work. They are familiar and, to the practitioners, easily recognized details of getting their work done under the constraints of getting it done with just what is at hand, just now, to make their lab experiment work. They are, in turn, part of the achievedly, specifiably yet unremarkably, indispensable work-site details of both shop-work and shop-talk. The contingencies we introduce here are thus details of the practitioners' work-site inquiry and theorizing that are unavoidably relevant yet unremarkable as such. By "talking" the contingencies with practitioners across a range of lab settings, our incessant local problem was to get them to tell us what we ourselves were talking about and, only by telling us, to teach us the discovering practices that are distinctive to that particular science. We are calling that process "analytic ethnography" (see below). The contingencies that make up the schedule, as will be seen throughout the discussion that follows, are not semiotic or semantic devices. Rather, they are locally lived constraints on the instructable reproduction of the phenomenon.

The following contingencies were collected in discussions with laboratory scientists.

> "Losing the phenomenon"
> "Wasting time"
> "Making an experiment work"
> "An issue can get settled"
> "Dread of, and provisions for, demonically wild contingencies"
> "Custom fitting imported methods and equipment to local, vernacular details of shop work and shop talk"
> "The local availability to 'our shop' of improvisational and bricolage expertise"
> "Zeroing in on the last jot and tittle"
> "The trivial, unremarkable, but indispensable technically specific skills of lab equipment's habitual body"

---

1 Garfinkel (2002: 95n) acknowledges that he first encountered the usage "Shop Floor Problem" while attending the Rockport Conference of the World Design Forum (August 7–12, 1993). He mentions that aerospace engineers spoke of the "Shop Floor Problem" during seminars at the meeting, which he summarily characterizes as "worldly, empirically local and specific, unavoidable real constraints of contingent facticities of 'shop floor' achievements in designed enterprises that must be done in and as the work of local, order production cohorts . . . [which] *somehow* escape from accountability with in-house front office certified methods of reportage and theorizing."

24 Respecifying the natural sciences

"The experiment in and as a laboratory's work-sites is a dense ecology of unforgivably strict sequences"

"Caution with, knowledge of, tracking, zeroing in on, provisions for, and repairs of, standard contingencies"

"The local, singular particularities of experimental equipment are by design practice, desire, and achievement specifically unremarkable"

"Teaching your lab's 'ways of doing things' to tourists, novices, visitors, new hands, site visitors, adversarial rivals, collegial rivals, and the rest"

"Golden hands"

"Klutz, slob, ignoramus, flake, careless, etc."

"Knowing how to get the phenomena out of your data"

"Unavoidably and irremediably relevant chiasmically cogent* and chiasmically coherent* details*"

"Setting for a yield"

"You missed the point! What are the contingencies for?"

The last contingency is singularly cogent. We learned it when Phil Agre, a computing scientists at MIT[2] who is trying to specify a Heideggerian phenomenologically adequate computable representation of practical action and practical reasoning, after hearing us through a descriptive litany of contingencies, demanded it of us. Having demanded it of us, Agre answered with the vicissitudes of his own project in mind: shop floor contingencies were relevant to the tasks at work-site of providing with them for what he called "constraints on the truth of the matter."

We shall examine Agre's answer and set it aside. We shall remain indifferent to that claim, because we shall find, in opposition to it, the relevance of the contingencies to the task at work-site of providing with them, *as practitioners provide with them*, constraints on the real time* teachability of a local gang's work-site, science-specific skills, and as constraints on the real time* instructable reproducibility of the phenomenon. We shall replace "constraints on the truth of the matter" with the "praxeological validity of instructed actions." We do so because, we shall argue, "constraints on the truth of the matter" are nowhere ever available to a local gang as its work-site's inspectable and therein inexorably work-site details*, whereas their bench affairs are everywhere with inexhaustible density done, witnessed, examined for, exhibiting of, and inhabited with the "praxeological validity of instructed actions."

---

2   Phil Agre has become something of a mysterious and legendary figure in sectors of the information sciences. He was a graduate student at MIT in Computer Science and Engineering when Garfinkel met him in the late 1980s (Agre received his PhD in 1989). At the time, Agre and fellow student David Chapman were interested in developing a Heideggerian conception of robotic machines. Instead of a central program to maximally govern machines, the machines would be designed to be interactive with the human and non-human contingencies in particular situations of use. Agre and Chapman also were interested in Lucy Suchman's (1987) critical treatment of plans and in ethnomethodological studies of work. See Agre and Chapman (1990).

We shall make a lot of the relevance of contingencies as constraints on the local, shop floor, real time* teachability[3] of work site skills, and as constraints on the local, real time* instructable reproducibility of the phenomenon.

(2) Another excursion is needed to explain, albeit very provisionally, our insistence on speaking of the natural sciences as sciences of practical action

Mathematics and Galilean physics are our empirical* cases in hand. On the basis of ethnomethodological studies of mathematical theorem proving by Eric Livingston (1986), and on the basis of ethnomethodological studies by us of Galileo's inclined plane experiment,[4] mathematics and Galilean physics is each provided for as a distinctive *discovering science of practical action*. On the basis of these studies, but only with them at hand, will we be able to say adequately*[5] just what we are insisting on and just why we insist. Until these studies are discussed in Collections III to VII we can only choose to make do with several merely general points.[3]

First, our interests are confined to the natural sciences. Nothing will be said about the social sciences in this chapter, and nothing can be said until after empirical* materials for mathematics and Galilean physics have been examined and their cases are established and clear.[6]

Second, we are hunting animals.[4] We entertain the following as empirical*[7] possibilities.

(i) The natural sciences are discovering sciences. By this we mean that discovering work in a natural science consists at work-site of contingencies that are specific to that science.
(ii) The natural sciences are sciences of locally and endogenously produced, locally occasioned, only embodiedly and in real time* teachably skilled, and only embodiedly and in real time* instructably reproducible phenomena. For practitioners of a science its phenomena are only findable and only specifiable as structures of practical action. Each science is a science of practical action.

---

3 The reference to Collections III to VII is to a series of studies that Garfinkel proposed to follow the present manuscript (Collections I and II). They would cover further topics in the study of work in the sciences, the "shop floor problem," "hybrid studies," and comparisons with "classic" studies. These are outlined in Appendix 4 of Part I. This was one of many lists Garfinkel compiled of forthcoming collections. One of the later versions was a document dated April 26, 2002, which listed a series of 15 books. That document listed Book 12 as published in Garfinkel (2002), and Book 5 would include the present manuscript. Book 14 would be a revised edition of Garfinkel (1967). The other books were not completed, though Garfinkel drafted numerous writings on the topics listed in the outlines he prepared.
4 One sense of "hunting animals" that Garfinkel occasionally mentioned is "finding the animal in the foliage," as in the optical illusion diagrams that challenge the viewer to find outlines of various animals hidden in lines and textures used for drawing foliage and other features of a scene. Such optical illusions were popular illustrations of gestalt principles such as figure-ground relations. Gestalt themes are discussed at length in the 1980s seminars Garfinkel convened on "the work of the sciences," the transcripts of which were edited for the present volume (see Part II).

(iii) The different sciences are not interchangeably discovering sciences. Instead, each is a distinctive discovering science of practical action. The different sciences are incommensurably distinctive sciences of practical action.
(iv) That each natural science is a distinctive discovering science of practical action we entertain as only witnessable and as only inspectable phenomena, and as instructable achievements.

Finally, and with utmost emphasis, discoveries *of* practical action does not mean discoveries that are made *because* actions are taken that are practical. Most emphatically, discoveries of practical action does not mean discoveries made by actions that are sufficiently practical, or effectively or in any other way adequately practical. We shall make no use of essential invariants of practical action or other generics with which to assess "particular cases" of practical action as candidate instances of a purported class of practical action. Nevertheless, we are *not* courting much less recommending the circumstantial morass of a plenum. We are concerned with the "universality" of the natural sciences, their awesome practical achievement, and not with anything else. In our later studies we specify with the structures of practical action of Galilean physics and with those of Euclidean geometry, the generality, the universality, and the transcendentality of their phenomena for each of these two sciences distinctively. We cannot take up that topic in this paper because to do so requires case materials. Collections III, IV, V, VI, and VII treat that topic *in extenso*.

We have come upon the animal twice. We report it in two sets of ethnomethodological case studies: those headed by Eric Livingston's studies of the work of mathematically proving Gödel's theorem,[8] and studies by Garfinkel, Robillard, and associates of the work of Galileo's experimental demonstration of invariants in the phenomena of bodies in free fall.[9]

[2] Contrasting ethnomethodological studies by Michael Lynch and Eric Livingston furnish our studies a structure of inquiry and argument

This chapter[5] announces a program and policies of ethnomethodological studies directed to respecifying the natural sciences as discovering sciences of practical action. It does so by reporting the first two of seven collections of studies in that program. In this chapter the procedures and results of using ethnomethodologically motivated methods of analytic ethnography to carry out this program are described. The respecification was done ethnographically by administering a schedule of contingencies in discussions with laboratory scientists in several natural sciences and by hanging around their laboratories.

---

5 "This chapter" is Garfinkel's reference to the planned inclusion of the manuscript in the Zimmerman and Boden volume. The volume was published, but without the chapter (see editor's introduction to this book and the editor's introduction at the start of Part I.

The contrasting ethnomethodological studies of work in the discovering sciences furnish our inquiries with a structure of inquiry and argument: Michael Lynch, *Art and Artifact in Laboratory Science* (London: Routledge & Kegan Paul, 1985); and Eric Livingston, *The Ethnomethodological Foundations of Mathematics* (London: Routledge & Kegan Paul, 1986). Each is concerned with and each reports discovering work as specifics of work-site practices. Each is an exemplary ethnomethodological study. However their methods and their findings are incommensurably alternates. Lynch obtained the material details of discovering work without being competent with the science he was studying, and providing for these details with various methods of analytic ethnography. Livingston spent seven years in graduate training as a mathematician and with this preparation conceived the work of proving mathematical structures and gathered analytically descriptive details of it.

In this chapter our purpose is to develop respecifying studies that were done via analytic ethnography, *not* as flawed or ersatz ethnomethodology, *but as a condition for finding and explicating dissatisfactions that in turn provide the respecifying studies in Collections III to VII with an agenda*.[10]

For our program the relevant contrasts are these: Lynch's study specifies the lived work of discovering axon sprouting in a neurobiology laboratory.[6] (a) It does so with the methods, and as the findings, of analytic ethnography. (b) The practices, equipment, measures, instruments, places, conversations, local staff, laboratory documents, lab results and the rest are literary objects. (c) His study specifies the work of discovering axon sprouting even though he *was* not taken seriously by the researchers and *could* not be taken seriously by them. (d) It does so even though he could not satisfy the unique adequacy requirement of methods. (e) His study describes the technical specifics of discovering axon sprouting though he did not know that work and could not recognize it for himself. (f) Moreover, he describes work-site specifics in which local staff are teaching each other, but he was not able to exhibit the analyzability of their craft as the details★ of its work-site specific teachability, and in no case was he able or required, as practitioners are able and required, to do as a deliberate pedagogic effort directed to upgrading the practitioners' accounts, and to teaching and elucidating the practitioners' craft and making it secure, which are preoccupying, omnirelevant shop work interests of practitioners. (g) Further he describes their discovering work in the local specifics of shop work and shop talk even though as a condition under which he was permitted to proceed with his studies he was not able to exhibit the analyzability of neurobiological

---

6 The main focus of Lynch's (1985) study was on a set of projects in a university laboratory in which the members investigated the extent to which neurons whose axons terminated in a layer of dendrites in the stratified hippocampus of the mammalian brain (with Sprague-Dawley rats as the model organism) "sprouted" new axons to partially re-enervate an adjacent layer of dendrites following the experimental destruction of neurons whose axons had terminated in that layer. Relying on earlier studies, the project treated the anatomical "sprouting" of axons and axon terminals as a given, and the lab's "discovering work" aimed to explore and characterize further anatomical, physiological, and chemical aspects of that regenerative process.

phenomena as the work-site details of their reproduction, nor was he ever required to do so, nor did he require it of himself. I will count very heavily in our studies that his findings are not results in neurobiology, nor was it ever imagined that they *could* be, nor as a condition of their adequacy were they ever required to be.

By contrast, Livingston's study required for the adequacy of his findings (a) that he know the mathematics he was talking about and that his findings be taken seriously by mathematicians; (b) that his analysis be constrained in recognizing and describing findings by the unique adequacy requirement of methods; (c) that his *findings* exhibit the analyzability of the proof accounts of mathematical structures (i.e. the schedule of theorems and their proofs that make up Gödel's theorem) as the details of their work-site-specific teachability; (d) that his *findings* do so by upgrading those accounts and by upgrading the mathematicians' craft of mathematical proving in and as the work-site-specific teachability of proof accounts; and (e) that his *findings* exhibit the analyzability of the phenomena of the work of evidential mathematical proofs[11] as the work-site detail* of their instructable reproduction.

- His study specifies the lived work of mathematical proving as the identity: Gödel's theorem, an ordered schedule of thirty-seven theorems and their proof accounts, is identical with the lived work of proving them. Consisting of a discovered *Lebenswelt* Pair,[12] the identity is specified with the mathematical identifying details of his seminal result: the proof account, the first segment of a *Lebenswelt* Pair, is a precise description of the *Pair*, [the proof account/the way of working to which it is irremediably tied]. Stated in the vernacular, Gödel's schedule of theorems and proofs are instructions that, in the hands of the practitioner, *in situ*, becomes precisely descriptive[13] of the instructed actions[14] that are glossed as "following them."
- This identity cannot be imagined, or stipulated, or obtained by any formal analytic, or inferential, or interpretive explication of theorems and their proof accounts. Nor can it be constructed.
- This identity is only inspectably the case.
- It has to be discovered.
- Livingston *can* be taken seriously.[15]
- Livingston's findings are mathematical results.[16]
- Livingston's findings, which are mathematical results, are cogent* and coherent* details of the *hybrid*, ethnomethodology/mathematics.[17]

"Being taken seriously" is critical in the arguments of this article. We offer explanatory remarks by considering the claim that for their adequacy Livingston's findings would need to be taken seriously by mathematicians. This is an abbreviation for a condition of the adequacy of Livingston's study. Spelled out the phrase should read: Livingston *required of mathematicians* as one of several conditions of adequacy of his findings that he have *exhibited* work-site-specific practices in the properties of proving's local production and natural accountability. *And, further, that* adequacy of Livingston's findings required that their work be this: as conditions under which mathematicians permit each other to proceed without corrections, *actually* and not imaginably or supposedly they "orient to" his findings – they "orient to" the Livingston-found properties of their practices of proving – and they for their part and relevantly to them inspectably incorporate Livingston's findings about their work into their work, and wherever it is the case, and without exception, that they not so they give reasons for putting them aside.

Livingston's findings that mathematicians at their work of proving Gödel's theorem "orient to" consisted of the lived work of mathematically proving Gödel's theorem. That lived work is specified in Livingston's book as (1) the practices that mathematicians gloss as Gödel's Schedule of Theorems and Their Proofs. (2) These practices are described and collected by Livingston as an "evidential proof" of Gödel's theorem. (3) The practices that compose an evidential proof of Gödel's theorem have the properties of their local production. (4) Among their properties of local production is their natural accountability.[18]

[3] "Shop floor" contingencies of the day's work specify discovering work in the natural sciences

For bench sciences in the natural sciences the day's work has familiar, easily recognized contingencies. They are specific to the particular science, and they specify a particular natural science as a distinctive discovering science. We introduce them with "Losing the phenomenon," "Wasting time," Making the experiment work," and "An issue can get settled."

J.K.,[19] a lipid chemist, told us how she and her colleagues once *lost their phenomenon*. Her story: For several years her lab entertained the possibility that a certain enzyme they worked with consisted of two enzymes, not one. One day, after running a solution through a filtering column, the solution responded spectroscopically to show two peaks. It being Friday afternoon they laid out a program of experiments for the following week. Monday morning they start the week's new work. They prepare the solution, pour it into the filtering column, and they get one peak. During the next hour, that day, the following day, the days after that, into the next week they get one. The question haunts them: Where are the two? What happened to the phenomenon? Did they have a phenomenon in the first place? The phenomenon is not reproducible so. It is lost. Do what they can, they cannot demonstrate it *again*.

Late in the second week a salesman from the manufacturer of the filtering column happens to come by. "I forgot to tell you. We changed the manufacturing procedure." He gives them the column they had used previously, and with that the phenomenon is there again.

We came to speak of another contingency as *wasting time*. You can have undertaken the formulation of a problem. You mobilize your friends and your resources of staff, stamina, money, and wit with which to specify the problem so as to bring it along to a solution. After a while it can happen as the worksite appearance of what you're doing that it has this about it: via the locally witnessable historicized character of just where you are, and given what you started with and for how long it has been going on, *what you are doing looks like this*: it is going to come to nothing. It is counted a contingency of the work, witnessable as work-site details, that you've been wasting your time. Witnessably, you have findings perhaps. But no results. Of what you have been doing in *its* witnessable specifics, you have wasted your time.

Moreover, at the beginning of a contemplated project, you can *imagine* that it can come out like this: though time will have been spent, it will come to nothing. It *can* come to nothing; it's not guaranteed to come to nothing.

Here's a variation.[20] In 1946 Aron Gurwitsch was hired at the newly established Brandeis University as a mathematician and philosopher. Abraham Sacher, the new president of Brandeis, urged his faculty to bring in money for their research, and reminded several that the US Army Air Force was a cornucopia. When Sacher told Gurwitsch, "Apply for money," Gurwitsch replied he would not do it. Sacher was enraged, and Gurwitsch had to find justification to withstand Sacher's plans for him. Gurwitsch complained to HG, "If I get money from the Air Force I will not be able to throw away papers. I will not be able to work on a problem and finally have the problem I've been working on come to nothing. Into the waste basket. I will not be permitted to do that. Instead, I will have to give reasons for whatever I am going to do next with or without it. If I turn away, I must give reasons. But above all I must preserve the history of the work I have been doing, and I am not going to be bound by that."

Laboratories offer many variations on the theme of *making the experiment work*. K.E., a distinguished academic chemist, assured us that graduate students in chemistry in their first term of graduate work learn about themselves that they can make experiments work, or they learn there is something less they have as skills. They can make experiments work up to a point. They have a skill of some sort, but they understand that a career in a lab doing experimental chemistry is not for them. Their instructors recognize that a student can find he is not good with experiments. It is not that students can either make experiments work or they can't. They can retain impressive literacy, and lab skills of sorts. But they can be faced with the prospect that in the workplace they are not able to develop a competence that promises a career in experimental chemistry. However, it's not that they must give up chemistry. As we understand it, they must give up the chemistry that requires *technicians'* skills that yield precise results with only locally and "practically" specifiable, equipmentally affiliated bodily techniques and their local vicissitudes.

A variation on *making the experiment work* plays on the theme of virtuosity and improvisation. Fermi was supposed to have been a virtuoso. A documenting story[21] depicts the early days of nuclear physics (Holton 1978a). He and his crew needed a beam of slow electrons. Just there, in that place, just then, with just the equipment at hand the beam was too fast. The story tells the delighted amazement of his co-workers when he reaches for a ball of wax, holds it in front of the neutron beam and gets the needed rate of flow.

In our discussions with bench scientists we use this story to speak of making do with just what is at hand, with just who is here, in just the time you have *with which* to make the experiment work. We use the story about Fermi to speak to the local availability in a laboratory, in particular persons, or as distributed skills, of *bricolage expertise*.[7]

A facet of *making the experiment work* is the indispensability of local *bricolage expertise*. That mean the indispensability as of the local gang's working together of making do with just what is at hand, under the constraints of just the time they have to get it done, to improvise with just what is at hand to bring the experiment through. To make it *work*. We always ask bench people, "Can you tell us a comparable story? But don't tell us a story of heroics. Don't tell us about the Fermi in your lab. Tell us about the machinist who bailed you out. Tell us about the person you turn to when a whatsoever won't work. So there is an expertise around to bring the experiment home."

We have yet to meet a bench person who gave us more than a blink for recall. "Of course." Then come the stories. Their question is, when do we want them to stop?

W.J., a former graduate student in microbiology, furnished another emphasis on *making the experiment work*. We paraphrase his remarks: They never do an important experiment without first doing dry runs. A lot of money can be committed to the experiment. The experiment is certain to be delicate. If it's a long sequence they don't want to find themselves in the midst of it, let alone coming to the end without having developed confidence that they know the minutiae of those sequences. They rehearse the experiment. They do a dry run, from the beginning to end, and as many times as are called for to take the set up smoothly from beginning to end. After rehearsals with which to master what the experiment could consists of as a workable experiment, *then* it is done.

In the natural sciences it can happen that an issue gets settled. This contingency was called to our attention by Gerald Holton, and was luminously specified by his analysis of the Millikan/Ehrenhaft dispute (Holton 1978b).[22] Robert Millikan and his gang proposed that there was a unitary charge of the electron. Felix Ehrenhaft, a distinguished Austrian physicist, and his gang proposed that the charge was one of distributed values. The two gangs were each at each other's throats, and the quarrel went on for seventeen years. Then Millikan did the oil drop experiment, after which physicists took it that Millikan had settled the issue, which, locally historicized and developingly was understood like this: In light of Millikan's findings you could no longer carry on that quarrel in its former terms. Further, and perhaps relevantly, Millikan got the Nobel prize: Ehrenhaft was denounced by colleagues, deserted by friends and students, and ended his career discredited.[8]

---

7 Levi-Strauss (1966) famously drew an ideal-typical contrast between the engineer, whose tools and skills are fitted to specific projects, and the *bricoleur*, a tinkerer, handyman, or jack-of-all-trades who adapts tools and materials to open-ended tasks at hand. As Garfinkel points out here, bricolage is no less indispensable in science than in traditional crafts.

8 Holton's (1978a, 1978b) account of the Millikan-Ehrenhaft episode became a source for a long-term debate among historians and philosophers of science about the propriety of Millikan's procedure of selecting among runs of the oil drop experiment to preserve results that confirmed the unit-charge on the electron while discarding and discounting anomalous results for technical reasons. Holton examined Millikan's notebooks and found handwritten notations that provided brief (apparently ad hoc) reasons for accepting "good" results and discarding others. Holton noted that Millikan's selective procedure supported his presuppositions about the unit charge, whereas Ehrenhaft's procedure

32 Respecifying the natural sciences

That an issue can get settled in the natural science[s] but not in the social sciences was brought to our attention in a story about – possibly by – Thomas Kuhn. When he was at the Center for Advanced Study in the Behavioral Sciences,[9] he asked his social science colleagues, does it happen in the social sciences that an issue gets settled? He was told that to the best they knew, no. They couldn't come up with any study *with which* an issue got settled.

[4] Some points "about" the contingencies in the previous examples with which to understand the descriptions of those that remain and with which to follow their discussion

Making up the day's work the contingencies are only locally witnessable. That they are only locally witnessable is so in ways that can only be found out, and cannot be imagined. Further, they are only locally witnessable as first-person-by-hands-on witnessable work-site stuff. And then they are only locally witnessable on the local "our gang's" behalf.

As of work-site details they specify the obstinacy and the recalcitrance of objects to instructable reproduction. As of work-site details they specify as unavoidably and irremediably relevant details the praxeological validity of instructed action.

Being only locally witnessable: only available as hands-on first person witnessable stuff: unavailable if they must be imagined; and specifying of the obstinate recalcitrance of the reproducible object that is accounted for as an instructed action, the contingencies are only available as revealed details★ of practitioners' *work site* theorizing.

But details★ – asterisked details★ – are not just any details. Nor are details★ any of the matters that details have been taken to be. (a) They are unavoidably and irremediably relevant *and* unremarkable. (b) They identify discipline-specific work-site's practices of teaching and inquire – i.e. work-site theorizing. (c) In both respects, which are material matters with respect to their local production and to their only-local-specificity-in-their-relevance-to-the-parties, they are unavoidable as irremediable specifics of work-site's instructed actions *as of which* alone and entirely the reproduced phenomenon consists.

Our idea has been to use these slogans – "losing the phenomenon," and "wasting time" – as Mooersian descriptors[23] with which to discuss with bench scientists their practices of shop work and shop talk, their uses of instruments and equipment,

---

of using all results in his calculations provided evidence of a continuous charge, evidence consistent with his preconception of "sub-electrons." Ironically, as Holton points out, Ehrenhaft's procedure was consistent with canons of experimentation that warn against confirmation bias. But, as Holton also points out, it would be a dubious procedure indeed to accept any and every result, regardless of the presumed adequacy of the experimental setup and the competency of the experimenters. Nevertheless, *just how* Millikan selected among runs remained to be specified, and continued to be a source of debate about, either or both, the ethics of Millikan's procedure and the adequacy of conventional experimental canons for accounting for the actual practices required to make experiments work.

9 This is a reference to the Center for Advanced Study in the Behavioral Sciences at Stanford, CA. Thomas S. Kuhn was a Fellow in 1958–59. Harold Garfinkel was a Fellow in 1975–76.

teaching's work-sites, lab architecture, and the rest. We present them with the contingencies for their recognition and further elaboration. In our discussions each contingency is offered with an accompanying story. We ask our discussants for explicating stories-in-turn. We ask the person whether the story is recognizable in his work, and if it is to tell us out of their actual workplace experiences, what our story is talking about. Our aim is to learn from the discussion and story exchanges what we are talking about.

For example, introductory remarks to T.C., a neurochemist, like this:

HG: "I'll tell you a story that was told to me by J.K. about how the people in her lab once 'lost a phenomenon.' I don't know what I'm talking about. I'm not a chemist. Is it recognizable? It if rings[,] will you tell me a story in turn[?] Will you, with stories from your experience in your lab, tell me what I could be talking about in your lab[?] I wouldn't know because I wouldn't know it to see it for myself. I 'know' what I'm talking about only in that I have it to *tell you* what somebody *told me*. So, would you tell me what I could be talking about as it may point to what *you* know at first hand as what that way of talking actually looked like in the actual places where it might have been encountered by you[?] Don't spare the details. Give me details. I'll be reminding you to tell me as specifically as you can."

Professor Arthur Yuwiler,[24] a neurochemist, after listening to our request, recognized what we were asking of him by calling our descriptors "coat hangers." His observation furnished us a cogent resource. An explanation of "coat hangers" is this: You can't tell, and you would not *want* to tell from the fact that you *have* a coat hanger, or from what you can do to it, what will hang on it. A descriptor – e.g., "losing a phenomenon," or "wasting time," or "dependence upon bricolage expertise" – used conversationally will have served as the condition for coming upon its definite sense, or its definite reference, or its unequivocal correspondence to an object. However, just what sense it will come to have been speaking of, or with what reference, or to what object, can't be decided and should not be decided by explaining the descriptor's meaning *a priori*.

The contingencies were searched for, collected, enriched, corrected, and the list of them was extended, as a collection of "coat hangers." We administered[25] the contingencies as a schedule of "coat hangers." That they are "coat hangers" is a phenomenon in its own right. We speak of that phenomenon as administering* the schedule of coat hangers. The phenomenon of administering* coat hangers is critical to our equipment.

[5] Shop floor contingencies (cont'd). The schedule of "coat hangers." The dread of and provisions for demonically wild contingencies

The soliciting story was told to HG by James Olds. "We had been graduate students together. When I arrived at UCLA in 1954 he was already there. We meet. What's new? "Harold, I'm a success. I made a discovery." We were meeting in his brand-new lab in the brand-new Brain Research Institute in the brand-new UCLA

Medical Center. The discovery: He had been a research nobody in Hebb's lab at McGill when he implanted an electrode in a rat's brain thinking to further map out what at that time was standard knowledge about where in the brain you could get aversive stimulation. Olds' implanted rat goes for the corner of the box, Olds gives him the jolt looking for the rat to turn away because of the painful stimulation, but no, the rat can't get into the corner fast enough. Olds sees that rat's behavior with "it's pleasure, *not* pain! And in a place where there's not supposed to be pleasure!" In frenzied weeks he, his wife and collaborator, and their friends exploit the finding, mapping the brain: there, and where else?[26]

Because of his discovery, UCLA hires him from McGill to the brand-new Medical Center. They give him large sums of money, a fresh new lab, equipment, connections, and assistance. They only want him to work miracles. And he's prepared to do it.

One day he comes into the lab. His brand-new assistant is on a ladder, carefully and thoroughly wiping the shelves, moving the equipment to get every speck. Olds: "I told him, you sonofabitch, I want you to get down from there, right now. I want you to get out of here. I never want to see you around here again."

What's the anger about? Olds explained. Having gotten the phenomenon "I had a low cost, high production mine." Anybody coming into the lab who had an idea [was] assured a research and an article. If someone proposed to heat the hypothalamus, "Let's heat the hypothalamus." "Let's give it this drug?" "This drug." "That drug." "That drug."

Said Olds: "Here is this guy moving the equipment. I had no idea that moving the equipment would make *any* difference to whether or not I could get that phenomenon again as I needed it, but I wasn't going to find out: I didn't know whether it would make *any* difference that the equipment was where it was. I didn't know that it made any difference, but I didn't want to learn."

That would be called the dread of and provisions for demonically wild contingencies. That dread of a demonically wild contingency, the dread of that thing that looms as Hubert Dreyfus said of the dumbwaiter in Pinter's play, as "an intrusion on a fragile island of order."[10] It's not that it's that fragile. Well, who knows about the fragility of it? As far as the practitioner is concerned, he is confident – though not in abandoned exuberance – until it happens that the phenomenon exhibits itself with obstinate recalcitrance to being reproducibly so for another first time. At that time, he sees what he can be up against as the local work-site contingencies of carrying on with the questionable matters in hand, i.e., of carrying on at work-site the combined teachable and instructed reproduction. The teachable and instructed reproducibility are one thing with this gang of us, here, engaged *as of* each other's skills, and as of our local histories and our shop talk with work in hand.

We use Olds' account to speak of taking cognizance of, of being attuned to, even of making provisions for demonically wild contingencies. Frequently, a lab person

---

10 Garfinkel provided no citation for the quotation, but see the discussion of Harold Pinter's play *The Dumb Waiter* by Dreyfus and Dreyfus (1964: xv). Garfinkel also mentions this line in his May 27, 1980, seminar (see Part II of the present volume).

has responded to the Olds story with chagrin, leaving us with the impression that it's not anything to own up to. M.F., a neurochemist, who does similar studies reprimanded us. "Don't think I'm a magician, or that I don't know what I'm doing, or that I don't have what you call the craft, or that I don't have the procedure under control." Whatever their reasons, recognition and agreement were immediate. Yes, it can happen. Not only that you can lose a phenomenon, but demonically wild contingencies are dreadful, and they are vicissitudes of the day's work.

In contrast to Olds' rage in the face of demonic contingencies is T.C.'s self-styled "paranoia." T.C. who directs a neurobiochemistry lab told us, when he had to decide procedures that the people in his lab would be using for an important experiment, and when he had to assign these procedures to particular persons and had to review their implementation, if he anticipated that problems would be encountered in reproducing a phenomenon, "I get practically paranoid." He explained his "paranoia" with a prevalent, vernacular meaning of paranoia; viz., a heavy, obsessive preoccupation with locally knowable, possible socially organized workings of the things in their minutia, and whereas Anyone Sees and Anyone Settles For Ordinary Motives, *he* was tracing out in his all too knowledgeable detail what he knew local persons could be doing as an organized division of work such that there *could* be a screw-up coming from these details, theorized details, *unreasonably* theorized details. He could be accused: "You're *unreasonable.*"

Gerald Holton[27] told us about a characteristic phenomenon of laboratory physics and suggested that we examine it. Equipment is frequently custom build and cannot be exported to other labs. Using custom equipment local gangs obtain reportably comparable results. We took it *that* local gangs of us obtain universal results from just this equipment speaks of the transcendentality and universality of methods and results as local, practical achievements.

By using Holton's suggestion as a guide in our discussions we learned to ask about *the unexportability of methods between laboratories*. In discussions with bench people our questions went to the point that methods travel between labs only insofar as the receiving lab custom fits the imported method so as to find via the local, specific, unavoidably vernacular details of just how, just us, just *this gang* of us, here, in this place, do just the things we do[28] for which a way of describing, and in other ways accounting, what we do as an instructed action might be found in published articles and in other lab documents – ours and others'. These articles stand curious proxy for just what the local gang of us do here to make those instructions come true as a precise description of the locally collaborated practices of which our work of following that consists. The articles stand proxy for just what the local gang of us do to make those instructions come true as a precise description of the instructably reproducible phenomenon, – i.e., the phenomenon.

The unexportability of method is a contingency of the day's work. For example, this can happen. For years Ben has been working in a light lipid lab.[29] Evenings and weekends Ben runs a short order restaurant, during the day he works in the lab. There it is the case with Ben, and it is known to the gang of us about Ben, that he doesn't label his solutions. Not that his solutions won't work. Rather, if you're to know what is in those solutions, when they were prepared, what he did to prepare them ask Ben. Question: Under what circumstances do you use Ben's preparations? Those circumstances will not be specifiable. Only if you are there, in that lab, and there you are to get done the instructably reproducible results promised in the publications that are being read to carry on the projects of this lab then *that* you know of Ben, and that you and others know, in each other's way of knowing about Ben, "Oh, that's Ben," how Ben works with these solutions becomes indispensable, vernacularly detailed, locally knowledgeable ways of talking, locally knowledgeable ways of exhibiting in solutions what they contain.

Where methods in the natural sciences are concerned a contingency of work in the local lab is this: methods travel between laboratories only insofar as the receiving lab custom fits the methods to the local, vernacular details of just how "our shop" does the work. Unless you can provide the custom fitting, methods won't travel.

Our slogans drew a range from a puzzled, "Yes, of course" to emphatic agreement. No one disagreed. We would say, "tell us what we're talking about, and of course tell us whether we are all wet. Methods travel between labs *only* to the extent that the receiving lab custom fits the method so that it becomes a method in the hands of just who is at hand, in this place, with this schedule of projects to make the method, as of its details, workable here with just how we do things."[11]

Our idea was to get stories with which to work out the hunch that "just how we do things in our shop" is identical with just as of our histories with each other, the just what we know of each other, includes the worksite specific how we get along *through*, let alone *with*, each other. Lynch[30] reported in specifics how, in the lab he studied, shop work consisted of ongoing, developingly embroiled vernacular details of locally organized and locally "historically" accountable projects.[12]

Knowing how to get the phenomenon out of the data. Gerald Holton's article on the Millikan/Ehrenhaft dispute[31] added brilliantly to his program of studies of work-site details of scientific imagination. In it he wrote with thoughtful and seminal emphasis that when Millikan published the results of his oil drop experiment he reported that he was publishing *all* his results. To prepare his study Holton had examined Millikan's

---

11 A related matter frequently comes up in interviews with scientists, which is that collaborations between labs often are mediated through exchanges of research students and postdoctoral researchers. Many of the main points that Polanyi (1958) makes about "tacit knowledge" are well known to scientists and, of course, Polanyi was drawing upon his experience as a chemist. Although some researchers were familiar with Polanyi's writings on the subject, regardless of what they may have read in the philosophy of science, Polanyi articulates "vernacular" understandings among researchers. This is a specialized "worksite-specific" variation on the theme of commonsense understanding. It certainly draws upon more widely shared competencies with the use of natural language, as well as embodied handling of tools and machinery, but it is distinctive to specialized laboratory work. A source that Garfinkel recommended on the subject was Senior (1958).
12 "Historically" is placed in quotes here to, among other things, point to what Garfinkel et al. (1981) refer to as "local historicity" – not the history of science as usually understood but the place of the current phase of a project in a temporally developing array of laboratory projects performed in a particular laboratory as well as reported (or otherwise known) research in other laboratories that the project builds upon and/or contests.

papers. He paid close attention to Millikan's lab notes. Some were annotated: "Beautiful," "Publish this one," "Something's wrong." Holton examined Millikan's entire corpus of observed trials. Many more trials were recorded than were published. Nevertheless Millikan wrote of the published trials that he was publishing all his results.

In the course of writing his article at the Center for Advanced Studies in the Behavioral Sciences in 1975–76, Holton presented his materials to a colloquium.[13] Describing the discrepancy in detail Holton was reflective about it but he was not disturbed. An historian of science in the front row *was* disturbed. "Isn't there a sense in which Millikan was wrong?" The point of the question was that Millikan was reporting his results inappropriately and incorrectly. He was not representing truthfully and correctly what he had done.

Holton disagreed. "Somehow these people know how to get the phenomenon out of their data." And *that*, Holton argued, is a practical achievement, though it is a mystery to those who do it. Bench scientists will acknowledge that they get the phenomenon out of their data, *some* how they get it out of their data, and they are obliged to do so. But when the emphasis turns away from *some* how to *just* how, the "skill" is dependent upon but it escapes specification. A work-site contingency, getting the phenomenon out of the data is "made to happen." As of the workplace it consists of organizational *things* searched for, produced, recognized, and understood as findings, reportable findings, and results.

Holton, in his reply, urged that this achievement's work-site specifics be studied. He insisted that if you count getting the phenomenon out of the data a faulty procedure you'll be left with a facile judgment of the work of a science. You'll leave unexamined getting the phenomenon out of the data and knowing how to do so as a day's unavoidably relevant and unremarkable practices.[14]

The trivial, unremarkable, uninteresting but indispensable technically specific skills of lab equipment's habitual body are smooth, technically specific to the science as a science of practical action, interactionally specifying "our local gang," costly to produce, depended upon, and unremarkably observable.

Y.R. a microbiologist we were visiting for the first time, was excited with the discovery he had confirmed just before we arrived.[32] When we walked in, he had the new gel in his hands. He introduced us to the undergraduate he had trained. "She helped me" to the discovery. He called her over, and in her presence praised her, "I trained Linda. When I first met Linda she didn't know anything." He picked up a platinum rod with a loop at the end. "I showed her. One of our jobs

---

13 During the 1975–76 academic year, Garfinkel also was a fellow at the Center for Advanced Study in the Behavioral Sciences at Stanford University.

14 As noted in editor's note 8 above (pp. 31–32), Holton's published account of Millikan's oil drop experiment touched off a dispute among philosophers, historians, and sociologists of science that lasted decades. As the anonymous comment from an historian of science that Garfinkel quotes suggests, some readers of Holton's account of Millikan's notebooks understood it to be exposing a bad or even fraudulent methodological practice of cherry-picking "good" data in order to save the phenomenon. For a concise account from the point of a physicist/philosophical realist who defended the "cosmetic surgery" that Millikan deployed when discarding anomalous results, see Franklin (1997).

will be to dip the wand in this fluid and mark these agar dishes. When you prepare these platinum rods, I want you never to hold the rod in the Bunsen flame like this. Never do that. You must always hold it like that. From now on I want you to do it exactly like that, without fail, in every case, and I want you to give me a solemn promise that indeed you will do it just like that."

On another occasion Y.R. remarked, "I look for persons in my lab who have *golden hands*. I have golden hands. I once had a student: *he* had platinum hands – but I lost him to medical school. . . . Harold, *I'm* a very good technician." Y.R. is a distinguished professor of microbiology.

One contingency seemed to inhabit every episode we discussed. It consisted of attention paid by bench workers to *unforgivingly strict sequences* – unfailing attention to, respect for, and omniprevalent concern with *unforgivingly strict sequences*. We're *not* talking about and we're *not* settling for standard versions of habitual actions, or standard accounts of the achieved amnesia for the reproducibility of a technique. Instead, as of *a* lab's embodiedly local procedures, bench work consists of an ecology of unforgivably strict sequences.

For example HG had been hanging around for the afternoon in Y.R.'s lab. Y.R. had been at the bench transferring DNA from a microdispensing syringe into iced vials. After he finished, he demonstrated for HG and criticized several techniques to rid the tip of the syringe of excess fluid, emphasizing in the course of showing a technique which technique he preferred and why. Later HG watched him at the sink as he washed and inspected a gel. Throughout each of those "watched" activities HG "heard" Y.R. speaking about the fine, embodied reproducibility and sequentially organized technical ways that can be counted on by everyone in the lab to satisfy them again, and with everyone dreading the costly consequences of anyone's small departures.

Another example, Y.R. recognized and insisted upon treating an experiment in his lab as embodied skills affiliated to equipment. That equipment is *located* in the "lab's and the equipment's *places*" got the same recognition and treatment. These are affiliations to working equipment that consists of extraordinarily detailed embodied skills that are delicately specifiable in locally done and locally recognized bench sequences. Later HG was told that microbiologists are notoriously that because they require antiseptic conditions. But then a chemist offered flat assurance that no matter what chemists' labs look like – slum closets or prepared for surgery – chemists *see* just what as of "the looks of the place" their sequentially organized projects consist of. Friedrich Schrecker[33] reported how in introductory lab chemistry undergraduates see just what they are doing and see just where they are only as of their afternoon experiment's tight, locally produced and, via its local historicity, its observable, equipmentally specific sequential organization.

Limited space prevents further discussion of the contingencies. We have deliberately avoided ranking the contingencies or assigning them priorities of relevance.[34]

[6] Administering* the schedule of contingencies

Administering★ the schedule of contingencies is a gloss for local, interactional particulars that we collected from our taped discussions when, in light of the requirement in our study that *lab scientists and we teach each other coherent* details of THEIR work*, these particulars were examined as our inquiries' adequate details. These particulars will be reviewed in light of Phil Agre's demand, "You missed the point! What are the contingencies for?" (See page 24.)

For his dissertation problem in the Artificial Intelligence Laboratory at MIT, Agre is trying to specify a Heideggerian phenomenologically adequate computable representation of practical action and practical reasoning.[15] After listening to our litany of contingencies, Agre described from his own project several features of attempted solutions to the problem of computability that bespoke a solution's failure. For example, while working out a programming problem mathematically, he might come upon the runaway exponential growth of a decision tree as an unavoidable consequence. Pointing out that these were work-site contingencies of his project, he collected them as "constraints on the truth of the matter." That features of an attempted solution made up such constraints was their point when speaking of them as contingencies.

"What are the contingencies for" he demanded.

The final contingency in our list of contingencies, it is singularly cogent. We shall speak of it with Agre's demand. The remainder of this article addresses that demand, as do the remaining collections of studies.[35] In the remainder of this article two questions are examined:

(1) We are indeed preoccupied with the contingencies, but why? What are they for? What's to be done with the contingencies? What's to be gained from such preoccupation?
(2) In any actual case of discovering work, there is what *needs* to be settled about the contingencies. Given what needs to be settled about them, just what *can* be settled by "saying so?"

The aim of our research was *via discussions* with bench scientists to ask for and get from them an explicit explanation of the coat hangers. Remember, we didn't know and we wouldn't know to see for ourselves what we were asking the scientists do describe for us, in detail. Given the foregoing particulars, and in their light, we pose the question: In any actual case of discovering work in a natural science, just what can be settled by "saying so?"

The following procedural specifics are glossed as administering* the schedule of contingencies. They explicate our aims as questionable aims. They explicate our aims as unavoidably, without remedy, and unremarkably questionable aims. The procedural specifics, glossed as administering* the schedule of contingencies, are collected and presented in the following topics:

(1) What are the contingencies for that "saying so" would ever specify?
(2) What did our incompetence consist of?

---

15 A monograph by Agre (1988) presents the argument Garfinkel summarizes here.

(3) The idea in *talking* the contingencies, and our incessant local problem, was to get practitioners to teach us what we could be talking about with which we would thereby be teaching them as well. Teaching what? Teaching them the coherent* and cogent* details of THEIR work. And certainly *not* teaching them to recognize their work's features as standard topics of sociology.[36]
(4) The crux of our task is to specify the discovering sciences with work-site *unmotivated observables*.[37]
(5) Various "relativities" accompany the administered* schedule of coat hangers.

(1) What are the contingencies for that saying so would ever specify?

What are the contingencies for that *saying so* would ever specify? What are the contingencies for that just talking the contingencies would ever provide for? What were we asking of the scientists we talked to? What did we hope to learn by *asking* them? What did we plan[38] they would teach us by our asking this of them: *tell* us?

We were asking them to *tell* us: As witnessable stuff, what makes up the day's work that is only witnessable? that makes up the day's work and is only witnessable in ways that cannot be imagined but that can only be found out? ways that are only inspectably so, and not being imaginably so, and not being imaginably the case would only be discoverably so? ways that would only be locally witnessable as first person hands-on witnessable work-site stuff, and *then* they would only there be witnessable as first-person work-site stuff where the first person is "doing witnessing" on the local gang's behalf, and in the local gang's immediate, actual presence? and *in* the local gang's presence, *there* everything that the profession could possibly consist of *generally speaking* – as for example in speaking of a professional community – would be encountered in what it looks like? Finally, at that work-site the contingencies would *there* specify the "obstinacy and the recalcitrance" of the reproducible phenomena of the particular science – and *there* not to their reproduction but to their *instructable* reproduction.

Further, we were thinking to find a *collection*[39] of such contingencies in what we had discussed. We were thinking that by being *told* we would find a collection, and by being *told*, with that collection we would enrich and correct the collection and in various consequential ways upgrade the collection so as to sharpen the bearing of the collection's items on the distinctive work of a particular science.

We thought we would get this from our discussants under the following conditions of our discussions:

First, we didn't know what we were talking about. In no case did we know what we were talking about. That doesn't mean we were stupid or ignorant in usual ways. It means we could not see for ourselves just what we were asking them to tell us. We were soliciting talked contingencies with the aim of searching for an analytic gist of their remarks. *We* would extract the gist from the discussions. We would find the gist for ourselves. We even reserved a theorist's privilege to find in the transcripts and to *say* on the grounds of examined excerpts what it consisted of as a contingency of the day's work that one could "lose a phenomenon," could "waste time," "could settle an issue."

We could find – i.e. we were able to find – the analytic gist of what we asked them to tell us. We could have documented stories. We could have analytic just so stories. We could have anecdotally documented arguments, and with any of these we could specify their practices of discovering work as reasoned or documented *conjectures*. With our stock of descriptions we did not need to fail to specify as practices the discovering work of a particular science – lipid chemistry or microbiology. But we could not examine for ourselves the work they described, consulting their descriptions as instructions with which to see of that work and to ask of it, what does it consist of as the just how, in just this place, with just what is at hand is it done to be coming upon just this instructable reproducibility of the phenomenon for just this, another, next first time?

We asked the scientists to tell us their practices, and by telling us to make their practices explicit, given that they could not take us seriously. Meaning, nothing of what we said to them, and nothing of what we proposed as their work or about their work, were they required either to incorporate into their day's work or give reasons for putting aside. In that way, although we were welcome visitors, we were not part of the local gang. Not that we did not *want* to be taken seriously. We *could* not be taken seriously, and for material reasons. Instead, we talked with them under the auspices of interdisciplinary interests, suggestively.

In short, we offered to learn, and we proposed to specify the discipline-specific practices of discovering work of a particular science by listening for them, though we were not taken seriously, and we could not be taken seriously, and everyone, us included, knew it. We were courting miracles.

The point: We could not depend upon discussions with scientists to specify the discovering work of a science as work-site stuff. No matter how carefully our discussions were done, and no matter that we hung around their labs, we could only get that stuff as stories for the professional folks back home.

(2) What did our incompetence consist of?

Issues were posed and distractions were introduced by everyone replacing examinable practices with glosses. Troubles were assured because we had to obtain, by talking with scientists, descriptions of discovering practices that are distinctive to the practitioner's particular science. But these descriptions need to satisfy the requirement of descriptive precision.[40]

However, four conditions of practitioners' work are omnirelevant to their work that we were not able to satisfy:

1. We cannot be taken seriously.
2. We cannot satisfy the unique adequacy requirement of methods by what we know of the discipline's practices.
3. We are not capable of teaching the local gang of practitioners their practices in and as of teaching's work-sites of *their* science particularly.
4. We are not capable of reproducing for and with the local gang their practices in and as of *smoothly* embodied, and locally, essentially occasionally emplaced, equipmentally affiliated, interactions "skills."[41]

42   Respecifying the natural sciences

To summarize our incompetence: We were unable to reproduce their phenomena as local, interactionally instructed actions, and, in and as those instructed actions exhibit their reproduction as locally teachable details★.

(3) The idea in TALKING the contingencies. And our incessant local problem was to get practitioners to teach us what we could be talking about with which we would thereby be teaching them as well

- We didn't do *interviews* of lab scientists.
- We presented them with *unmotivated observables*.
- A standing thematic point to a discussion was "tell me what I'm talking about," i.e., *only by telling me*, teach me what I'm talking about.

We offer further elaboration of these with the following relevancies and cautions that accompanied them.

(i) In 1959 Saul Mendlovitz and HG, together were going through a schedule of questions with the Dean of Harvard Law School, asking him how he went about writing an article for the Law Review. Mendlovitz, with a law degree from the University of Chicago, and at Harvard Law School on a fellowship, couldn't risk asking questions of the Dean if the Dean could assume he knew the answers. HG, a sociologist, *could* ask "dumb" questions with no risk. So HG asked the questions, and, where it seemed called for, Mendlovitz explained what H had in mind.

(ii) From a respondent's glances and side remarks during discussions[42] we often find we are talking better than we know, in unknown ways, "by rote."

(iii) Lynch[43] has described the differing relevancies to the local gang in requests that they receive from "tourists," "novices," "visitors," "adversarial rivals," "collegial rivals" and other "social types" when local members of a lab seek to describe "what we do here and how we do it."

(4) The crux of our task was to specify the discovering sciences with work-site unmotivated observables

The crux of our task was to specify the discovering sciences with the *unmotivated observables*[44] of work-site equipment, places, architecture, methods, persons, skills, shop work, and shop talk. We think of unmotivated observables as something like achievedly, specifically unremarkable and indispensable work-site details of shop work and shop talk that are interactionally known to and are mutually required of the local gang, that no one in his right mind would dare to call attention to.

To specify the discovering sciences with unmotivated observables is the crux of our task: It is the crux of our procedures; the crux of cautions and difficulties in administering the coat hangers; the crux of the news that administering★ the contingencies delivers; and, with respect to our procedures, the crux of our craft glossed as "analytic ethnography."

(5) Various "relativities" accompany the administered★ schedule of coat hangers

It is important to note that the contingencies that make up the schedule are not simply semiotically available. They do not "refer" to phenomena. Neither do they "represent" the phenomena that they are "used" conversationally to "speak of." They are not "appresentationally paired"[45] with phenomena. They are not signs, symbols, marks, or indicators of objects. They do not "reference" objects. They are not constituent elements of sign functions.

Similarly the contingencies are not available as of the coherence★ and cogency★ of details as *representations* of details. They are conversational "coat hangers." Speaking in procedural specifics, various "relativities" accompany their use. Thus, the following different "performative" meanings of "I don't know what I'm doing" were encountered.

(i) HG introduced the second meeting with T.C. like this: "I'm going to speak about various contingencies of the day's work, and specify each with a story. Tell me, from the details of your actual experiences in your lab, what I'm really talking about."
(ii) The unique adequacy requirement of methods.
(iii) We *were* not taken seriously by the scientists we talked to and we *cannot* be taken seriously.
(iv) HG's experience with U.M watching movie videos. The following is an excerpt from HG's notes.
U.M. writes a column for *Cash Box*, a trade journal in the record industry.[16] I had taken up his offer to give me a guided tour through an afternoon of movie videos. In order to find matters to comment on in the video clips, and while we're watching, I'm explaining to him some work-site advice that is used in the advertising industry, "make it look like what it is." I'm suggesting that this work-site advice in making video commercials might hold in making movie videos. I'm suggesting, too, that if it does hold, then that one crew member is giving that advice to another, or that it is enforced as the work-site maxim are tied to in-house issues of manageable, recurrent and stable, cost-accountable operations of the producing company, and of course there are ties of those issues to the vicissitudes of the market. In his replies to my remarks U.M. acknowledges the cogency and the correctness of my remarks,

---

16 *Cash Box* was a weekly music industry trade magazine from 1942 until 1996. After a ten-year lapse, it was revived as an online publication, www.cashboxmagazine.com/.

thanks me for new angles, etc. in re: what is seeable by him in and about the witnessed video episodes. But *I* don't see and I *can't* see, I'm not *able* to see anything in the clips of what I'm talking about. Moreover, I wouldn't know where in the clips to look for it or where to find its details. I can't see what I'm talking about that's going on before my eyes. Yet I don't *need* to see what I'm talking about in order to be making praiseworthy observations, probative remarks, serious suggestions for his future columns, etc. I'm *teaching* him to see what's going on as the industry's cogent details, visibly, and on screen. But I have no idea what it looks like.

(v) Finding, recognizing, following up, teaching, being taught and learning what we are talking about – i.e. talking plain English – by glossing.[46]

To summarize:

(1) The coat hangers are talking about discipline specific practices in and as of work-site details, but their definiteness of sense and reference in these respects is only available relative to the local, discipline-specific vernacular of shop practices and shop talk.
(2) Actual practices were glossed by our list of descriptors, by our stories, and by our discussions of the contingencies.
(3) Talk *about* contingencies masked the strong relativizing conditions or recognition in, and as talk *about*, the following: the contingencies are not interchangeable between disciplines.
(4) The "relativities" accompany the use of the coat hangers unavoidably, and without remedy or alternative (i.e., "essentially"). More consequentially, the relativities accompany the use of the coat hangers *e-wise*.[47]

[7] A singularly cogent contingency: "What are the contingencies for?"

(A) Having heard us describe the contingencies, Agre, understanding that he had a rival enterprise, was pleased to charge us with a fatal error: "You missed the point! What are the contingencies for?" Having demanded it of us, Agre answered with the vicissitudes of his own project in mind: shop floor contingencies were relevant to the tasks at work-site of providing with them just what about his project's details he collected and understood as "constraints on the truth of the matter." From his experience and reflections, Agre insisted, the contingencies of the work-site were variously relevant to, composed of, pointed to, offered sometimes opaque sometimes lucid messages about, the local, unavoidable work of addressing and overcoming "constraints on the truth of the matter." Agre understood the point we missed as this: Nowhere in the specifics of the contingencies that we described was provision made for "constraints on the truth of the matter."

Although we disagree with him we shall speak of the last contingency with his demand. When, for a particular science, his demand is specified and answered, it gathers and exhibits the others as specifics of a coherent phenomenon.

(B) It is true that we made no mention of "constraints on the truth of the matter." But throughout, and repeatedly, we emphasized the intractability of local, work-site specifically produced phenomena. Under his goading, and thanks to him, and with his permission, we'll claim that we took the intractability of the locally produced phenomena to be what the contingencies are for. We understood by the intractability of the phenomenon the contingencies of only locally producing the phenomenon as an instructed action, and of instructably reproducing the phenomenon for another next first time.

What are the contingencies for? *That* contingency is indeed a practitioner's work-site demand. *That* contingency is indeed demanded by practitioners not *at* work-site *as* a demand found at work-site, but a demand that *is* (i.e., it is identical with, it is as of) an unavoidable and changing work-site detail★. We take the point of *our* interest in the contingencies to be identical with the work-site interests of practitioners in the contingencies. We learn from bench scientists that the contingencies, as of work-site details★, are not constraints on the truth of the matter. *They are locally lived constraints on the instructable reproduction of the phenomenon.*

So we set aside Agre's answer. We shall remain indifferent to his claim, because we find, in contrary opposition to it, the relevance of the contingencies to the task at work-site of providing with them, as practitioners provide with them, and which they cannot avoid or escape or arrange time out from providing with them constraints on the real time★ teachability of the local gang's work-site, science-specific skills, and as constraints on the local gang's real time instructable reproducibility of the phenomenon. So, with the highest respect for Agre's alternative, we replace "constraints on the truth of the matter" with the "praxeological validity of instructed actions". We make this replacement because "constraints on the truth of the matter" are nowhere ever available to the local gang's work-site's inspectable and therein inexorable work-site details★ whereas their bench affairs are everywhere, with inexhaustible density done, witnessed, examined for, exhibiting of, and inhabited, inescapably, with the "praxeological validity of instructed actions."

It is because practitioners must do so that *we* must make a lot of the relevance of contingencies as constraints on the local, shop floor, real time★ teachability of work-site skills, and on the local real time★ teachability of work-site skills, and on the local real time★ instructable reproducibility of the phenomenon.

(C) Given our insistence on the policies of (B) we must pose the following questions for ourselves about the contingencies-in-and-as-a-science-distinctively – those contingencies being the prize we are after.

Do the contingencies that we have discussed with the use of the schedule of contingencies specify constraints on the instructable reproduction of the phenomenon?

46 Respecifying the natural sciences

Are the contingencies that we have described science-specific constraints on the instructable reproduction of the phenomenon? Are the contingencies that we have described *distinctive* constraints on the instructable reproduction of the object?

(D) For *us*, for Livingston, Lynch, Macbeth, Robillard, and Garfinkel, to answer these questions requires of us:

  (1) That we know the science we're talking about. To answer this question *with actual materials* requires that we can be taken seriously.
  (2) It requires that in our use of methods we satisfy the unique adequacy requirement of methods.
  (3) It requires that we exhibit the analyzability of the instructed actions (i.e. the phenomena) of the particular science as the details★ of work-site-specific teachability, and being addressed in that way to the phenomena of a particular science as its practical achievements, i.e. as its achievements of practical actions, that we upgrade the craft for the local gang.
  (4) It requires that we exhibit the analyzability of the phenomenon as the work-site details of its instructable reproduction.

But we can't meet any of these requirements. Thus we have a collection of dissatisfactions.

They are disclosed when we ask, as we must ask, and as we cannot avoid asking: Given (A), (B), (C), and (D), what are the contingencies for *that saying so can settle*?!

We recall that for a science particularly, in and as of distinctive technical details, the contingencies make up the day's work; they are only locally witnessable; this is so in ways that can only be found out and cannot be imagined; they are only locally witnessable as first-person by-hands-on-witnessable-work-site stuff; and then they are only locally witnessable on the local gang's behalf; and at the work-site they specify the obstinacy and the recalcitrance of the objects to instructable reproduction. We were reminded of these by having to reply to Agre. What we had been calling the obstinacy and recalcitrance of objects is identical with the *in situ* instructable reproduction of the phenomenon, *in situ, as an instructed action*. It is identical with the reproducibility of the phenomenon for another next first time in and as an instructed action.

We ask again: Given (A), (B), (C), and (D), what are the contingencies for *that saying so can settle*?

1. Given (A), (B), (C), and (D), saying so can settle nothing of what the contingencies are for. Saying so can *provide for* nothing that is *demonstrably* the case about what the contingencies are for.
2. *This holds wherever it is the case and holds without the possibility of remedy or alternative if the analyst is incompetent with the science he describes.* ("Incompetence" means that the analyst cannot satisfy the conditions described before in (D).)
3. This holds whether or not the analyst is competent, if the contingencies and the phenomena are provided for as literary objects.[48]

Respecifying the natural sciences   47

4. This holds if the analyst *is* competent, under any and all attempts to provide for the work-site teachability and reproducibility of the phenomenon with classic methods and as the details of a classic science.
5. Yet another dissatisfaction with "analytic ethnography" is that details* are unavailable, and cannot be witnessed, inspected, recovered, taught, or reproduced except as *a sense* of detail*.[49]

[8] A summary of dissatisfactions

Having provided for the work of a discovering science through the methods and as the findings of analytic ethnography we encountered several dissatisfactions. We tried to pinpoint dissatisfactions that cannot be avoided and are without remedy, and demonstrably so. To develop these dissatisfactions we started with the problem that we are trying to solve with the use of the contingencies: to learn as *in situ* details* of a particular natural science, that and just how work-site contingencies of its teachability and its inquiries specify that science as a distinctive discovering science of practical action.

We summarize our dissatisfactions as the following findings.

(1) The strongest case we can hope to make with the contingencies by administering* the coat hangers would be the case of a discovering science specified and elaborated as a merely reasoned and merely documented exposition of themes.
(2) Specifying the work of a discovering science as a merely reasoned and merely documented exposition of themes consists of this: issues of cogency* and coherence* of details are not dealt with as inspectables of discovering work. Instead they are only and unavoidably available in and as *a sense* of discovering work. That result is unavoidable if the analyst is incompetent.
(3) That *sense* is specified as of a signed object[50] and its properties.
(4) Discovering work, given in, and specifiable as, *a sense* of discovering work, ignores essentially[51] the cogency* and coherence* of locally produced, naturally organized and naturally accountable details*. On the same grounds the phenomena of a science that areas of those details* are not recoverable. On the same grounds, *that* they are not recoverable is unavoidably and irremediably the case.
(5) They are essentially unavailable to ethnography. More strongly claimed, they are *e-wise* unavailable to ethnography.

In light of these findings several procedures of "analytic ethnography" take on their specifics as the practical actions they consist of: (i) The coat hangers were administered* in discussions with practicing scientists with laboratory experience. (ii) With regard to issues of recognition, relevance, cogency, detail, facticity, etc. the coat hangers are Mooersian descriptors. (iii) We had undertaken as our task to specify the discovering sciences with the *unmotivated observables** of work-site equipment, places, architecture, methods, persons, histories, shop work, shop talk, etc.

[9] A second attempt to explain "sciences of practical actions" by detailing generalities

The following points make up the second of two attempts in this article to explain "Sciences of Practical Action." The first attempt will be found in the section, *Program and Policies*, pages 21 to 26. This try is not better than the first one. Like the first it pretends to describe a practice by detailing generalities. The only adequate explanation comes with, and after the Galileo studies in Collections III, IV, V, and VI.[17] Only with material cases of the actual natural science are we able to, *can* we, specify *the structures of practical action. That's the animal*. The present article only states to problem of specifying the discovering sciences, gives it a setting, examines a hands-on analytic ethnography, and announces an alternative.

For a particular natural science, and for that science distinctively, its discovered and discoverable phenomena are specified as only discovered and only discoverable structures of practical action. These are not available in the following generics and they cannot be recovered from them.

(1) The work must put up with the intractability of its phenomena. The work can never fail to suffer the constraints of the recalcitrance and perversity of its phenomena.

These constraints are suffered without the possibility of remedying them with time out, promises, postponement, evasion, sell outs, say-so's, hiding places, or word play. Curiously, only work-site phenomena in the natural sciences can betray the urgencies of publication, importance, schedule, sponsorship, funding, cleverness, place, praise, or friendships; and more curiously, these betrayals cannot be prespecified.

(2) To accompany its intractability (recalcitrance) (perversity) the phenomenon is done in detail★; it is done only as of what detail★ could possibly be; it is done only in and as of cogent★ and coherent★ detail★.

(3) The phenomenon is done in and as of technical detail★ that offers itself to inexhaustible, further, specifying exploration. Therein the phenomenon is "done" in and as of "detail★ really"; "detail★ actually and not supposedly"; "detail★ evidently"; and these ordinarily.

(4) The phenomenon is reproducibly the case for whosoever. It is reproducibly the case anonymously with respect to particular persons and singular authorship but *only with the full quiddity of its local production and natural accountability*. The phenomenon is to be gotten out of just *this* equipment, and out of just *these* instruments, in just *this* place, in *just* the time at hand with just *these* people;

(5) *to make the phenomenon reproducibly the case*.

(6) Yet not only reproducibly the case, but *instructably reproducibly the case*

---

17 These "Collections" were not published or completed as outlined in Appendix 4. However, a chapter on efforts to perform, or at least mock up, Galileo's inclined plane demonstration of a free-falling body is included as Chapter 9 of Garfinkel (2002).

(7) in all quiddative details, and in every respect of the quiddity of its local production.[52]
(8) For the bench scientist the animal he is searching for, the sought after "discovery," the only-discoverable phenomenon, is a phenomenon that is instructably reproducible for another next first time. The animal to be searched out is the unavoidable and irremediable relevance of reproducing the phenomenon for another next first time, doing so as of the instructable quiddity of the phenomenon's local production,
(9) and all of (1) through (8), without the possibility of avoidance or remedy, is only come upon first time through[18]
(10) in embodiedly real time★.
(11) We shall borrow a metaphor from Merleau-Ponty who spoke of the chiasm of "body and the world."[53] WE shall use the chiasm as a characterizing gloss of embodied, local, interactional, equipmentally affiliated practices lives as the phenomenon's locally produced, naturally accountable, cogent★ and coherent★ details★.
(12) Finally, all of these, (1) through (11), are achievedly unremarkable.

[10] A synopsis of the argument restated by calling ahead upon the finished seven collections of studies for a point of view

This article announces a program and policies of ethnomethodological studies directed to respecifying the natural sciences as discovering sciences of practical action. It does so by reporting the first two of seven collections of studies in that program. In this chapter the procedures and results of using ethnomethodologically motivated methods of analytic ethnography to carry out this program are described. The respecification was done ethnographically by administering a schedule of contingencies in discussions with laboratory scientists in several natural sciences and by hanging around their laboratories.

Work-site contingencies in the natural sciences were collected and examined. "Losing the phenomenon," "wasting time," "making an experiment work," "the dread of and provisions for demonically wild contingencies," "settling an issue" are examples. The contingencies specify a discovering science as the local, unavoidably and irremediably relevant and unremarkably observable details of the local gang's real time, work-site teachability of discipline-specific skills, and the instructable reproducibility of discipline-specific phenomena.

In our discussions the contingencies were called "coat hangers" with which to emphasize, for us and for the scientists we talked with, that we sought to specify

---

18 Garfinkel et al. (1981: 134) discuss the theme of "first time through" in relation to "discovering work" with observatory equipment, which took place at Kitt Peak Observatory in Arizona in 1969, when two astronomers and an observatory night assistant were credited with the first discovery of an optical pulsar. "Discovering work" is the central topic for a series of seminars that Garfinkel convened in 1980, which are reproduced in edited form in Part II.

the contingencies when we did not know the science we were asking about (or *any* natural science). We could not recognize, watch and follow, read, teach, or reproduce the practice we sought through discussions to specify. More, we *were* not and we *could* not be taken seriously by the scientists who we asked to teach us what we were really talking about, as they recognized what we were really talking about in their work affairs, by *telling* us *about* the contingencies of their bench work – in detail. Local and interactional details of these discussions were collected and glossed as administering★ the schedule. A phenomenon in its own right, administering★ the schedule yielded the details of discovering work of a science as a *sense* of discovering work's details. That *sense* of work-site details was specified as properties of a signed object. We call that object a "profusion of themes."

We report several general results.

(1) The procedure and findings of administering★ the schedule are those of analytic ethnography.
(2) When analytic ethnography is used to specify discovering work in the natural sciences strong★ dissatisfactions accompany its practices and findings. The dissatisfactions are essentially unavoidable and are essentially without remedy.

These results were obtained as follows.

Administering★ the schedule of contingencies is a gloss for local interactional particulars that we collected from our taped discussions when, in light of the requirement in our study that *lab scientists and we teach each other coherent and cogent details of THEIR work*, these particulars were examined as our inquiries' adequate details. These particulars were collected and presented in the following topics:

(A) Procedural specifics in administering★ the schedule of contingencies.
(B) Four identifying details of the "local gang" of practitioners' work-site competence.
(C) Our standing task was to get practitioners to teach us what we could be talking about, given that in the details of work-site science-specific competence these consist of unmotivated observables.
(D) We are not practitioners of the sciences we discussed. For us several distinct meaning of "I don't know what we are talking about" accompanied the administered schedule of coat hangers.

Given these particulars, and in their light, we pose the question: In any actual case of discovering work, just what *can* be settled by "saying so"?

In order to answer this question, we first ask: What *needs* to be settled? From results obtained in the studies of Collections III, IV, V, and VI we show that what needs to be settled are instructably reproducible phenomena *specified as discovered structures of practical action*. These structures of practical action technically are both adequate and distinctive to a particular science.

That these *need* to be settled are principal research problems of studies taken up in Collections III through VII. These collections report and examine discovered structures of practical action for Gödel's proof and for selected theorems in Euclidean geometry, based on the work of Eric Livingston, and for Galileo's inclined plane demonstration of invariants in the motion of bodies in free fall [see Garfinkel 2002, Chapter 9]. Cases of discovered structures of practical action are (i) *Lebenswelt* pairs in mathematics, and in Galilean physics; (ii) instructions that consist of first segments of *Lebenswelt* Pairs in *Euclid's Elements*, in laboratory exercises in introductory chemistry, and in Robillard and Pack's corpus of instructions and medical curricula for medical students and residents in pediatrics at Michigan State University;[54] (iii) six rendering theorems; (iv) the "classically" accountable natural science of Galilean physics; (v) the phenomenal field of interchangeable details for Galilean inclined plane experimental demonstration of the motion of free falling bodies; (vi) classically accountable contingencies of the lecture demonstration of Galileo's inclined plane demonstration of invariants in the phenomena of free falling bodies respecified as properties of the phenomenal field of that experiment.

By referring to our experience of administering★ the schedule of contingencies we are able to ask: In *any* actual case of discovering work, what *can* be settled by "saying so"? Given what needs to be settled, answers are stated in the following theorems:

Theorem I: Of discovering work's details really and of these details evidently, and of these achieved details done locally and ordinarily, *nothing*. Analytic ethnography can provide for nothing that is *demonstrably* the case about contingencies.

"Done locally" is an abbreviation of "done locally, locally occasioned, naturally and reflexively accountable, and in all these respects ordinarily." Theorem I reads: "Of discovering work's details really and of these details evidently, and of these achieved details done locally, locally occasioned, and naturally and reflexively accountable, and in all these respects ordinarily, nothing."

This argument of Theorem I is *inserted* in Theorems II, III, and IV by using the italicized *Theorem I* as an abbreviating prefix.

Theorem II: *Theorem I* holds wherever it is the case that the analyst is incompetent with the science he describes. In that case it holds without the possibility of remedy or alternative. ("Incompetence" means that the analyst cannot satisfy the conditions described before in (B) "Four identifying details of the 'local gang' of practitioners' work-site competence.")

Theorem III: *Theorem I* holds if the analyst *is* competent, under any attempts to provide for the real time work-site teachability of skills and instructable reproducibility of the phenomenon with classic methods or as the details of a classic science★.

To summarize: we are able to specify strong dissatisfactions with our efforts, and with any efforts, that provide for the work of a discovering science through the methods and as the findings of analytic ethnography. By strong dissatisfactions is meant dissatisfactions specified by the conditions of their occurrence as phenomena that are essentially unavoidable and are essentially without remedy.[55]

The strongest case we can hope to make with ethnographically described contingencies exhibits the particulars of discovering work as a *sense* of practices. That sense of practices is found in stories to tell professional folks back home.

When, with the results in view, we recapitulate our program's aims, we obtain the following further results: (1) The maneuver discloses what the adequacy of this study of the work of a natural science consists of. (2) It discloses, too, that that adequacy is answerable to teaching the craft in real time★ instructable reproduction of phenomena for the local gang. (3) From this maneuver we see that in *any* studies of the natural sciences in which the real-world existence of a particular science is relevantly topical, *only* this adequacy counts. (4) From this maneuver we see that this adequacy was at stake in our study.

This adequacy is at stake in the studies that remain to be reported. These make up Collections III, IV, V, VI, and VII [see Appendix 4].

APPENDIX 1

Postscript and preface

Harold Garfinkel

What is this article on the natural sciences doing in a volume dedicated to talk and structure? We would want the article to be understood like this.[1]

Latter day CA which, since Harvey Sacks' death,[2] insists upon coded turns' sequentially organized ways of speaking of talk and structure, makes talk out as structure's mandarins: ruling it, insiders to everything that counts, dreaming science, all dignity,

---

1 As noted in the editor's introduction to the present volume, Garfinkel originally drafted the manuscript as an article to be published in a volume edited by Deirdre Boden and Don Zimmerman (eventually published in 1991, with the title *Talk and Social Structure*). As Garfinkel makes abundantly evident in this appendix, his vision of ethnomethodology was deeply at odds with the emphasis on "talk" in the title – an emphasis that carried through much of the Boden and Zimmerman volume – and a dispute with the editors led to his withdrawal of the article. Several years later (in approximately 1993), Garfinkel wrote an undated note, that he proposed as "a revision of the 'postscript and preface,'" which read, in part:

> Studies that are done with the policies and methods of canonical conversation analysis (hereafter referred to as CA) are specifically excepted from the EM corpus. For many years CA authors and EM authors have recognized that although and somehow their studies are massively agreed they are somehow and just as massively incommensurable. In no actual case of methods, policies, problems, findings, results, worksites, examinations, or pedagogies in specifics are they comparable, let alone interchangeable. CA studies are easily recognized by their authors to have everything to do with formal analytic studies in social psychology, communication studies, sociology, and sociolinguistics. EM and canonical CA are distinct disciplines. The two disciplines exhibit their occupation with locally produced, naturally accountable orderlinesses of everyday activities as two incommensurable, asymmetrically alternate technologies of social analysis and their relationships. Their relationships of asymmetric alternativity among which is the primordiality of EM are specified with the rendering theorems.

I'm grateful to Clemens Eisenmann for alerting me to this note from the Garfinkel archive in Newburyport, Massachusetts, and to Anne Rawls and Jason Turowetz for their help in finding the note and permitting it to be used here.

2 Sacks, the founder of Conversation Analysis (CA), died in an automobile accident in 1975.

pedantic, and corporately correct. These ways make talk out as really the just what all concerns with structure could have been about, and, to the point of these remarks, the just what ethnomethodological concerns with structure could have been about.

This note recommends a corrective.

Early in ethnomethodological studies, talk showed its relevance and found its development but *not* as the "We finally found topically where we can work and get results." Instead, through and through, talk has been topical as part of an array of phenomena that exhibit ethnomethodology's standing interest in the concertedly achieved and witnessable objectivity and observability of practical action and practical organizational reasoning. In these enterprises of research and teaching by ethnomethodologists, talk is only one member in a company of objects. The title to this volume leaves the impression that talk is the *sine qua non* of what ethnomethodological interests could possibly be.[3] Our article, in its concerns with science, speaks in part to the task of correcting that impression. It is a reminder to readers not to take the mandarin concerns with talk seriously as all or even interestingly what ethnomethodologists could be speaking of in seeking to make discoverable as practical action familiar society really, actually, and evidently.

Our article is a reminder. At the same time it *is* a study of the sciences – the natural sciences. What could be both a reminder and interesting about that? This. What ethnomethodologists have been studying in various real settings as locally produced, naturally accountable organizational things really, actually, evidently, comparably, reproducibly, and these in uniquely adequate detail of social facts as the most ordinary things in the world, come home to roost in stuff of the natural sciences. The ethnomethodological study of the sciences has been perspicuous, proving itself to be a collector of these phenomena.

A paragraph by Livingston introduces one of them.[4] In the course of explicating his findings in mathematics, he points out that the affairs of work-site proving that he describes are unspoken and yet *they are identical with* the curriculum of graduate mathematicians. Livingston's epitome collects for comparisons the findings by ethnomethodologists of a profession's work-site specific unspoken curricula in other sciences and professions: Robillard and Pack for interns and residents in pediatrics at Michigan State University;[5] Robillard and Robillard for training health counselors and mental health counselors from indigenous populations of Oceania to return to those populations;[6] Lynch for neurological diagnosis at UCLA;[7] Burns

---

[3] Garfinkel is referring to the title of Boden and Zimmerman's (1991) volume, *Talk and Social Structure* (see note 1).

[4] Garfinkel apparently is referring to Livingston (1986).

[5] Garfinkel did not provide citations or references to the studies by Albert B. Robillard or Christopher Pack, two former students of his who conducted studies in the pediatrics unit of Michigan State University Hospital. A later publication that may have drawn upon the research Garfinkel mentions is Robillard (1994).

[6] The study by Robillard and Robillard is very likely related to research published in the edited volume, Robillard (1992).

[7] Apparently, this is a reference to Lynch (1984).

for first-termers in civil procedure at Yale Law School;[8] Liberman for Scholarly debates of Tibetan monks on topics from texts of medieval Tibetan Buddhism;[9] and Wieder for professional performances of tricks and illusions.[10] Each of these studies is a study of talk, not however of the functionalist talk at work,[11] but talk-in-and-as-of-work's details* of a particular profession or a particular science. In each case, material detail* of professionals' talk inhabits the unspoken curriculum as a heavily consequential uniquely adequate competence of their work lives.

A second issue can be recommended if we recall that this article consists of studies I and II of a series of seven on the sciences.[12] Why the sciences? Phil Agre faced us unavoidably with the question: After listening to our recitation of work-site contingencies he found our findings questionable. "In your description of the contingencies you have missed the point. After all, what are the contingencies for?" Then, on the basis of his own research, he advised us that the work-site contingencies that he encounters in his attempts to devise a computable representation of practical action "provide constraints on the truth of the matter." We embedded Agre's question into the conduct of our studies and by doing so introduced the potential of a consequential dispute bearing specifically on the nature of discovering work in the natural sciences.

We could not avoid Agre's question. Therein it was indispensable for our studies. But although his question assured a dispute, it did not settle the terms of the dispute. What is consequential about the dispute are new *phenomena*. Named with strange phrases these phenomena are the terms of the dispute: detail*; the properties of a phenomenon's local production; that the properties of local production include the on-going achievement's natural accountability; the hybrid ethnomethodology/mathematics and ethnomethodology/Galilean physics; asterisked topics of order*; the praxeological validity of instructed action; sciences *of* practical action; ticked bracketed phenomena; classic studies; classic methods of studies; classic science of mathematics; constructive analysis; signed object; the rendering theorem, {[   ]} —>(   ); the locally achieved, locally occasioned coherence of objects; the ethnomethodological understanding of Aron Gurwitsch's seminal finding in his transcendental phenomenological examination of the received Gestalt theory of form: "Saliency of a group

---

8   Garfinkel apparently is referring to an unpublished paper (Burns 1986). A later publication on the topic of law school pedagogy is Burns (1997).
9   A book based on the study is Liberman (2004).
10 D. Lawrence Wieder never published his phenomenological investigation of stage magic tricks, but he did present talks based on the study, such as Wieder (1989).
11 This remark was possibly a reference to the title *Talk at Work* (Drew and Heritage 1992), a volume that was published a few years later but which, like the Boden and Zimmerman volume, promoted studies of "institutional talk" – applications of CA to talk in medical, legal, and other organizational settings. Such studies were well underway at the time Garfinkel wrote the present manuscript. By referring to such studies as "functionalist," he may have been alluding to the way studies of "institutional talk" treated courtroom interrogation, doctor-patient interaction, teacher-student interaction, news interviews, and so forth, as instrumental actions oriented to the goals of the respective institutions.
12 See Appendix 4.

of data so that this group emerges and segregates itself from the stream (of experience) is a feature not introduced into the stream, but yielded by the stream itself."[13]

Unfortunately, there is no place in this article to develop these topics. In Appendices II and III one of these topics, detail★, is annotated. Endnote 12 [pp. 83-87] discusses the topics of Pair and *Lebenswelt* Pair, and endnote 15 [pp. 87-89] the properties of local production and natural accountability of the evidential proof of Gödel's theorem.

Do not imagine that our study is to be taken straightforwardly as a study of science. To be sure, it *is* a study of science, but in the ways it is a study of science it is this: the straightforward stuff of a science, and of a particular science distinctively, comes home to roost as the phenomena named above with strange phrases. These are locally and reflexively achieved, locally occasioned, naturally accountable phenomena. They are brought to adequate specification out of lived shop floor "streams" of lived instructably reproducible phenomena. And this stuff, spoken of in these ways of the natural sciences, but only with the particulars of each science distinctively, specifies a science of practical action.

The phenomena we have discussed – the unspoken curricula, and the stuff of a science, stuff with strange names – point with the particulars of each to workings of immortal ordinary society that is more, other, and different than classic analytic explications of signed objects provide and can provide.

The stuff above, *for each science distinctively*, picks up such topics as objective knowledge, doing science by talking science, evidence, proof, generality, detail, real, reason, reasoned discourse, rational action, methods of study, rules, and instructions, but remains indifferent to them and even uninterested in them as departmentally taught topics of social science and intellectual history.

Instead, there is the curious business of finding as a resource with which to specify any of these topics the *authority of a particular science distinctively*, finding, too, with each science that the authority is both claimed as and accorded a *deserved* authority. But at *that* point the topics of evidence, proof, transcendental methods, universal results, objective knowledge, are lifted out of the discourse of classic studies and intellectual history. They are removed from talk in generics of Science, of The Sciences, of Scientific Method, of The Unity of the Sciences, of Adequate Theories of Good Science, or of A Central Method that Recovers All Actual Cases of Methodic Procedure, and no longer have anything seriously to do with them. For example, for the bench scientists and ethnomethodologists, evidence is no longer interestingly Evidence speaking in generalities and universally, but is evidence locally achieved and locally occasioned, witnessed, recognized, and understood in and as of a particular science distinctively in work-site specific coherence of detail★. Not findable without talk, but not in the talk, *that* evidence is *found* and is *given*, not and never as topics of mandarin's talk, but embodied, work-site specific, instructably reproducible genetic sequences and flying machines.

Consider the change.

The gorgeous topics of logic, reason, meaning, method, order, and of course the topics of a natural science, are around as specifically, unavoidably and unremarkable

---

13 Quotation from Gurwitsch (1964: 31); originally in italics.

achievements of members' ordinary lives together. Egon Bittner pointed out that these plain creatures – i.e., reason-, rules-, evidence-, demonstration-, each with its suffix – in-and-as-the-work-of-the-streets, went away to college and came back educated. After the Greeks you'd never recognize them.[14]

Ethnomethodologists have come upon the ways that members, *living* as they do, are producing the deep orderlinesses as of which the most ordinary organizational things of their everyday lives consist. According to policy, an academically fragile policy, these orderlinesses are only but always discoverably the case. A glimpse has been caught of what achieved organizational social facts the natural sciences and objective knowledge could be. Already studies in hand show that these could be come upon on behalf of practitioners, for their sakes, for more, other, different, and better than the celebrants of science have ever but only so thoughtfully imagined it.

Wherever natural sciences have been done they have been matters for epiphany. If its celebrants were from Athens the revelation of truth in the world could be found in the achievements of deep thinkers. If they were from Manchester the revelation of truth was to be found in the labs and factories.[56][15] On one matter both agreed: whether in the universals of thoughtful proofs or in the mysterious effectiveness of crafts and shop techniques the revelation of truth in the world was not to be searched for already in and as of the deepest, most familiar, most unremarkable lived possession of ordinary everyday activities. It was not to be found in and as local work-site achievements of the most ordinary organizational things in the world, in detail, for everything that the organizational thing was really, actually, evidently; and in each instructably reproducible phenomenon distinctively and uniquely, everything that detail and the coherence of objects *could* possibly be.

Ethnomethodological studies of the sciences offer the researchable possibility that the agreement between Athenians and Mancunians, like other achievements of practical action, is normally thoughtless.

---

14 Garfinkel's citation to Bittner here did not include any further information, and to my knowledge it was a personal comment.
15 See Garfinkel's endnote 56 [p. 93]. Gould (1988) discussed Freeman Dyson, *Infinite in All Directions* (Harper & Row, 1988), and singled out Dyson's essay "Manchester and Athens" for special praise for the way it used the two cities separated by millennia to contrast basic styles of science: the Athenian search for abstract unity beneath appearances versus the Mancunian attunement to materially diverse particulars available to hands-on exploration.

APPENDIX 2

Some notes on the play of basketball in its circumstantial detail

Douglas Macbeth

(Revised from previously published version: Macbeth [2012] "Some Notes on the Play of Basketball in Its Circumstantial Detail, and an Introduction to Their Occasion," *Human Studies* 35: 193–208.)

Introduction

These notes on the play of basketball were written around 1987, prompted by a conversation with Harold Garfinkel where the talk turned to a topic central to his program and corpus. One could imagine several instructive formulations of EM's program; this one is identifying, uncompromising, and so disruptive of the normative consensus of social science as to be inadmissible. My impression is that for many, and for some time, it was.

It has to do with ethnomethodology's [EM] treatment of the relations of local order to "formal structure." The rub begins with how modern social science and its precursors wrote the genealogy of local order – the presenting world of everyday life as any 5th grader or her parents might encounter it – in terms of distal structure. The disposition is venerable and deeply cultural. The seen is only a stand-in for the unseen hands that shape it. Whether by the work of pantheons, hegemonic complicities, or discursive formations, the seen is rendered a veiled expression of the un-seen, and at once, an analytic task is delivered: the unveiling.

The logic assigns an essential incompleteness to evident worlds. They cannot themselves account for the order, structure, and recurrence they evidence at every glance, and finding those things (order and the rest) elsewhere organizes the diverse forms of formal analysis (whose elsewheres are no less diverse: ideology, power, structure, agency, identity, "practices," alongside more conventional accounts of rules, roles and their internalizations).

The phrase "formal analysis" is familiar in Garfinkel's corpus over the last 40 years, and especially in his more recent writings and publications (Garfinkel

1996, 2002; Garfinkel and Wieder 1992; see Garfinkel and Sacks 1970, and Lynch 2019 on formal structures). We find throughout not only a critique of the formal analytic premise and promise, but a clearly formulated alternate: order, structure and recurrence, like meaning itself, are endogenous productions. Their evidence and accountability are occasioned. And as with every discernment of a distant landscape, we find these things by local reckonings.

Meaning leads the finding – order, structure and recurrence follow – and though apparently easily missed, once seen, the work and achievements of common understanding are ubiquitous (Moerman and Sacks 1988 [1971]). Meaning underwrites intersubjective worlds, and common understanding – "shared agreement" (Garfinkel 1967: 30) – is meaning's work and achievement. When we set out to examine the evidence, we find the endlessly occasioned work of understanding's production. Common understanding is foundational to order and structure, though a kind of foundation that does not run "deep." Rather, it runs wide, and relentlessly, and at all points (Sacks 1984a, 1984b).

These are familiar EM programmatics, and they have nothing to do with indeterminacy or the vagaries of interpretation or transcendental categories. EM is writing instead on behalf of structure's occasioned achievements as "ordinary organizational things" (Garfinkel 2002). It is this *other* genealogy of formal structure that EM has been writing for these last 50 years. It is about how regularity evidences structure, and how regularity, like meaning itself, is occasioned. There is no time out from these production tasks (as we see in Sacks et al. 1974, and Sacks 1988/1989), no relief from the in vivo analysis of turn taking whether in rush-hour traffic or conversation. Within these fields of action's practical grammars of temporal and circumstantial detail, structure's evidences are the yield. In this way, structure is the yield of communitarian practice.

By these understandings, there is nothing contrarian about local order and social structure. Instead, the argument re-locates structure's provenance: rather than distal, structure is a local assemblage too. The argument is replete in Garfinkel's corpus. In his 1996 remarks on receiving the Cooley-Mead Award of the American Sociological Association, he observed:

> The central obsession in ethnomethodological studies is to provide for what the alternate procedural descriptions of achieved and achievable phenomena of order – methodologies – could be without sacrificing issues of structure. That means without sacrificing the great achievements – of describable recognizable recurrencies, of generality, and of comparability of these productions of ordinary activities – activities that carry with them the recognizable achievements of populations that staff their production, along with the interchangeability and surveyability of those populations. This is not an indifference to structure. This is a concern with structure as an achieved phenomenon of order.
>
> *(Garfinkel 1996: 6)*

These "Notes" were written as an exhibit on behalf of structure's occasioned production. At the time, Garfinkel was also speaking of "the catalog" (Garfinkel 1993).

My understanding was that he was speaking of a kind of alternate pedagogy (as indeed *Studies* was; see also Liberman 2013; Livingston 2008; Sacks 1992). Formal analysis tells us we need to distill synthetic and synoptic formulations from our studies. Garfinkel put his studies to work in an entirely different way. These "Notes" aimed to join the catalog.[1] They then became an appendix to an unpublished manuscript that Michael Lynch has now brought to press in the company of a collection of Garfinkel's illuminating seminar lectures.

There was some editing of these notes on the play of basketball over the years, and they subsequently appeared in a collection in honor of Harold Garfinkel in *Human Studies* (Endress and Psathas 2012, 35:2), the journal that was known informally for a time as "Ethnomethodology's journal." With some amendment, this is the iteration that appears here.[2]

Basketball notes: finding the sense and relevance of "detail*"[3]

In reading ethnomethodological studies, students will find an insistence on understanding the familiar topics of sociological study (order, structure a recurrence, power and rational decision-making, for examples) and their familiar settings (studies of work, the family, law, schooling, small and large groups) as local organizations, achieved as the competence of members to produce, recognize and render accountable their mutual affairs, in and as the circumstantial detail of those productions in their course.

Students may also find and complain of bedeviling formulations. The experience is familiar in my own readings, but I think I've been relieved of the complaint by the following understanding: Foundational works tend to be taken up with the makings of familiar worlds. They tend to topicalize familiar objects and affairs, hopefully without resort to mere ironies. This means speaking of things like suicide or "hotrodders," for example, that already possess a common currency. To topicalize them means to speak of them differently, and in speaking differently there is, it seems, ample grounds for complaints of "bad talk."

---

1 From Garfinkel's remarks on "the catalog," Dusan Bjelic began speaking of the "praxitorium," a collection of studies in their materiality, wherein, for having to master the release of the weights of Galileo's pendulum in your own hands, for example, one might find the dense embodiment that subsequent accounts of "discovery" erase (Bjelic 2003).

2 The decision to reproduce the 2012 text rather than the 1988 text in this volume was for the gain in clarity of presentation. There is also some editing. The 2012 "Introduction" included substantial passages from Garfinkel's Appendix 3, which is presented in its entirety in this volume. The editing does make for some schism in Garfinkel et al.'s (1988) remarks on the "Notes." The distance, however, is not great and does not obscure what use he had for them. The 2012 publication is available at www.springerlink.com.

3 Garfinkel's Appendix 3, reproduced in this volume, is titled "Detail*" and opens with a discussion of the asterisk he appends to this and other ordinary words to flag a "tendentious use". He does so throughout Appendix 3, and our discussions of the detail* of play follow suit.

Yet for those pursuing ethnomethodological studies (hereafter, EM), the task and prize remains to describe and understand familiar worlds for their production histories, and do so for matters about which everyone evidently and already "knows." The notion of *detail* exemplifies the difficulty. *Detail* is a central and recurrent formulation in EM studies. And we can read of it and nod an understanding of detail as-we-all-know-it, as, for examples, the detail of a map, or a crime scene or a journey – the detail of an object or course of action rendered as a list, writ long and small.

But something decidedly different is intended for this ordinary word in EM studies. Roughly, it turns on nothing having to do with attributes or inventories carefully specified. It points instead to the grammars of action whereby we assemble our affairs, and witness them materially as just these affairs, in their course, in the constitutive *detail*★ of their productions. (Generality arrives as our ways of speaking of them.) It is, for an example, as of the circumstantial *detail*★ of productions-in-their-course that we see and find a "pinched" greeting from a colleague, while walking down the hallway. Think of the developing *detail*★ of it: bodies in motion, eyes, gaze, gait, timing and the rest, and of course speaking across these closing temporal parameters, shaping next turns, or pre-empting them (the "pinch"). As ethnomethodology intends it, ensembles in detail★ are the makings of such things, and all things of action, meaning and structure. It is hard to imagine an exemption from this circumstantiality. EM argues there is none.

Though it probably won't do in the end to offer up an understanding of *detail* as "ensembles of detail," imperfect accounts can be useful for saying how we intend our words. What follows is a different effort to the same end. Rather than trying to write of it formally, I want to speak of detail★ through one of the ways or occasions in which its distinctive sense for EM studies is available to me, available from within a body of more and less competent practice. These notes will be particularly accessible to you if you can find from this account a body of competent practice that you too may own. Whatever the practice, it will not do to consult it in principle, or to consult it as someone else's competent affairs. It needs to be your own to find *in* those competent affairs the sense of EM's regard for *detail*★.

Playgrounds and Joneses

I have been playing basketball for over 30 years (as of the first writing, and still do). Since high school, I have played pick-up basketball in gyms and on playgrounds, after school/work hours and on weekends. These irregular settings and cohorts can be made out as different from the basketball of leagues and the like, with their schedules, officials, and clocks. But for everything that basketball consists of, pick-up is the same creature. As of its play, we recognize the game, take its measure, and witness its order, structure and recurrence.

There is a phrase from the American east-coast heroin culture that speaks of "having the Jones," i.e., having a compelling addiction. And on city playgrounds and elsewhere, you will find people possessed of the Jones for basketball. Occasionally, you'll hear someone say as much. As for understanding it, I've come to rely on a phrase from Vonnegut's *Slaughterhouse 5*, where he speaks of two army scouts caught behind enemy lines. They have for some days been entirely "thinking through their spines" – living by the embodied competence of what they do as wartime scouts, without much use or time out for all classic and familiar notions of rational action. (See Schutz 1962: 33, on the paradox of rational action.) Sustained periods of thinking through my spine, in the company of endorphins, no doubt, and others doing the same, is a big piece of the draw.

Another way of speaking of it is as a state of grace. Seldom do I feel as graceful as when playing well. It is a bodily sense of grace to be sure, but also a social grace – extraordinary moments of articulation with others who are, and this is no small point, virtual strangers. In my life, this grace and synchrony produced with other bodies in motion is unparalleled. Moreover, within it lies and lives the identifying detail of "playing ball," and I want to provide some description of how it is produced and found from bodies-in-play, *as* the play, as the sense of being well into the game "now," the lived affairs for which "playing ball" can only be, without complaint, a concealing gloss.

Local affairs

The business of grace is a serious one. It too is a gloss, but the real point is that it cannot be found from anywhere off the court, no matter how closely you sit to the sidelines. (This begs the question of how basketball has become such a spectator sport, for which I have no interesting clues. Conventional wisdom says 80% of the *professional* game is pre-specified playmaking. Perhaps that's part of its charm. Given the pace of today's game, loss of control can seem imminent for any next "now," and yet *somehow*, the order of pre-specification is leveraged from those edgy edges: a spectacle of rescue, from extremis. It may only be a confession, but as a spectator I tend to lose the play by the third pass of the ball.)

As I approach the court and wait for a next game, I study the play in progress. I try to assess the skills I'm seeing, and imagine which two of the ten players now on the court I will likely guard and be guarded by in the next game, depending on who wins and loses. Assessing skills from the sidelines is tricky, because the game seldom looks as good, powerful, agile, quick, precise, intense, i.e., *graceful*, off the court, to an observer, even a motivated, already sweating observer, as it does *on* the court, in the midst of play. This is where grace is produced and found. This is where discoveries of just who is agile, quick, skilled, etc. for the purposes of *this* play, these players, *this* time, are made. Practically, it means I am often in danger of under-estimating the powers of a potential opponent, and often do.

Knowing bodies

My play is routinely with virtual or actual strangers. The former are preferred; people whose names or nick-names I may or may not know, but whose basketball bodies I do know, for having found them in-play. If we have played together before, each knows and can find again the looks of alignment and synchrony, and not "generally," but rather in how the other sees, moves and beckons. If you know them in their gait and pivots, feints and looks, what they are doing is seeable for a developing course of action, for planfulness, misdirection, engagement, fatigue, etc.

Seeing is serious business on the court. The less competent player will "look," and in the look reveal next moves or the aim of a pass (and sometimes be told, "you're looking"). This seeing, in my experience, has to do with a peculiar field of view, much like looking at a landscape wherein the view is from edge to edge and yet provides for movement in the foliage. On the court the view *is* movement, and seeing finds its objects variously by voices, complexions, colors, grunts, squeaks, and, perhaps pervasively, the sounded durations of bodies in-play.

One finds teammates and opponents and what to do next – how to continue or disrupt the play-in-its-course – from within enveloping ensembles of such detail*. From within them, you see what carries and identifies offensive players and defensive players. You see and find who is orienting to the ball as something to receive or something to take, bodies-in-motion that affiliate to your own, those that challenge, and those that lead, knitted in fine temporal durations.

Said differently, purposes, for both the ball and bodies, live, and can only be found and joined, as creatures of pace, trajectory, on-sets, off-sets and the visibilities-in-detail of gesture and duration. They live this way not to be found by just anyone, found in principle or formally, but only in-their-course, as you and another jointly produce the developing coherence of a pass that begins with the release of the ball to a place on the floor where no one is yet standing, but is becoming, *as* this projectable course, the synchronous arrival of the ball and another, whose arrivals both evidence the play, and then revise the field for finding and producing next possibilities. The flow of the game, the "fact" of the game, of teamwork, competence, intensity, and exhaustion: these things are produced in their constitutive detail*, yet are nothing that can be rendered as a list of attributes. As a way of speaking, the identifying detail* of the play of the game possesses a half-life; it is revealed only in its course, as the play of a local gang engaged in producing it this time. Only sometimes can you see just what things will come to. Yet *what* they come to, of course, is basketball, complete with an order, structure and recurrence that most anyone can see.

This account has been intended as a suggestive, but not formal tour of the sense of *detail** as found in EM studies. But it has, I think, become taken up with general talk and formulations, so in the next section I want to describe some vignettes of play, to see if that order of account might be a resource to the same task.

An errant pass

Recently (as of the first writing, and countless many more before and since), I did just that. It went like this. If you were facing the basket from mid-court, you would see me facing you on the right side, with the ball and my back to the basket about ten feet away, closely guarded by an opponent. Playing from the "spine" – having no "plan" yet decidedly having a body in motion and a purpose to do something "next" – I spun quickly to my left [your right], and then, after half a beat, reversed direction, turning inward towards the center lane of the basket, still from the right side.

As the second spin began, and as the center lane came into view, two other players came into view as well. Though I am certain that more than two players were within my field of view, only two were seen. One was standing to the left of the basket, "down low" and relatively stationary. The other player was "higher up," farther from the basket, more centrally located on the floor, yet still to the left. And he, like me, was moving in an arc that was closing in on the basket, down the center lane. Thus, what I saw within the developing envelope of my movement was one player relatively stationary near the basket on the far side, and a second player whose pace and trajectory were *becoming* a mirror of my own – a mirroring that had the look of a discovered joint enterprise. As we closed together towards the basket, the arcs becoming more parallel in our turning in, and as the man guarding me stepped between me and the basket to cut off my inward turn, I passed to my "teammate" giving him both the ball and a sheltered path to the basket. Our bodies, moving in concert, were blocking out the other two players nearby. It was a lovely synchrony, save for the fact that this second player was not my teammate. He was an opponent, and the discovered and then cultivated synchrony of our inward turns became an errant pass. His surprise was first; mine came second (see Figure IA2.1).[4]

I would like to think that this "turnover" was for the very best reason in the world. Playing with virtual and actual strangers, the sense for teammates and opponents is shaped by bodies in motion and their orientational properties. These spectacles are available only in the *shaping* of them, and to find them is to be engaged in producing what you find. And what I found was a player whose course and acceleration were becoming complements to my own. We were, it seemed, jointly producing a play of the game, an attack on the basket. The lane, the floor, was opening up to us as we closed in; our closings were its opening. Such a floor does not "self-exist." It unfolds. One finds it and takes its measure in the course of its making. It will not stay there for you as the painted lines do. Floors are reflexive to the developing play, and each is produced within closely lived durations.

---

4 The graphics for Figures IA2.1 and IA2.2 originally were produced on a Mac Classic. In honor of this technical history, they have not been re-visioned.

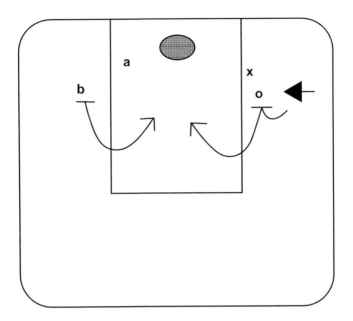

FIGURE IA2.1   An errant pass

So I passed the ball, and then found the first looks of an errant pass in the surprise that emerged from his inexpressive look of concentration. The synchrony of our pace and gait collapsed as he found his hands to receive the unexpected pass, and then his feet to turn away, and up-court. The floor I thought we were producing collapsed and dissolved. My 'teammate' dissolved too, and became nothing to look for, or miss. My end of the court, so recently filled with compelling, inspectably developing *detail**, suddenly became only the other end of things, the one out of play, a field of painted lines only. For the game, there was simply nothing there to see, and no one was looking: a nice place to catch your breath and feel something less than competent, or graceful.

Trailers and stalkers

The first of these terms is a basketball term, and if you hang out near courts you will hear it shouted or said softly sooner or later. The second term I've inserted to suggest that the makings of trailers, who emerge on offense, are a resource for defenders as well.

Trailers are creatures of fast breaks. One side suddenly comes into possession of the ball and quickly moves to offense, with one or more players pushing the ball down court against an equal or lesser number of defenders, who are just as quickly trying to cut off the penetration. (The last vignette may have become such a break.) Their movements, all of them, are quickly paced. As they move down court together, offense and defense, they fill and empty the floor space as they press forward, creating something of a "whoosh," and with it a sense of a trailing vacuum.[5] Trailers fill the void. It works like this:

In hustling down court, in possession of the ball, the orientational properties of bodies, arms, and gaze are forward looking. Floor space is quickly filled and emptied. The floor-in-play hops and shifts with the running and the passing, leaving a "mere" floor in its wake. Unlike set plays, or one-on-one contests, where defenders engage bodies as much if not more than the ball, in breaks the ball leads the push, and the play usually ends in close and relatively sure shots. In its course, but not only there, you can discover that two floors are in play: the floor as a fixture – drawn lines framing a rigid basket – and the floor shaped by the temporal flow of bodies and the ball. The play of the break produces the latter as the relevant floor-in-play. The trailer's find, and his call of "trailer," resurrects the former.

The trailer is never engaged in the forward edges of the play. Rather, s/he "fills" the floor vacated by the force of the break. It is an inserted position, behind the push of the ball, in its wake. Depending on how deeply the play has penetrated the area of the basket, the open, unattended floor may permit a shot of 10–15 feet, unobstructed by defenders. The transformation of the floor from the fury of the leading edge of a break to this backwater of quiet lines and varnish is palpable, first in the call of "trailer," and then in the looks of the pass it calls for, a pass against the grain of movement, a pass to the seeming barrens of a space no longer encompassed by the floor-in-play. As of the call, the shape of the "whoosh" and the play in-play seeabiy bends, distorts and compresses. From the offensive side, hearing the trailer's call transforms the floor from one for pressing forward to one of finding positions relative to the basket. Whereas the pending shot of the break is one of quick movement and close quarters, the shot in the hands of the trailer is patient in its looks. The play of the trailer and the pass it calls for transforms the floor to the settled terrain of a fixed rim.

The experience of measuring pace, producing and finding one's place of insertion, calling for the ball, witnessing the transformation of the floor in the course of this pass of a different kind – these "features" are not tellable incidentals to the play of a trailer. They are its living presence, for and as their durations. They are of its constitutive detail★, and also its structure. Trailers trade on structure. They see and measure it so as to place themselves "off" the floor of the break, using its very structure to stand behind. They reveal and further their project only on the call "trailer," and in such moments structure is revealed too, for everyone else, as the structure we hadn't quite noticed we were producing. Structure is reflexive to the play, and each next play is leveraged from it. The rules of the game of course account for none of this. And knowing rules speaks nothing of one's competence to produce the game and the structure of its play evidently, and in concert with strangers even.

---

5   I am borrowing the "whoosh" from John Horwitz and his collaborators in their study of pedestrian street crossings as graduate students at UCLA. The "whoosh" was a gloss for how pedestrians, on either side of the street, waiting for the signal to turn, begin their traverse, and somewhere in the middle, negotiate their passage through and between one another. The "whoosh" is an observer's phenomenon. Those who are so engaged, do it. Their eyes are fixed elsewhere, yet the "whoosh" is their production. On the floor, trailers trade on it.

To stalk, to hide, to steal

The notion of stalking points to another kind of play that finds shadows, literally and materially un-noticed places. To stalk, either on offense or defense, is to hide. And that one may hide in full and public view ties to how it is that never in my playing experience have I ever seen nine other players engaged in play at once: never, irrespective of their evident, objective presence, for any third grader to count. Basketball shows ten players only diagrammatically. From the inside, the field of view admits of no counts, and is filled only with emergent, tendentious engagements. To stalk is to find positions slightly to the side of those nascent places.

To stalk is to imagine where things might go next, the horizontal "heres" and "theres" projectable from the looks of things at hand.[6] Stalking defenders thus trade on the finds of others. The trading is delicate. It entails standing in the shadows of the play, just to the side of the sight lines and bodily orientations that yield it. Those material positions, shadows included, are creatures of fine duration. Stalkers can show themselves too soon, show themselves engaged with the play rather than masked by it, becoming then formative of the field they are hoping to exploit. Alternatively, you can stalk from too far afield, finding that your emergence from the shadows, e.g., the reach for a pass intended for another, falls short by a bodily measure. You know from within the reach as it uncoils, as of its duration, that the ball, and the play, is now elsewhere. Relevant distance and duration for stalkers, and for the play of the game generally, are immeasurable. They are embodied instead, made of half-steps, shoulders and forearms, opening and closing pathways, and pace. The concert of the floor-in-play is seeable in these ways, to be stood next to, stalked and penetrated, or missed, as of these constitutive details.

Often, but not only, in the context of fast breaks, offensive players take the ball into the air under close guard from defenders, close to the basket, and release a shot (a layup, a finger roll, a fade, hook, jump hook, etc.). As a defender in those moments, I try to look for and measure the bodily extension of the driving opponent. It's a peculiar looking and measuring (though not so exceptional; people with fly swatters know it too). Full extension only happens once, for me and for him. Anything less is likely a feint. So, I look for measures of extension. And what that could be can only be found, though not certainly found, in the looks of bodily comportment in the air. I do that looking even when the driver is not my direct, engaged responsibility. I do so to the end of a stalk.

In a recent game with very big people, I watched a driver paired to a defender, my teammate. A shot seemed near to hand, and the issue for my play was where, if not through the hoop, the ball would go next (seeing those trajectories is a useful skill to cultivate). In competent play it is the issue for everyone engaged in the near vicinity of the driver – offensive and defensive players alike. Offensive players, however, can be looking not only to rebound, but to provide a potential "outlet" target for a failed drive, to provide an alternate "where" that the ball could go next. Those possibilities

---

6 In truth, these things can't be imagined, and they aren't. They are rather produced and found in the emerging and receding coherences that constitute the play of the game. We shape them as we look for them.

68 Appendix 2

are shaped by the players across fields of view reflexively produced in the air. As a grounded party, I orient to what that field is becoming as well, finding in the detail of indefinite alignments, places to stand next to, as in the produced locales of "outlet targets," candidate recipients for a last-moment pass. As a stalking defender, you trade on those productions, and wait for them to be found by others, first.

In the play at hand, the driver and the defender, my teammate, are in the air, close to the right side of the basket. The driver is right-handed, and as his right hand reaches its extension, lifting the ball near the backboard, he finds his "trailing" teammate, a few feet out from the rim, still to the right side, and releases a pass to him. It is a looping pass over the outstretched arms of the defender-in-the-air.

Closing in on the play before the pass, my position is to the left of the basket and to the left of the outlet target. I am closer to the basket than he, within its "shadow" as a fixture, and within the developing shadow of my teammate defender in the air. That the pass is a looping pass in its release and pace provides the metric of my move, stepping into the play, inside of the outlet target, across his left shoulder, into the clear space between him and the players in the air, for an aptly called "steal." As with "driving fast" (Sacks 1988) steals trade on normative structures. (See Figure IA2.2.)

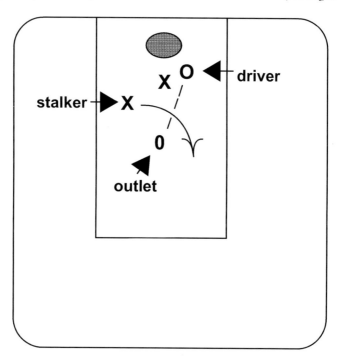

FIGURE IA2.2 A steal

So what?

This question has been known to and heard by the EM community for a very long time. It is a familiar retort to every descriptive program. (I first heard it, produced with a laugh, as "The BIG so what?") The question reminds us of the great divide between programs that promise causatives – explanation – and those that describe and thereby elucidate, instruct, and perhaps dissolve conceptual confusions (see Wittgenstein 1981: 314). Aside from the pleasures of speaking of affairs we know well (and there are serious issues for every effort to study affairs that we do not, serious for the character of access a tourist could have, notwithstanding the assurances of formal methods), the point to these notes is that the *detail** they speak of, in this description and that one, is fully, and for what the play of basketball could be, nothing less than a description of just *what* its play could be. These are not "details" of play. They are, rather, the identifying, *constitutive* details* of the game, the material organizations of just what every playground player is looking for as he or she walks onto the court, wondering if, again, it will be produced and found. This order of detail is not available generally. It can't be sampled or parsed, and is only produced in the company of a gang of players. "Basketball" is a gloss for these on-going communitarian productions. They afford its structure, regularity, reproducibility, and also the possibility of its instruction. Embedding ourselves in the contextures of our own handiwork, we find the play of the game and produce its every evidence of structure in bodily crafted durations. Pick-up basketball, alongside queues, freeway traffic, shopping malls and public spaces of every kind, is yet another standing miracle of strangers-in-concert. For the analysis, in Garfinkel's phrase, of "ordinary immortal society" in its endlessly profuse expressions, EM studies take interest in things like science, juries, checkers, air traffic control and the rest as the artful achievements of communitarian practice. They – those practices and practitioners – are what leverage order, structure and recurrence into view. We live by their achievements, and just what practices they are, in their order-productive details*, is more than a formal-analytic account can say. EM takes interest there. Harold Garfinkel and his students have written a radically alternate and uncompromising account of order, structure and recurrence in the lived world. Roughly speaking, that's the so what.

References

Bjelic, Dusan (2003) *Galileo's Pendulum: Science, Sexuality and the Body-Instrument Link*. Albany, NY: SUNY Press.
Endress, Martin and George Psathas (eds.) (2012) *In Memorial of Harold Garfinkel*. Special issue of *Human Studies* 35(2).
Garfinkel, Harold (1967) *Studies in Ethnomethodology*. Englewood Cliffs, NJ: Prentice Hall.
Garfinkel, Harold (1993) "A Catalog of Investigations with Which to Respecify Topics of Logic, Order, Meaning, Method, Reason, Structure, Science, and the Rest, in, about, and as the Working of Immortal, Ordinary Society Just in Any Actual Case. What Did We Do? What Did We Learn?" Unpublished manuscript (17 October), Department of Sociology, UCLA.
Garfinkel, Harold (1996) "Ethnomethodology's Program," *Social Psychology Quarterly* 59(1): 5–21.
Garfinkel, Harold (2002) *Ethnomethodology's Program: Working Out Durkheim's Aphorism*. Lanham, MD: Rowman & Littlefield.
Garfinkel, Harold and D. Lawrence Wieder (1992) "Two Incommensurable, Asymmetrically Alternate Technologies of Social Action," in G. Watson and R.M. Seiler (eds.), *Text in Context: Contributions to Ethnomethodology*. Newbury Park, CA: Sage, 175–217.

Garfinkel, Harold, Eric Livingston, Michael Lynch, Douglas Macbeth, and Albert B. Robillard (1988) "Respecifying the Natural Sciences as Discovering Sciences of Practical Action, I & II: Doing so Ethnographically by Administering a Schedule of Contingencies in Discussions with Laboratory Scientists and by Hanging around Their Laboratories." Unpublished manuscript, Department of Sociology, UCLA.

Garfinkel, Harold and H. Sacks (1970) "On Formal Structures of Practical Actions," in J.C. McKinney and E.A. Tiryakian (eds.), *Theoretical Sociology: Perspectives and Development*. New York: Appleton-Century-Crofts, 337–366.

Liberman, Kenneth (2013) *More Studies in Ethnomethodology*. Albany, NY: SUNY Press.

Livingston, Eric (2008) *Ethnographies of Reason*. Aldershot: Ashgate/Routledge.

Lynch, Michael (2019) "Garfinkel, Sacks and Formal Structures: Collaborative Origins, Divergences, and the History of Ethnomethodology and Conversation Analysis," *Human Studies* 42(2): 183–198.

Macbeth, Douglas (2012) "Some Notes on the Play of Basketball in Its Circumstantial Detail, and an Introduction to Their Occasion," *Human Studies* 35: 193–208.

Moerman, Michael and Harvey Sacks (1988 [1971]) "On 'Understanding' in the Analysis of Natural Conversation," in M. Moerman (ed.), *Talking Culture: Ethnography and Conversation Analysis*. Philadelphia, PA: University of Pennsylvania Press, 180–186. Originally drafted in 1971.

Sacks, Harvey (1984a) "Notes on Methodology," in J.M. Atkinson and J. Heritage (eds.), *Structures of Social Action: Studies in Conversation Analysis*. Cambridge: Cambridge University Press, 21–27.

Sacks, Harvey (1984b) "Doing 'Being Ordinary'," in J.M. Atkinson and J. Heritage (eds.), *Structures of Social Action: Studies in Conversation Analysis*. Cambridge: Cambridge University Press, 413–429.

Sacks, Harvey (1988/1989) "On Members' Measurement Systems," *Research on Language and Social Interaction* 22: 45–60.

Sacks, Harvey (1992) *Lectures on Conversation, Vols. 1&2*, edited by Gail Jefferson. Oxford: Blackwell.

Sacks, Harvey, Emanuel A. Schegloff and Gail Jefferson (1974) "A Simplest Systematics for the Organization of Turn Taking for Conversation," *Language* 50(4): 696–735.

Schutz, Alfred (1962) *Collected Papers, Vol. 1*. The Hague: Martinus Nijhoff.

Wittgenstein, Ludwig (1981) *Zettel*. Oxford: Blackwell.

APPENDIX 3

Detail*

Harold Garfinkel

In this chapter we use details★ (and several other terms) "tendentiously," i.e., with a deliberately abiding, corrective, but concealed tendency. Appendix 2, *Basketball Notes: Finding the Sense and Relevance of Detail*★, by Douglas Macbeth describes the detail★ of "lived basketball." We urge the reader to read Appendix 2, and then return to consult Macbeth's case of detail★ when mentions occur in our text.

Macbeth's "case study" of lived basketball is deeply and accurately instructive of the most critical aim of our argument: We use detail★ tendentiously in order to remain faithful to the essentially unavoidable and essentially achieved quiddity of lived organizational *things*, and with that achieved quiddity, to make discoverable and to respecify the awesome achievements, in and as the lived orderliness of practical action, of *structure* – i.e. of the great recurrencies, their reproduceability, their comparability, their produced and accountable independence of the local staff engaged in their production, and their accountability.

In speaking "tendentiously" of detail★ we use the term knowing that we mean by detail★ something other and different than the reader would explain with any of detail's many "straightforward" meanings, or *can* explain with any classic methods to justify straightforward meanings; thus at the same time knowing that we use detail★ as a corrective on the reader's understandings and sometimes as a radical corrective; knowing, too, that we are deliberately delaying an explanation; doing so on the grounds of later studies; and knowing that an explanation will be forthcoming at an appropriate place in the argument, although not in this chapter but as the argument develops over seven Collections of Studies.

Detail★ is not the only term we shall use tendentiously. Other terms are adequately★, administer★, classic science★, cogent★, coherent★, constructive analysis★, empirical★, instruction★, instructed action★, phenomena of order★, provide for★, real time★, structure★, topics of order★, unmotivated observables★, descriptive precision★ (i.e., as in "the first segment of a *Lebenswelt* Pair precisely describes the Pair"). Terms used tendentiously are spelled with an asterisk.

An interest in detail★ – asterisked detail★ – detail tendentiously used – has been recurrent and fundamental to ethnomethodological enterprises from their outset. In their earliest studies ethnomethodologists insisted on detail's★ importance, not only for ethnomethodology's program, but for all studies of practical action, lay and professional. Their insistence has been obstinate. However, to established sociology just what was being insisted upon remained mysterious, and over the years ethnomethodologists voiced that insistence at the risk of not being taken seriously, or worse.

The job of explaining detail★ in a few words is luckless. Even with 20 lectures and goodwill galore detail★ has been *very* hard to teach. Discussions of detail★ – the experienced detail★ – are apt to summon bewilderment, conservatism, exasperation, fear, and contempt.

An excerpt from Macbeth's "Basketball Notes" in Appendix 2 furnished a masterful synopsis of just what detail★ is all about, and by showing what needs to be taught gives some idea of why it should be so tough to teach.

> . . . For those pursuing ethnomethodological studies . . . the burden (of complaints about "bad talk") remains to find and speak of the familiar differently – foundationally. And the burden is worsened by speaking of affairs about which everyone evidently and already knows. The notion of *detail*★ exemplifies the difficulty. It is a central and recurrent formulation to ethnomethodogical studies. And we can read its references and nod an understanding of "detail" as-we-all-know-it – as, for example, the "detail" of a map, or of assembling or riding a bicycle, serving dinner, word processing – "detail" as the detail of the object of [a] course of action rendered as a list, writ long and small.
>
> But something decidedly different seems intended for *detail*★ in ethnomethodological studies. Roughly, it turns on nothing having to do with attributes or inventories carefully specified. *It is more nearly something like the ensemble of affiliations whereby we recognize our affairs, and can only find and recognize them, in their midst, for their duration, as we produce them, materially, and not in some semblance, but only as just these affairs we are engaged in, in their course, as their detail, this time through.* (Our italics.)
>
> . . . Rather than trying to speak formally of the notion of *detail*★ I want to *talk* it for one of the ways or sites in which its distinctive sense for ethnomethodological studies is, I think, available to me, available from within a body of practice for which I have some competence.
>
> I've been playing basketball . . . for nearly 30 years. These notes will be particularly accessible to you if either you too share this competence, or if you can find in this account ways to inspect a different body of practice for the relevance and production of its identifying detail. It won't do to consult them in principle, or to consult affairs as someone else's competent affairs. They need to be your own, to first find them *as* their produced *detail*. [This quoted passage is from the version of Macbeth's paper in Appendix 2 of Garfinkel et al. (1988), Garfinkel's emphasis added. The relevant passage in the present volume is on pp. 60–61, though Macbeth has revised it.]

The italicized paragraph contains a synoptic collection of descriptors. They are descriptors (see endnote 23 [p. 89]) which means they are only available to the search for and recognition of their sense and relevance when they are consulted from within the in-course on-site practices that the analyst is competent with. Therein, *only* therein, their use to recognize, describe, follow, or teach the practices of basketball consists of this: they reveal the phenomena of "lived basketball" as disclosed details of observable and reportable play, – real play, actually done, and evidently. These phenomena are glossed as "playing basketball." In contrast, the following ways of understanding these descriptors – the well-known ways of formal analytic social science – in the very same ways that these understandings are familiar, and technical, and skillfully and carefully carried out, will waste the analyst's time. Thus the analyst's efforts will be a waste of time when the descriptors are used as "dimensions" of the phenomenon, or as names for variables or as instant values for variables. Further, the analyst will miss the aim and point of their use when the descriptors are administered as abstract formal properties of the phenomenon; when they are "mapped" into the phenomenon as the phenomenon's corresponding schema; when they are used as models of essential invariants of the phenomenon, or as the phenomenon's parameters; when they are used to provide in propositional formats for the decidable sense, reference, correspondence to objects, truth, relevance, and other issues of adequacy such as observability, description, effective procedure, reasoned specification, instructable reproduction, or teachability.

When the descriptors in Macbeth's paragraph are understood in these familiar ways of classical social science studies – we'll collect them by speaking of the methods of "constructive analysis" and their affiliated "logic of induction" – those understandings guarantee that everything that methods for the study of practical action is and could be, and everything that is thereby offered as results and their warrant, will be hopelessly distracted, and wrong, in its specifics.

Then, of what use is Macbeth's paragraph given the prevalent respect for the aims and tasks, the problems, and the evident achievements in the social sciences, via the methods of constructive analysis of empirical description, generality of results, comparison, demands for evidence, and the rest?

Macbeth uses the paragraph of descriptors to exhibit "lived basketball" in and as revealed identifying detail★. His paragraph of descriptors may also be used to exhibit other phenomena that ethnomethodologists have described. They may be used, but of course only with changes in their availability to sense, observation, recognition, teaching, demonstration, etc., since that availability accompanies the analyst's competence in the phenomenon's production. The analyst's on-site competence is required of the analyst to do the jobs that are glossed as description, observation, understanding, etc. Only in the analyst's embodied competence is the phenomenon's availability that of revealed detail★ of a witnessed and teachable "organizational *thing*" whether that thing be an "individual" achievement or a "concerted" one.

Macbeth's descriptors illuminate "lived phenomena" that other ethnomethodologists have described as locally produced, natural accountable detail★. These are found in studies by Beryl Bellman, Stacy Burns, Kenneth Liberman, Douglas

Macbeth, Lois Meyer, Albert B. Robillard, Jr., Christopher Pack, Wesley Sharrock and Robert Anderson, Friedrich Schrecker, and others.[1]

Ethnomethodological studies of detail★ require that analysts motivate talk of detail★ with ethnomethodology's policies and methods. Note *some* talk of detail★ but *all* talk of detail★ must be motivated by ethnomethodology's policies and its methods of study. For example, two policies are "ethnomethodological indifference," and the analyst's required uniquely adequate embodied competence with the locally occasioned production and natural accountability of the phenomena.

By contrast, *nothing* of detail★ is available with the use of the paired distinctions between *generic representation* and *detail*. In all their astronomical number and variety they are useless. Despite their omniprevalence in endlessly many arts and sciences of practical action, and familiar as they are, none of these pairs of generics and detail, offering for examination, and specifying as empirical observables the organizational *things* as propertied classes of objects, will locate, collect, identify, permit the recognition of, describe, or analyze detail★. None will demonstrate inspectable and criticizable detail★, and none *can* do so.

Similarly worse than useless are the familiarly practical reductions of detail★ that are the matter-of-course achievements of classic social theories of action (e.g., Lewin's field theory; Parsons' unit act; Simon's rational action; theories of "talk in interaction" of symbolic interaction, cognitive science, of the different social psychologies of Psychology and Sociology Departments; of minds of all sorts; of medicine's various bodies; of analytic philosophy's theories of objective knowledge; of theories of signs; of formal analytic sociologies whether their emphases are "businesslike" or "romantic"; and of post-World War II's philosophies, histories, and other theories of good science.[2]

Through the exercise of the same analytic skills that make up the stock in trade of professional social sciences, the detail★ that is described in Macbeth's article is reduced by being rendered as the properties of signed objects.

Their distinctions of generics and detail, administered over the exigencies of inquiry and argument, lose to their accompanied and theorized "concreteness of things," they lose to the plenums that they need with which to speak of "real worldly organizational things," the locally achieved, locally occasioned, unremarkable real worldly practical actions of immortal, ordinary society. That loss is unavoidable and without remedy or alternative.

---

1 Garfinkel did not cite specific sources by the authors he lists here, though published and unpublished writings by Burns, Liberman, Macbeth, Meyer, Robillard, and Schrecker are mentioned elsewhere in the text and appendices. In addition, his original reference list included a draft of a paper by Anderson, Sharrock, and Hughes that later was published (Anderson et al. 1990); two publications by Bellman (1975, 1984); as well as by Heap (1986a, 1986b), Morrison (1976), Wieder (1974), and Zimmerman and Whalen (1987).

2 Garfinkel did not provide references here to particular works by Kurt Lewin, Talcott Parsons, or Herbert Simon, but the relevant papers and volumes are well known. When Garfinkel mentions "theories of 'talk in interaction' of symbolic interaction," it might seem that this is an allusion to Conversation Analysis, since Emanuel Schegloff often referred to "talk-in-interaction" as CA's domain of investigation, but Garfinkel more likely is referring to schematic treatments of social interaction in the tradition of Symbolic Interactionism associated with the Chicago School of Sociology.

Appendix 3 **75**

In its concerns with detail and generality, ethnomethodology seeks a big prize: Can you have produced and reproduced organizational objects specified in the achieved coherence of detail and still have detail provided for without generic representations of the phenomenon; indeed, without *any* "exterior" representations of the phenomenon, and that means without any representations other than those that are local and endogenous? Inquiry and their results furnish the grounds for the following current policies in answer to this question.

It cannot be done if these issues for their adequacy are made decidable when they are found, recognized, collected, observed, recorded, or analyzed with the polices and methods of constructive analysis and their affiliated logic of inductive inference. (Abbreviated as classic studies.) Nor can it be done if for their adequacy these issues are made decidable with any of the well-known (and perhaps *any* of the available) alternatives to constructive analysis and their accompanying logic of inductive inference. Alternatives, although they are attractive, are wrong, or they do not or cannot deliver the empirical goods, or they lose the issues or settle them with definitions, or they introduce bowdlerizations or use tropes without motivating the trope's interpretation by the phenomenon's observed details, and other distractions. Some alternatives are Pierce on abduction; Caws on the logic of discovery; Goguen on the logic of fuzzy set theory; formal theories of indexical expression; the programs of leading authors in the current micro/macro controversy in sociology; experience-based theories of practical action, e.g. Polanyi, applied sociology, operations research, risk analysis, and cost-benefit accounting methods.[3]

Similarly, insofar as mandarin studies of talk and structure consist of an analysis of signed objects their claims are questionable. In many cases their claims are wrong.[4] What if these issues for their adequacy are made decidable for whatever in the world, when using the methods of ethnomethodological research, adequacy and decidable could be found to be. Then the *topics* of order – i.e., adequacy, decidable, methods, research, analysis, observation, inductive inference, non-inductive inference – would be examined as locally achieved, locally occasioned *phenomena* of order.

Endlessly many texts in intellectual history speak of logic, order, purpose, consciousness, reason, rational action, evidence, identity, proof, meaning, method, and the rest.

Ethnomethodology's standing task is to respecify *topics* of order as locally produced, locally achieved and locally organized, naturally and reflexively accountable *phenomena* of order★.

To carry out its research policies ethnomethodological studies developed as research sites, and make use of, a collection of "perspicuous settings." These provide for the discovery of, the specifications of, and, in the results that are obtained with their use, the lessons learned and learnable about locally achieved phenomena of order★. These

---

3 Garfinkel did not include citations to mentioned authors (Charles S. Peirce, Joseph Goguin, Peter Caws, and Michael Polanyi), or to the theories and controversies listed. Polanyi (1958) is listed in the references, and Garfinkel could be referring to any of the many relevant sources by the others.
4 See Appendix 1 on "mandarin studies of talk."

order★ phenomena are exhibited as the locally produced, naturally accountable coherent★ details★ that compose *as instructed actions* the phenomenal fields of ordinary human "jobs," – "jobs" such as typing thoughtful words, teaching introductory sociology, talking conversational English, finding and counting conversations, joining and standing in line, following a sketch map, playing chess, or proving the Pythagorean theorem.

Many *topics* of order★ have been studied by ethnomethodologists as locally achieved, locally occasioned, naturally and reflexively accountable *phenomena* of order★. Detail★ is one of them. Other topics are rules, instructions, signs, spatiality, analysis, accounts, logical properties of indexical expressions, rational action, reasoning, and practical reasoning.

Each of these terms identifies a topic of a particular ethnomethodological study and each topic is explicated in a study, but not as one-for-one. Instead a particular topic takes on a technical sense as locally produced phenomena of order in studies of various perspicuous settings and their differently affiliated order topics. Thus: the *in situ* practices of consulting occasion maps in the course of the work of a way-finding journey is a perspicuous setting for "signs," "spatiality," "analysis," "logical properties of indexical expression," and "reasoning." Playing chess while wearing inverting lenses is a perspicuous setting for "spatiality," "analysis," and "reasoning." Formatting in queues is a perspicuous setting for "reification," "rational action," "accounts," "indexical expressions," "sedimentation," "Heideggerian thing," "macro- and micro-structures," "sameness" and "spatiality." Games-with-rules elucidate as order phenomena received topics of "rules," "collections of rules," "completeness of collections [of] rules," and "game-grounded demonstrations of formal structures of social interaction." The Mooersian catalog elucidates the order phenomena of "practical organizational reasoning."[5] Inverting lenses are used to elucidate "the apt and familiar efficacy of specifically ordinary activities," and "an-object-evidently." Michael Lynch [1985], in his book, examined neurobiologists at the work of discovering axon sprouting as a perspicuous setting for the locally produced order phenomena of "demonstrable fact" and "demonstrable artifact," "methodic procedure," "research planning," "shop talk," "technical detail," and "the community of scientists." Eric Livingston [1986] used the work sites of competent mathematics as a perspicuous setting as of which to formulate and solve as a phenomenon in the production of order the foundational problem of mathematics: What explains mathematical rigor?

These ethnomethodological inquiries and their affiliated topics have their origins in the *Lebenswelt* studies that were instated by Edmund Husserl and carried on by scholars in phenomenological philosophy. Ethnomethodological studies are continually renewed in the masterful writings of Husserl, Heidegger, Merleau-Ponty, Gurwitsch, and Schutz. The renewal is obtained by the shop practice of deliberately "mis-reading" these texts in the interests of directing the discovery of the *Lebenswelt* to discovering the phenomena of embodied practices that compose as its production and analyzability the miraculous familiarity of the ordinary society.

---

5   This is a reference to a mechanical filing and retrieval system for engineering document descriptors developed by Calvin Mooers (1919–1994), an American computer scientist. Mooers called the system "Zatocoding." Garfinkel also discusses Mooers' cataloguing system in Part II of the present volume.

APPENDIX 4

Collections of studies I–VII respecifying the natural sciences as discovering sciences of practical action

Harold Garfinkel

Seven collections of studies are arranged and enumerated as steps of an argument. With this format I hope to provide researchers' further studies an initiating specificity, aims, some direction and origins, warrant-of-sorts, and to situate further inquiries in the current state of science studies. The argument is an occasioned feature of work in progress.

I

Program and polices

A provisional explanation of the ethnomethodological policy that each natural science is to be discovered and is only discoverable as a distinctive *discovering science of practical action*.

II

Respecifying the natural sciences as discovering sciences of practical action, doing so ethnographically by administering a schedule of contingencies in discussions with laboratory scientists and by hanging around their laboratories. Strong dissatisfactions.

III

That an issue can get settled is a specifying detail of discovering work in the natural sciences, – i.e., the works' probativeness – and a contingency of that work. Our problem is: What explains the probativeness of experiments in the natural sciences?

IV

Ethnomethodology's standing task is to respecify topics of order* as locally produced and locally organized, naturally and reflexively accountable phenomena of order★. To carry out its research policies ethnomethodological studies developed as research sites, and make use of, a collection of "perspicuous settings." These provide for the discovery of, the specifications of, and, in the results that are obtained with their use, the lessons learned and learnable about the locally produced, naturally accountable coherent★ details that compose *as instructed actions* the phenomenal fields of ordinary human "jobs."

What is the relevance of phenomenal fields of ordinary human "jobs" for the problem? What explains the probativeness of experiments in the natural sciences? What we did and what we learned with perspicuous settings in studies of instructed actions pose this problem and permit its solution.

V

The phenomenal field and its properties of Galileo's experimental demonstration of the motion of free-falling bodies.

VI

The following studies explicate findings about the phenomenal field of Galileo's inclined plane experiment as results in foundation problems in the natural sciences.

(A)

Discovered structures of practical action of Galilean physics

1.0 The phenomenal field of fungible details of Galileo's inclined plane experimental demonstration of the motion of bodies in free fall. (Abbreviated as "PHI GXPT")
2.0 Explicating the ties between the contingencies and the phenomenal field, PHI GXPT.
3.0 The tie between the contingencies and the phenomenal field that consists of: PHI GXPT *specifies* the motion of free-falling bodies.
4.0 Identifying structures of the phenomena of Galilean physics.
5.0 The lawfulness of the phenomena of the motion of free-falling bodies.
6.0 The collection of left-hand and right-hand ways, in starting with Galileo's report in *The Two New Sciences*, of arriving at s/t^2; and that collection's properties.

(B)

Lebenswelt physics

7.0 The phenomena in topics 1.0 through 6.0 are empirical★ phenomena. When they are specified they are specified [as] structures of practical action.
8.0 That Galilean physics is a distinctive discovering science of practical action is explained by demonstrating these structures.

Appendix 4 **79**

9.0 These structures are only h–sociologically★ discoverable and h–sociologically★ demonstrable★.
9.1 They specify and demonstrate a domain of phenomena in physics that are results in physics.
9.2 That domain is only discoverable.
9.3 (i) These phenomena:

   (ii) that they are results in physics;
   (iii) that they are only discoverably the case;
   (iv) that they are only h-sociologically★ discoverable;
   (v) that they are only h-sociologically★ demonstrable;
   (vi) that they specify a domain of results; are collected by speaking of that domain of results as *lebenswelt physics*.

(C)

Lebenswelt mathematics

10.0 A comparable domain of only h-sociologically★ discoverable and only h-sociologically★ demonstrable results, collected as *lebenswelt mathematics*, is demonstrated in the studies by Eric Livingston of the work of proving Gödel's theorem.

(D)

Respecifying mathematics and Galilean physics as discovering sciences of practical action

11.0 The structures of practical action in topics 1.0 through 6.0 are distinctive to Galilean physics.
12.0 A second and distinctive set of structures of practical action is the case for mathematics.
13.0 Each set preserves the universality, generality, and transcendentality of results of its science in technical details of work-site practices.
14.0 The two sets are incommensurable.
15.0 Our program's aims, announced in the topic, Program and Policies are the beginning of this article, which reports Collections I and II are satisfied in these two cases.
16.0 These aims are uniquely satisfied by these two cases.
16.1 These aims are not satisfied and cannot be satisfied ethnographically.
16.2 Neither are they nor can they be satisfied with classic studies of science, or as properties of a classic science.

VII

Prizes from our studies of the Galileo experiment. An annotated list of discovered and only discoverable "real animals."

Questionable matters: reservations, uncertainties, incompleteness, equivocations, "fancies and good *nights!*," etc.

Some consequences and big issues.

ACKNOWLEDGEMENTS, NOTES AND REFERENCES

Harold Garfinkel

Author's acknowledgements

Many of the policies that we depend on were originally developed in other studies by ethnomethodologists. For example, the unique adequacy requirement of methods was worked out by Melinda Baccus. Stacey Burns is responsible for teaching's properties of local production, which includes that work's natural accountability. For their generosity we are grateful to Melinda Baccus, Beryl Bellman, Egon Bittner, Stacey Burns, James Heap, Kenneth Liberman, Lois Meyer, Christopher Pack, Friederich Schrecker, D. Lawrence Wieder, and Ernst Wieltschnigg.

We extend thanks to Bennetta Jules-Rosette; Bernard Giesen; Dierdre Boden and Don Zimmerman; Louis Quéré; Bernard Conein, Patrick Pharo, and Donald Watson; and George Psathas and Jeff Coulter for invitations to present some of these materials at their conferences.

We thank Ann Marcus, our superb research assistant, and Perry Taka for discussions and joint work in Haines 225 [UCLA office] on the Galileo stuff. Murray Leaf and Hubert L. Dreyfus could be counted onto spend their time reading our materials with the rare talents of candid and loyal opposition.

The studies reported in this chapter and our further studies of the sciences could not have been done without the help of Phil Agre, Gerald Holton, Louis Narens, and John Weiler. They made available to us their enormous expertise as practicing scientists and their own original concerns with discovering work in the natural sciences. They are not responsible, of course, for what we have done with their work.

We could not have learned our own study were it not for the hours that lab scientists spent teaching us by telling us what we were talking about as the contingencies in their labs. Arthur Yuwiler and Nikki Olds were splendid colleagues. We have identified with masking initials the lab persons we cite.

Thanks are due to the Center for Advanced Study in the Behavioral Sciences for a year during which it became clear that laboratory experiences in the natural sciences were perspicuous settings for ethnomethodology's interests. This focus was the precious outcome of conversations with Gerald Holton.

Notes

1. See Appendix 1, Postscript and Preface; Appendix 2, Basketball Notes: Finding the Sense and Relevance of Detail* by Douglas Macbeth [later published as Macbeth (2012)]; and Appendix 3, Detail*.
2. This chapter reports the first two of a series of Studies (Collections I through VII), entitled *Respecifying the Natural Sciences as Discovering Sciences of Practical Action*. For a Table of Contents see Appendix 4.
3. We entertain as a working prejudice that in the natural sciences an experimental laboratory offers to local practitioners the identity of shop work/shop talk and teaching's work-sites. From the point of view of a local gang's day's work it is distracting to *them*, and because it is so, therein it is pointless for *us*, to mark out, let alone require that they distinguish in their local work between "inquiry" and mutual work-site science-specific teaching. We take it as our research maxim that in the natural sciences an experimental laboratory is inexhaustibly dense with teaching's work-sites. The local "gang of us," "our shop," staffs those sites.
4. See Section 10, A Synopsis of the Argument Restated by Calling Ahead upon the Finished Seven Collections of Studies for a Point of View, and Appendix 4, Section VI.
5. Here we can only talk *about* "adequately" and *about* its relation to a family of terms. Adequately* takes on just what it is talking about in Collections V and VI. [See Appendix 4.] There Lebenswelt Pairs are described* for Gödel's proof and for Galileo's inclined plane experiment. In V and VI *Lebenswelt* mathematics and the *Lebenswelt* Galilean experiment are exhibited *not* as "evidence of Gödel's theorem" and *not* as "evidence of the law of falling bodies" but each, distinctively, in Livingston's seminal observation, "as revealed details* of a witnessed demonstration."
   In V and VI adequately* is exhibited as classically accounted structures of practical actions of a phenomenal field: for Gödel's proof; for Heath's visual proof of the Pythagorean theorem; for Euclid's proof of the Pythagorean theorem in *Euclid's Elements*; and for Galileo's inclined plane experimental demonstration of invariants in the motion of bodies in free fall.
   This chapter, which consists of Collections I and II, only speaks *about* adequately* and *about* family members – i.e. *about* detail*, coherence of objects*, topics of order*, locally achieved phenomena of order*, real time*, structure*, observable*, empirical*, and others. This chapter treats these achievements merely as mentions of these achievements. Only the work-site practices of V and VI can provide adequately's* particulars, and only these can provide the reader its examinable and criticizable explanation. These practices are available only in case studies, and therefore this chapter is deliberately proleptic. Unavoidably, it borrows ahead for its sense upon the studies in Collections V and VI.
6. The social sciences are discussed in Collections VI and VII.
7. We call attention to the asterisked spelling of empirical*, which is another case of tendentious usage. It should be noted that we are not recommending any established school of empirical inquiry. Empiricism understood as a tradition is not an issue here. Our reference has nothing to do with the "school" of empiricism as it is understood in academic circles. For the time being we shall insist on empirical materials – i.e., we shall insist upon "empirical's" emphasis on actual experience, on practical observability, on practical objectivity, on accounting procedures, on record keeping, on care with notation, and on warranting methods of study, – but without being responsible for empiricism as an operating rationale. An explanation of empirical* is deferred to Collections IV, V, and VI.

Acknowledgements, notes and references

8   See endnotes 12 and 16.
9   Collections V and VI. See Appendix 1 and Acknowledgements.
10 Livingston's study and Lynch's study were not done simultaneously. While it would be misleading to say that Livingston's study developed from Lynch's, Livingston did have the advantage of appropriating the "dissatisfactions" expressed and/or evident in Lynch's study while pursuing his own. [Livingston – email message to Editor, 2 March 2020 – said that this note is not consistent with what he did or did not know of when writing his dissertation.] By the end of [this manuscript] it should be evident that the differences in their studies raise several general issues: What is the relation of analytic ethnography to the respecifying studies of Collections III to VI? How is analytic ethnography found to work in them? Is analytic ethnography to be treated as a viable ethnomethodological project? Or is it to be treated as a discarded alternative? Is it an historical or genealogical antecedent? Or is a variation within our program?

Although [this manuscript] never states in so many words that analytic ethnography has its virtues, it has exhibited such virtues in public discussions of the contingencies. Audiences at colloquia and seminars, composed for the most part of social scientists, found the list of "coat hangers" and their exemplary stories absorbing and informative. More compelling for us, so did practicing scientists. So did scholars, scientists or not, who study the sciences. So we do not know just how our discussions of the contingencies engage us in teaching colleagues, and particularly in teaching scientists *about* their work, but that teaching has been going on.

Further, the analytic ethnography ties into, while developing further, current science studies of experimental practices. And added to these virtues, the discussed work of analytic ethnography reveals in the contingencies of their generic sense, relevance to, and resonance with not just *this* particular scientific practice we discuss, but with *that one* as well. And this "sense" of pertinency accompanies and holds despite our assurances to audiences that *we*, the authors and researchers, have no idea what we are serving as witnesses to, have never seen it at first hand, and *could* not.

More. The "virtues" of ethnographically discussed contingencies are, of course, not different than the "dissatisfactions." As "virtues" or "dissatisfactions" the contingencies discussed ethnographically point to their generic applicability: they point to the congruency with science studies topics, with literary cogency, and with disengagement from work-site identifying details.

11 The term "evidential proof" is explained by Livingston (1986) in *The Ethnomethodological Foundations of Mathematics*. There the work of an evidential proof for Gödel's proof is described while satisfying the requirement of ethnomethodological adequacy of mathematical detail★. In "Notation and the Work of Mathematical Discovery" (Livingston and Garfinkel 1983), evidential proofs are similarly described for the Pythagorean theorem and several other theorems. Extended discussions of evidential proofs will be found in endnotes 12 and 15 and full citations in endnote 16.

12 *We urge the reader to read Appendix 2 before reading this note and then in conjunction with it.* [Editor's note: this note goes on to discuss Livingston's work, whereas Appendix 2 is a paper by Macbeth on playing basketball, which discusses "detail★" and not *Lebenswelt Pair*. Garfinkel leaves it to the reader to work out the relationship between the two, and perhaps intended to include a different "Appendix 2" in a future draft of the manuscript.] Livingston's (1986) book is concerned with the lived work of proving Gödel's theorem. His achievement consists in having discovered and specified the identity: Gödel's theorem, which consists of a schedule of 37 theorems and their proof accounts, is identical with the lived work of proving that schedule. Livingston specifies that identity as a *Lebenswelt Pair*.

A synoptic account of Lebenswelt Pair: In the hands of a practitioner, Gödel's schedule of theorems and their proofs is read as hierarchically arranged instructions. At the local work-site the schedule of theorems and proofs, in and as the unavoidably and irremediably relevant work-site details★ of working out the schedule, becomes precisely descriptive of the work of following it. In metaphoric characterization, the schedule is "attached" to the lived work of following it. It is "attached" without possibility of remedy or alternative.

Just how, in the quiddity of revealed details★ of a witnessed demonstration, each theorem and/or each proof account becomes precisely descriptive of the work of following it is what a practitioner has to do at a work-site. It is only, exactly, entirely, and *just* what a prover has to do at a work-site.

Only locally achieved and only locally occasioned, and naturally accountable, the "just what a prover has to do," the lived work of proving Gödel's theorem, *is* (i.e., is identical with) the *Lebenswelt Pair*, Gödel's theorem.

The Constituent Segments of a Lebenswelt Pair. We shall write Pair as an abbreviation for: (A theorem and/or proof account/the way of working to which it is unavoidably and irremediably tied).

We offer the following observations:

(i)   A Pair is composed of constituent segments.
(ii) The parentheses exhibit the evidential proof of Gödel's theorem, the Pair, as the lived work of proving it. Its constituents are (i) a first-segment-of-the-Pair, i.e., in the case of Gödel's theorem, the Schedule of 37 theorems and their proofs, and (ii) an affiliated second-segment-of-a-Pair, i.e., in the case of Gödel's theorem the-way-of-working-to-which-the-Schedule-to-which-the-Schedule-is-irremediably-and-unavoidably-tied.
(iii) A Pair of constituent segments specify Gödel's theorem in and as the lived work of proving it.
(iv) The Pair specifies Gödel's theorem as an evidential proof.
(v)   The Pair specifies Gödel's theorem.
(vi) The Pair specifies Gödel's theorem as a mathematical object.
(vii) The Pair specifies Gödel's theorem as a lived organizational thing. The Pair specifies Gödel's theorem as the practices of proving it.

We shall use "praxis" or "a practice," to gloss Gödel's theorem specified as a Pair.

Five required features of Lebenswelt Pairs. When, in order to collect cases of Pairs, we restrict the requirement for *Lebenswelt* Pairs to Pairs with features found in mathematics' Pairs, we observe the following features of *Lebenswelt* Pairs.

(1) The first segment is only discovered, and is only discoverable. It cannot be imagined or stipulated. It cannot be "recovered" as properties of a signed object.
(2) *As a discovery* the first segment consists in its materials details★ of this: it precisely describes★ the *Pair*.
(3) The *Pair* is classically accountable.
(4) The first segment is a classic account of the *Pair*. That means, the first segment is a classic account of the "lived" work-site practices – "the work" – of proving the theorem. The first segment speaks on behalf of the proof-as-a-practical-action. The first segment *renders* the lived work of proving as the properties of that work's classical accountability. So, the first segment ignores the *reflexive accountability* of the work of proving. It ignores the details★ of the proof; it ignores the reflexively, naturally accountable details★ of the proof which are *only* reflexively naturally accountable details★ of the proof. You cannot find the work of the proof, and you cannot *teach* the work of the proof, you cannot teach the evidential proof, if you address only the first segment to do so. To find or specify the work of the proof you must "recover" the Pair.
(5) The Pair specifies the details★ of an evidential proof.

Some Notation

Square brackets with an enclosed text will refer to the first segment of a Pair, e.g., [Gödel's theorem].

Square brackets enclosed with ticked brackets will refer to the Pair of constituent segments, e.g., {[Gödel's theorem]}.

Observation about first segments

(i) Gödel's schedule of 37 theorems and their proofs is a first segment.
(ii) *Euclid's Elements*, in its availability as an arranged presentation of theorems, their proofs, and accompanying commentary, is a compendium of instructions, and therein is a catalog of first segments.
(iii) Mathematical treatises are catalogs of first segments. It is the present state of affairs in mathematics that with no exceptions its treatises consist of catalogs of first segments. Included among those treatises are the many accounts of Gödel's proof.
(iv) Several Lebenswelt pairs in mathematics are described in ethnomethodological studies. Except for these no other descriptions exist at present in the entire corpus of mathematical treatises.
(v) It is the present state of affairs in mathematics that *nowhere* in Euclid, and *nowhere* in the corpus of mathematics is there provision for, let alone is there available *as findings in their own right*, a domain of Lebenswelt Pairs that are mathematical results, really, actually, and evidently. The news from Livingston's work is that there exists, *demonstrably*, a domain of Lebenswelt Pairs for mathematics. We speak of that domain as Lebenswelt mathematics.

The following results are in hand

(1) There exists a discovered and only discoverable domain of Lebenswelt mathematics. That the domain exists; that it was discovered; and that it is only discoverable are demonstrable with several *Lebenswelt* Pairs: a Pair for Gödel's theorem, and Pairs for several theorems of Euclid.
(2) We offer as a matter of praxeological validity of published theorems and proofs in a mathematical treatise that every mathematical treatise is a catalog of first segments.
(3) On the grounds of the praxeological validity of a treatise's theorems and proofs, a treatise testifies to the existence of a domain of *Lebenswelt* Pairs, and therein testifies to an only discoverable domain of *Lebenswelt* mathematics.
(4) Thus, we offer as *our* claim's praxeological validity that each treatise testifies to the existence of a domain of *Lebenswelt* mathematics.
(5) However, the domain cannot be read off the page no matter how talented a reader the mathematician is. Nor can it be imagined, no matter how talented a mathematician the reader is. There remains the work of seeing/showing, in and as of the work-site, as the local synesthesias of proving's phenomenal fields, or *just how* a theorem consists of the instructed action of a Pair – of *just, only, distinctively, and entirely how* a theorem consists of the work of proving in that, and as, the *in situ* synesthesias are unavoidably relevant and unremarkable details★ of practices whereby the theorem becomes a *precise description*★ of the Pair, really, actually, and evidently. Gödel's proof is for us an emblematic case of that because just *that* is provided in the schedule of 37 theorems and their proof accounts; the first segment of the Lebenswelt Pair. The structure of detail★ provides for endless further exploration of *the Pair* in inexhaustible detail★ of the Pair, and without loss of the coherence and the cogency of the Pair, (i.e., really); these details★ are only available in the "lived doing," (i.e., actually); and only in detail★ really and actually are they available to autonomous criticism, (i.e. and only therein, evidently).
Livingston points out a seminal detail★ of Gödel's proof that bears on the matter of Gödel's proof *really*: A prover can only work out the proof in that there comes a point when embodiedly, with paper and pencil as a work-site, the prover must write it out notationally. That is because only in and as the embodied-course-of-writing *does* the prover and *can* the prover overcome the abbreviations so as to be able to sees how in and as the notational followability just what s/he is doing that

makes up the locally seeable, followable structures of the argument as its material *details*★ – details★ that are developingly and endogenously coming to be described precisely★.

(6) The domain of Lebenswelt pairs in mathematics is identical with what mathematics, as the coherence of unavoidably and irremediably relevant and unremarkable details★ really, actually, and evidently, and these as the-most-ordinary-organizational-*things*-in-the-world, consists of as the day's work.

(7) We have recommended a mathematical proof as a precise description of a mathematical object, distinctively and in mathematical particulars. The idea of precise description is this: Disputing the matter that is described, i.e., in and as the disputed matter's "followability," *in and as revealed details★ of a locally historicized, witnessable demonstration*, the disputed matter exhibits itself in the specific pointlessness of the dispute as the disputed matter's unavoidably relevant detail★.

(8) The demonstrable Lebenswelt Pairs in mathematics specify mathematics as a distinctive discovering science of practical action.

(9) The compendia of first segments that compose the current contents of mathematical treatises identify the existence and the practice of current mathematics as a *classic* science of practical action.

Cautions and reflections

At the time of this writing we propose, but only as an ethnographically recommended argument, and thus with no greater strength than a documented conjecture, that Pairs with the characterizing label Lebenswelt Pairs are to be found for the other discovering sciences of practical action. We conjecture that there exist, but only discoverably, and only for the natural sciences, domains of Lebenswelt chemistry, Lebenswelt physics, Lebenswelt molecular biology, etc., just as there exist the discovered domain of Lebenswelt mathematics.

We believe that Lebenswelt domains cannot be demonstrated for the social sciences. We entertain that belief on the grounds that the first segment of a Lebenswelt Pair is only discoverable and can always be discovered. It cannot be imagined or stipulated, nor can it be provided for as a signed object or in an interpretation of signs. The domain cannot be represented, or theorized, nor can it be provided for because its provisions are inferentially necessary inductively or deductively, or because its provisions are needed in, for, or as some "all practical purposes." The first segment is only available paired in and as the coherence and cogency of inspectable details★ really, actually, and evidently.

A caution. We have been very insistent that Lebenswelt Pairs occur in the discovering sciences but not elsewhere. Nevertheless, the grounds for our insistence are not stronger than documented conjecture. We insist for the *merely* good reason that endless cases of first segments can be found that do not satisfy the five requirements of Lebenswelt Pairs in mathematics. Examples are occasion maps, computing manuals, industrial and academic job descriptions that depend for their specifications upon the entries in the *Dictionary of Occupational Titles*, store-shelves-full of how-to-do-its, rules in games, freeway signs, occupational codes of ethics, contracts, and the Ten Commandments. Social science treatises, by their endless use of constructive analytic methods, offer a cornucopia of first segments as their professional stock in trade. Their treatises report first segments of *Pairs*. In no actual case have we found a treatise that offers the first segment of a Lebenswelt Pair. This can be demonstrated in any particular case if the treatise is read "praxeologically" as instructions by following which phenomenon is reproduced.

On the question of whether the social sciences are discovering sciences we prefer to proceed "conservatively." In studying the arts and sciences of practical action we believe that clear ground can be won by exploiting the consequences of the strength of Lebenswelt Pairs in mathematics. In that way we shall look for results that are

Acknowledgements, notes and references

demonstrable and interesting, possibly consequential, and even deep, without imagining that news in these matters is to be won anywhere except in and as the lived, first-person presence and availability of horizonal phenomena.

13   See endnote 12.

14   Instructed actions are fully described in Collection IV. The term "instructed actions" can be explained by briefly characterizing ethnomethodological studies of the essentially occasioned incompetence of other logical properties of occasion maps. Maps such as those that persons draw for each other, are called "occasion maps" when (i) the lived work of consulting the map is an unavoidable and irremediable detail of the way-finding journey that the map is consulted to get done, and when (ii) under that work-site condition the map's consulted relevant-to-the-user, inspectable properties of logic, order, meaning, reason, facticity, or method — we shall collect these topics by using order★ as a proxy — are topical and problematic for the user. Under these conditions the occasion map exhibits *in situ* such work-site specific order★ properties as *only locally achieved* and *only developing and naturally accountable* completeness, clarity, consistency, factual accuracy, omissions, mistakes, errors, equivocalities, followability, definiteness of sense and reference, unique correspondence between map notation and territorial features. No topics of order★ *need* to be excused.

Drawing upon ethnomethodological studies of the logical properties of occasion maps comparable properties of software documentation were specified by examining a manual's work-station affiliated details of the lived work of following its instructions. In and as the locally historicized lived work at the computing console of making a manual's instructions "come true" the manual "becomes" a description of the lived work of following it. In each case the Pair, i.e., "Instructions" and the "affiliated work of following them," are glossed as Instructed Actions. These two — the lived way-finding journey a detail★ of which is the consulted occasion map, and the lived work at the console of "using a software application" — are perspicuous settings for extensively detailed case studies of distinctive Instructed Actions. Each exhibits *only* as work-site specific and *only* in and as locally historicized details, its observable properties of incompleteness, inconsistency, omissions, factual errors, equivocal expression, and other "complainables." Similarly, each exhibits its "virtues."

Key structures are the *only* work-site locally inspectable correspondences between the manual's text and the keyboard-and-CBT's gesturally organized and organizable places and the manual's very own significant territory of embodiedly unremarkable, embodiedly effective computing practices and procedures. Comparable structures are demonstrable for the occasioned map as an unremarkable embodied detail of the way-finding journey.

The studies in Collection IV describe instructed actions in re: occasioned maps; formatted queues; the use of inverting lenses with which to accompany ordinary tasks; side-one delay demonstrations; blind-specific tasks and troubles; and intractable problems in designing computable representations of practical actions. For each set of materials the questions are asked, what have we done? What have we learned?

15   Endnote 12, a discussion of *Lebenswelt* Pair, needs to be read, along with its required prior reading, in order to understand this note.

Livingston's findings about the mathematical practices that make up the lived work of proving Gödel's theorem are findings that mathematicians at the work of proving Gödel's theorem "orient to." His findings are mathematical results. His findings consist of the *lived work* of mathematically proving Gödel's theorem. That lived work is specified in Livingston's (1986) book, *The Ethnomethodological Foundations of Mathematics*, as the work-site practices that mathematicians gloss as Gödel's Schedule of Theorems and their Proof.

In his book Livingston carries out these practices. He exhibits them in coherent★ and cogent★ details★ as observable and inspectable manifestations of mathematical phenomena. He collects these practices as technical details★ of an *evidential proof* of

Gödel's theorem, and recommends them to the reader's autonomous examination and criticism.

The adequacy of the reader's autonomous grasp and criticism requires the reader to carry out the proving *by reading Livingston's descriptions of these practices as instructions for doing so. By doing the proving in this way* – ONLY *by doing the proving in this way* – CAN *the reader encounter the evidential proof as work-site specific practices.*

Only by actually doing the proving, and doing it *in this way*, can the reader encounter these practices so as to autonomously assess the following claims:

(A) That thereby encountered and inspectable practices are constituents of an evidential proof of Gödel's theorem.
(B) As such they have the properties of their *local production*, and that
(C) Among their properties of local production is their *natural accountability*.
(D) Livingston's findings include that their properties of local production and natural accountability are essentially unavoidable and without remedy or alternative, *and* from the point of view of classically accountable mathematical proving they are *uninteresting*, – that is to say, for the practical demonstrability and followability of a course of mathematical proving their existence is depended upon, made use of, and ignored. They are "seen but unnoticed."

By the properties of their *local production* is meant that the work-site practices of an evidential proof are not available by adhering to prespecified procedures. Rather, for their cogency and coherence the specifics are locally occasioned. For their cogency and coherence they are "hidden" in and as their apt and familiar efficacy. They are only available to practitioners in and as of embodied work-site equipmentally-affiliated "skills." They are *only* available to practitioners, and *only* to their vulgar competence. They are done unwittingly. They are developingly objective and developingly accountable. In any actual case they are unavailable to "situationally" disengaged, let alone to *a priori*, analytically reasoned reflection. Nor in any actual case are they available to introspection, to ethnographic reportage, to the analysis of ethnographic documentation or to documented arguments except, and at best, as documented conjectures. They are done in detail★ and they consist of what detail★ *could be* in technical, material contents. They are real worldly. They are only discoverable: they cannot be imagined. *And they are naturally accountable.*

The natural accountability of provings' practices of Gödel's theorem is the crux of the lived work of mathematically proving Gödel's theorem. That work's natural accountability permits Livingston to specify the lived work of proving Gödel's theorem as a real worldly phenomenon in and as mathematics. Via its natural accountability that work permits him to claim on behalf of mathematics what *in the world*, – what *practical action* – Gödel discovered that made up an "object" of mathematicians' technical competence and achievement.

The evidential proof of Gödel's theorem, hereafter {[Gödel's theorem]}, includes as an identifying detail★ its natural accountability. By provings' practices' natural accountability we mean that the evidential proof of Gödel's theorem, i.e. {[Gödel's theorem]}, as an endogenously produced identifying detail★ of it, and as a condition under which it gets done,

(i) comes to provide in the properties of Gödel's Schedule of Theorems and Proofs, [GT&P], for itself as a publicly verifiable object.
(ii) The evidential proof, {[Gödel's theorem]} comes to provide in the properties of [GT&P] for {[Gödel's theorem]}'s *own* observability. The evidential proof comes to provide in the properties of the Schedule of Theorems and Their Proof for the evidential proof's observability. The evidential proof exhibits in the properties of the Schedule [GT&P] the evidential proof's observability. The evidential proof comes to exhibit in the properties of [GT&P] what the observability of the evidential proofs *can* be taken to be.

(iii) The evidential proof, {[Gödel's theorem]}, comes to provide in the properties of the Schedule of Theorems and Their Proofs, [GT&P], for the evidential proof's *own* topicality.
(iv) {[Gödel's theorem]} comes to provide in the properties of [GT&P] for the analysis of the evidential proof, {[GT]}. {[Gödel's theorem]} comes to provide in the properties of The Schedule for an analysis of itself.
(v) The evidential proof, {[Gödel's theorem]}, comes to provide in the properties of the Schedule of Theorems and Their Proofs, [GT&P], for reasoned discourse about the evidential proof of Gödel's theorem, and for what reasoned discourse about {[GT]} could possibly be.
(vi) The evidential proof {[GT]} comes to exhibit, in the foregoing practical respects, in the properties of the Schedule, [GT&P], the Schedule's transcendental orderliness with respect to the identifying details of the evidential proof, {[Gödel's theorem]}.
(vii) And the evidential proof {[GT]} comes to provide in the properties of the Schedule, [GT&P], for the Schedule's incorporation into a current situation of mathematical inquiry as a *corpus* of mathematically warranted grounds of inductive or deductive inference, and of further inquiry, and action.
(viii) Finally, the evidential proof of Gödel's theorem {[GT]} comes to provide, in the properties of Gödel's Schedule of Theorems and Their Proofs, [GT&P] for all of the foregoing in institutionally established terms as matters of competent membership in a technical, esoteric, though nonetheless natural language community.

It is in light of the foregoing that the adequacy of Livingston's study can be summarily stated in the claims:

- Livingston's findings *can* be taken seriously.
- Livingston's findings are mathematical results.
- Livingston's results, which are mathematical results, are details★ of the *hybrid*, ethnomethodology/mathematics.

16   That Livingston's findings are mathematical results, and what his results consist of, are discussed at length in his book (1986). Other findings that were obtained ethnomethodologically that are results in mathematics are discussed in Livingston and Garfinkel (1983) and Garfinkel (1986).

17   It is necessary to make a lot of "hybrid." One reason: hybrid is new for both sociology and for mathematics. Hybrids have been demonstrated by ethnomethodologists for mathematics (Livingston 1986), Galilean physics (Garfinkel et al., [n.d.; not listed in references – Ed.; see Garfinkel (2002, Ch. 9)]), teaching civil [law] procedure (Burns 1986 [also see Burns 1997 – Ed.]), curriculum design and evaluation in pediatrics (Robillard and Pack 1976–1982; Robillard 1983, 1984, 1986a, 1986b; Robillard et al. 1987), classroom bi-lingual education (Meyer 1988), analytic video recordings of classroom authority in high school (Macbeth 1987); and playing and teaching improvised jazz piano (Sudnow 1978/2001).

18   Discussed in Endnote 15. See also Garfinkel et al. (1981).

19   Pseudonyms and pseudo-initials have been used throughout these sections. Exceptions in the use of names will be obvious from the context.

20   From notes of HG.

21   From Holton (1978a: 155–156).

22   From Holton (1978b).

23   Our knowledge of Mooersian descriptors is based on the following sources by Calvin N. Mooers (Mooers 1951, 1956a, 1956b, 1958, 1960). H.G. had several conversations with him during a sabbatical year in 1969–70 about his work, and innumerable discussions before that with Dr. Anatol Holt, to whom we are heavily indebted for having introduced us to Mooers' studies. Mooers must be counted the author of a brilliant and original corpus of studies of practical reasoning.

24 Neurobiochemistry Laboratory, Veteran's Hospital, Westwood, Los Angeles, CA, V.A.M.C. Brentwood Division.
25 See below in section, Administering* the Schedule of Contingencies.
26 [Blank – note redacted by H.G. in original manuscript.]
27 Conversation in 1975 at the Center for Advanced Study in the Behavioral Sciences, Palo Alto, CA.
28 Senior (1958) is certainly a neglected classic.
29 From Notes of H.G.
30 Lynch, "Projects and the Temporalization of Lab Inquiry," Chapter 3 of Lynch (1985: 53–80).
31 We are indebted to Professor Holton for many instructive discussions of the issue, and for his generosity with his original and expert observations (see Holton 1978b).
32 The examples from the discussion with Y.R. are from H.G.'s notes.
33 Schrecker (1980). [Editor's note: Garfinkel cited Schrecker's study as appearing in H. Garfinkel (ed.), *Ethnomethodological Studies of Work in the Discovering Sciences*, Routledge and Kegan Paul, in press, 1987. The volume was never published. Schrecker's study is summarized in Lynch, Livingston and Garfinkel (1983: 225–229), and is available in the Garfinkel archive.]
34 In a provisional cut that is not stronger than reasoned and documented conjectures we offer a distinction between (I) *locally occasioned contingencies* and (II) *standing contingencies*.

> (I) "Losing the phenomenon," "Wasting time," "Making the experiment work," "Depending upon the availability in the lab or bricolage expertise," "Dread of and provisions for demonically wild contingencies," "Zeroing in – e.g., on the last jot and tittle," "Settling for a yield," "The experiment is a dense 'ecology' of unforgivingly strict sequences," "Teaching 'our shop's ways of doing things' to various types of visitors where some critical part of just what we know and just what we do is none of somebody's business: e.g., tourists, novices, new PhDs, site visitors, adversarial rivals, collegial rivals, etc.," "Having golden hands," "Klutz, slob, ignoramus, flake, careless, etc.," "Tracking, specifying, teaching building, making available to other members of the local gang the trivial, unremarkable, but indispensable technically specific skills of lab equipment's habitual body," "The local, singular particularities of experimental equipment are by design, practice, desire, and achievement specifically unremarkable," and "Knowing how to get the phenomenon out of the data."

These contingencies are collected by their common, real time* property: they are in and as the local occasions of which they consist. Each, as a phenomenon, is produced, detected, recognized, and understood in and as the real time* and manifestations of its locally occasioned details*.

As Lynch (1985) and Macbeth ([2012]; in Appendix 2 of this manuscript) have so elegantly described them, these are only locally historicized details*.

> (II) The locally occasioned contingencies are accompanied by several *standing contingencies*. Like the locally occasioned contingencies the standing contingencies are uniquely contingencies of work in the natural sciences. They are:
>
> (1) Discovering work is done "first time through."
> (2) An issue can get settled by an experimental demonstration of a phenomenon. In and as of work-site detail* issues can be compellingly settled through experimental demonstrations. We call this contingency the "probativeness" of experimental demonstrations in the natural sciences. Just as practitioners are compelled to ask, we ask: What explains the probativeness of experimental demonstrations in the instant case?
> (3) Methods travel between laboratories only insofar as the receiving laboratory custom fits the method to the local, vernacular details* of the gang's "local culture" and to the gang's local work-site specific histories of projects, persons, shop talk, etc. The awesome achievements in the natural sciences

of transcendental methods, objective knowledge, teachable, reproducible phenomena, and universal results in and as a natural science distinctively are assured as the local gang's work-site equipmentally affiliated achievements of practical actions and practical reasoning.

(4) Similarly, to assure as local practical achievements the transcendentality and universality of results, experimental equipment is *only* with overwhelming frequency custom manufactured, but it is *always*, only, and then entirely exactly and certainly custom fitted to the local, vernacular, embodied histories of the local gang's experimental shop practices, and to its embodied vernaculars of shop talk. This is done to obtain the locally and practically achieved adequacy of a demonstrated phenomenon, a phenomenon that the equipment *is used via custom fitting* to *demonstrate* as instructably reproducible across work-site vicissitudes *and* in independence of the phenomenon's local production and of its naturally accountable manifestations.

(5) Only as work-site practices in their details★, only, entirely, and exactly in their details★, do the victories of a natural science – e.g. transcendental and universal results, comparability of findings, decidedly adequate reproduction of results, indifference of methodic procedure to particular users, standardization of equipment – take on their specifics and their inspectability as the work of a particular science.

We speak of these as standing contingencies in order to collect their following common properties.

Each, given to a local gang of bench scientists in the specifics of the practices it glosses, is obvious in its specifics to that gang. Each is recognized immediately, and all gangs are unanimous in recognizing each. Further, they know each to be unavoidable, without remedy, and without alternative. More, each accompanies their work-site practices without time-out, buy-outs, hiding places, or evasions. It inhabits the gang's practices, being omnirelevant. Each is all these "essentially" – i.e., every attempt to escape, alter, or remedy its omnirelevance makes use of the identical features for which the remedy was sought with which to demonstrate the cure. Finally, each is tied to the inexorable relevance of equipment; it is tied in the way a laboratory's bodies are "chained" to equipment.

Each of the above standing contingencies speaks in the case of *a* science of that science distinctively and singularly. What it speaks of is (a) the relevance to each other of details★, generally, local craft, and results; and (b) that their relevance for each other is essentially unavoidable, without remedy, *and* unremarkable.

The locally occasioned contingencies are accompanied by the standing contingencies. The locally occasioned contingencies are *somehow* tied to the standing contingencies. But we don't know how, and only knowing how generally speaking is worse than useless. We don't know *just* how.

Several settings present those ties to bench scientists as explicit problems as encountered troubles. Because they are this for scientists they promise to specify and elucidate those ties for us. It is our purpose to become knowledgeable about how the two sets of contingencies may be related by examining these settings and settings lie them in which for a gang the ties between details★, generality, local craft, and results are troubled.

35 See Appendix 1.
36 Some examples are the reward system of science, its normative structures, institutionalized patterns of evaluation, Blum and McHugh's (1984) thoughtfully revealed judgments of scientific reasoning, and the topics of Merton's (1973) program in the sociology of scientific knowledge.
37 See below, endnote 44.
38 Not what we imagined or hoped, but what we counted on and planned for by exercising the theorist's privilege: Whatever was going on in their laboratories that made up the contingencies of their work was being produced, recognized, and understood by

them in order to make it possible for us to ask and answer a theoretical question. Our vanity in seeking to specify the contingencies of their work by exercising the theorist's privilege is of course the point that is being made.

39   By "collection" we mean that the contingencies would lend themselves to strong conditions of inclusion and comparability.
40   See endnote 11, p. 83.
41   We add "skills" to a list of cognate metaphors, e.g., "embodied work," "work-site practices," "practices," "effective procedures," "constructive procedures," and "chiasmically embodied practices."
42   From H.G. notes.
43   See Lynch (1985: 147–150).
44   The term "unmotivated observables" is borrowed from Sacks et al. (1974: 699) but we have changed its sense. We use it to speak of practices of such unquestioned efficacy and banality that no motive ordinarily exists, either in commonplace settings or professional inquiries to make an issue of their methodic character. In the social scientific search for routine, predictable, standardized, and orderly states of affairs in the society, as well as in the search for such affairs by local laboratory methodologists in the natural sciences in the instant laboratory, these practices are overlooked, while at the same time their routine, predictable, standardized and orderly production or real worldly matters of fact and conjecture incessantly "works for" the local inquiry. Members of a local gang know very well and avoid the risks of attending them. To call attention to these is to invite a curious undermining of locally available theoretic interests in and insistence on "empirical problems." "Members" is not a matter of secrecy but of constituent identifying details of unremark-able availability. "Members" speaks of being efficaciously and witnessably known in common without saying, and therein unworthy of remark, specifically unnotice-able as a practical and local achievement.
45   Compare to Schutz (1962).
46   See Garfinkel and Sacks (1970: 364–365), "Notes on Glossing." Also see Liberman (1985) for a most instructive, experientially informed discussion of the theme "Understanding properly proceeds through a milieu of potential signification which is indeterminate."
47   By e-wise we mean about the relativities that:

   1. They are cause for members' complaints: they are faulted; they are nuisances; troubles; proper grounds for corrective, that is, remedial, action.
   2. They are without remedy in the sense that every measure that is taken to achieve a remedy preserves in specifics the features for which the remedy was sought.
   3. They are unavoidable: they are inescapable; there is no hiding place from their use, no moratorium, no time out, no room in the world for relief.
   4. Programmatic ideals characterized their workings.
   5. These ideals are available as "plain spoken rules" to provide accounts of adequate description for all practical purposes, or adequate explanation, adequate identity, adequate characterization, adequate translation, adequate analysis and so forth.
   6. Provision is made "in studies by practicing logicians" for each ideal's "poor relatives," as indexical expressions are the poor relatives of objective expressions; as commonsense knowledge is a poor relative of scientific knowledge; as natives' practices and natives' knowledge are poor relatives of professional practices and professional knowledge of natives' affairs, practices, and knowledge; as Calvin N. Mooers' descriptors are poor relatives of sets, categories, classes, or collections in formal logic; or, as formal structures in natural language are poor relatives of formal structures in invented languages. For "poor relatives" we understand "embarrassing but necessary nuisances," lesser versions," "non-phenomena,"

"no causes for celebration," "ugly doubles" that are relied on by members to assure the claims of the relatives that went to college and came back educated. Ideals are not the monopoly of academics and neither are their poor relatives confined to the streets. Always in each other's company, they are available in immense varieties for they are as common as talk. Being theorized out of existence by members' ironic contrast between commonsense knowledge and scientific knowledge, they are also difficult to locate and report with the use of that contrast.

7. Members are unanimous in their recognition of the foregoing six characteristics of specific practices: they are also unanimous in their use of these characteristics to detect, sense, identify, locate, name – that is, to formulate – one or another "sense" of practical activities as an "invariant structure of appearances." [Editor's note: Up to this point, the endnote's elaboration of "e-wise" is a slightly re-worked version of a discussion of constraints satisfied by "*essentially* contexted phenomena" in Garfinkel and Sacks (1970: 356–357).]

"Temporal Order in Laboratory Work" by Lynch et al. (1983) takes up ethnomethodological "themes" that serve as ethnographic detailing "devices" with which to elaborate this topic. One example of such themes is the local historicity of projects.

48 For some objects questions of adequacy – e.g., adequacy of description, relevance, fact, sense, reference, correspondence to real world events, and the rest – can be considered and decided without having to leave the page of text. We call such objects "literary objects".
49 See endnote 50 re: sense of detail★.
50 [Garfinkel redacted the endnote from the text. See Appendix 3 on detail★ and endnote 11 on "signed object" – Ed.]
51 "Essentially" is an abbreviation for "to its practitioners, unavoidably without remedy or alternative." See also *e-wise* in endnote 47. We use *e-wise* as a strong version of "essentially."
52 See Garfinkel (1988). Again, we urge the reader to read Appendix 2, Douglas Macbeth, "Basketball Notes: Finding the Sense and Relevance of Detail★".
53 See Chapter 4, "The Intertwining – The Chiasm" in Merleau-Ponty (1968: 130–155).
54 [Endnote redacted by author – Ed.]
55 Further cases of strong dissatisfactions are examined in Collections V to VII as part of the studies of Galileo's inclined plane experiment. By doing Galileo's experiment we take up the problem: What explains the probativeness of experimentally demonstrated phenomena in the natural sciences? With it we obtain a result that provides strong dissatisfactions with available science studies, for all studies, with specifics for each, for studies that take Galileo's account in *Two New Sciences* (Galilei 1974), as a point of departure and proceed from there to exhibit in "classic ways," the analyzability of bodies in free fall as the details of arriving at the lawfulness of those phenomena.
56 We found this metaphoric contrast in Stephen Jay Gould's (1988) charming review of Freeman Dyson's essays.

References to Part I

Editor's note: In addition to sources listed by Garfinkel in the text and endnotes of the "Respecifying" text, this reference list includes sources from the editor's footnotes to that text. Many of the latter sources were added to complete, correct, or supplement cited names and sources in Garfinkel's text and endnotes. A separate reference list is included in Appendix 2, an article written by Douglas Macbeth which was later published (Macbeth 2012) and then revised for publication in the present volume. Part II of the present volume (the series of Garfinkel's 1980 seminars) includes a separate reference list.

Agre, Phil (1988) *The Dynamic Structure of Everyday Life* (Technical Report 1085). Cambridge, MA: MIT Artificial Intelligence Laboratory.

Agre, Phil and David Chapman (1990) "What Are Plans For?" *Robotics and Autonomous Systems* 6(1–2): 17–34.

Anderson, R.J., W.W. Sharrock, and J.A. Hughes (1990) "The Division of Labour," in B. Conein et al. (eds.), *Les Formes de la Conversation* (volume 2). Paris: CNET.

Bellman, Beryl (1975) *Village of Curers and Assassins: On the Production of Fala Kpelle Cosmological Categories*. The Hague: Mouton.

Bellman, Beryl (1984) *The Language of Secrecy: Symbols and Metaphors in Poro Ritual*. New Brunswick, NJ: Rutgers University Press.

Blum, Alan and Peter McHugh (1984) *Self-Reflection in the Arts and Sciences*. Atlantic Highlands, NJ: Humanities Press.

Boden, Deirdre and Don Zimmerman (eds.) (1991) *Talk & Social Structure: Studies in Ethnomethodology and Conversation Analysis*. Cambridge: Polity Press.

Burns, Stacy (1986) *An Ethnomethodological Case Study of Law Pedagogy in Civil Procedure*. Unpublished manuscript, Department of Sociology, University of California, Los Angeles.

Burns, Stacy (1997) "Practicing Law: A Study of Pedagogic Interchange in a Law School Classroom," in M. Travers and J. Manzo (eds.), *Law in Action: Ethnomethodological & Conversation Analytic Approaches to Law*. Aldershot: Dartmouth Publishing Co., 265–287.

Drew, Paul and John Heritage (eds.) (1992) *Talk at Work: Interaction in Institutional Settings*. Cambridge: Cambridge University Press.

Dreyfus, Hubert and Patricia Allen Dreyfus (1964) "Translators' Introduction," to Maurice Merleau-Ponty (eds), *Sense and Non-Sense*. Evanston, IL: Northwestern University Press, ix–xxvii.

Franklin, Allan (1997) "Millikan's Oil-Drop Experiments," *The Chemical Educator* 2(1): 1–14.

Galilei, Galileo (1974) *Two New Sciences*. Stillman Drake (trans.). Madison, WI: University of Wisconsin Press.

Garfinkel, Harold (1967) *Studies in Ethnomethodology*. Englewood Cliffs, NJ: Prentice Hall.

Garfinkel, Harold (1986) *Lebenswelt Mathematics: Its Discovery, Its Specifications, and Some Consequences*. Unpublished manuscript, Department of Sociology, University of California, Los Angeles. [Editor's note: Garfinkel listed Eric Livingston as second author of this item, but in an email to the Editor (21 May 2020), Livingston said that he had not been invited to be co-author, had never seen the manuscript, and did not want to be listed in the reference to it.]

Garfinkel, Harold (1988) "Evidence for Locally Produced, Naturally Accountable Phenomena of Order, Logic, Reason, Meaning, Method, etc. in and as of the Essential Quiddity of Immortal Ordinary Society (I Of IV): An Announcement of Studies." *Sociological Theory* 6: 10–39.

Garfinkel, Harold (2002) *Ethnomethodology's Program: Working Out Durkheim's Aphorism*, edited with introduction by Anne Rawls. Lanham, MD: Rowman & Littlefield.

Garfinkel, Harold, Michael Lynch, and Eric Livingston (1981) "The Work of a Discovering Science Construed with Materials from the Optically Discovered Pulsar," *Philosophy of the Social Sciences* 11(2): 131–158.

Garfinkel, Harold, and Harvey Sacks (1970) "On Formal Structures of Practical Actions," in J.C. McKinney and E.A. Tiryakian (eds.), *Theoretical Sociology: Perspectives and Development*. New York: Appleton-Century-Crofts, 337–366.

Gould, Stephen Jay (1988) "Mighty Manchester", review of Freeman J. Dyson, *Infinite in All Directions*. *The New York Review of Books* (27 October).

Gurwitsch, Aron (1964) *The Field of Consciousness*. Pittsburgh, PA: Duquesne University Press.

Heap, James L. (1986a) "Sociality and Cognition in Collaborative Computer Writings." Paper prepared for discussion at the University of Michigan School of Education Conference on Literacy and Culture in Educational Settings (7–9 March).

Heap, James L. (1986b) "Collaborative Practices During Computer Writing in a First Grade Classroom." Paper prepared for presentation at the annual meetings of the American Educational Research Association, San Francisco.

Holton, Gerald (1978a) *The Scientific Imagination: Case Studies*. New York: Cambridge University Press.

Holton, Gerald (1978b) "Subelectrons, Presuppositions, and the Millikan-Ehrenhaft Dispute," *Historical Studies in the Physical Sciences* 9: 161–224.

Levi-Strauss, Claude (1966) *The Savage Mind*. Chicago, IL: University of Chicago Press.

Liberman, Kenneth (1985) "The Hermeneutics of Intercultural Communication," in Kenneth Liberman (ed.), *Understanding Interaction in Central Australia: An Ethnomethodological Study of Australian Aboriginal People*. London: Routledge and Kegan Paul.

Liberman, Kenneth (2004) *Dialectical Practice in Tibetan Philosophical Culture: An Ethnomethodological Inquiry into Formal Reasoning*. Lanham, MD: Rowman & Littlefield.

Livingston, Eric (1986) *The Ethnomethodological Foundations of Mathematics*. London and New York: Routledge and Kegan Paul.

Livingston, Eric, and Harold Garfinkel (1983) "Notation and the Work of Mathematical Discovery." Unpublished paper, Department of Sociology, University of California, Los Angeles.

Lynch, Michael (1984) "Turning Up Signs in Neurobehavioral Diagnosis," *Symbolic Interaction* 7(1): 67–86.

Lynch, Michael (1985) *Art and Artifact in Laboratory Science: A Study of Shop Work and Shop Talk in a Research Laboratory*. London: Routledge and Kegan Paul.

Lynch, Michael, Eric Livingston, and Harold Garfinkel (1983) "Temporal Order in Laboratory Work," in K. Knorr-Cetina and M. Mulkay (eds.), *Science Observed: Perspectives on the Social Study of Science*. London: Sage, 205–238.

Macbeth, Douglas (1987) *Management's Work: The Social Organization of Order and Troubles in Secondary Classrooms*. PhD Dissertation, School of Education, University of California, Berkeley.

Macbeth, Douglas (2012) "Some Notes on the Play of Basketball in Its Circumstantial Detail, and an Introduction to Their Occasion," *Human Studies* 35(2): 193–208.

Merleau-Ponty, Maurice (1968) *The Visible and Invisible*. Evanston, IL: Northwestern University Press.

Merton, Robert K. (1973) *The Sociology of Science: Theoretical and Empirical Investigations*. Chicago, IL: University of Chicago Press.

Meyer, Lois (1988) "'It Was No Trouble': Achieving Communicative Competence in a Second Language," in Robin Scarcella, Elaine Anderson, and Stephen Krashin (eds.), *Development of Competence in a Second Language*. Newbury House.

Mooers, Calvin N. (1951) "Zatocoding Applied to Mechanical Organization of Knowledge," *American Documentation* 2(1): 20–32.

Mooers, Calvin N. (1956a) "Zatocoding and Developments in Information Retrieval," *Aslib Proceedings* 8(1): 3–22.
Mooers, Calvin N. (1956b) "Information Retrieval on Structured Content," in Colin Cherry (ed.), *Information Theory, Third London Symposium*. London: Butterworths, 121–134.
Mooers, Calvin N. (1958) "A Mathematical Theory of Language Symbols in Retrieval." *International Conference on Scientific Information*. Washington, DC: National Academy of Sciences, National Research Council.
Mooers, Calvin N. (1960) "Some Mathematical Fundamentals of the Use of Symbols in Information Retrieval." *Information Processing, Proceedings of the International Conference on Information Processing*, UNESCO, Paris, 15–20 June 1959. London: Butterworths.
Morrison, Kenneth (1976) *Reader's Work: Devices for Achieving Pedagogic Events in Textual Materials for Readers as Novices to Sociology*. PhD Dissertation, Department of Sociology, York University, Toronto.
Polanyi, Michael (1958) *Personal Knowledge*. Chicago, IL: University of Chicago Press.
Robillard, Albert B. (1983) *Pacific Island Mental Health Counselor Training Program: A Final Program Narrative and Evaluation Report*. Honolulu: Department of Psychiatry.
Robillard, Albert B. (1984) *Pacific Islander Alternative Mental Health Services: A Project Summary Report*. Honolulu, HI: Social Science Research Institute.
Robillard, Albert B. (1986a) "Mental Health Services in Micronesia: A Case of Superficial Development," in Carole E. Hill (ed.), *Current Health Policy Issues and Alternatives: An Applied Social Science Perspective*. Athens, GA: University of Georgia Press.
Robillard, Albert B. (1986b) "Community-Based Primary Health Care: Reality or Mystification?" in Trinidad S. Osteria and Jonathan Y. Okamura (eds.), *Participatory Approaches to Development: Experiences in the Philippines*. Manilla: De La Salle University Press.
Robillard, Albert B. (ed.) (1992) *Social Change in the Pacific Islands*. London and New York: Kegan Paul International.
Robillard, Albert B. (1994) "Communication Problems in the Intensive Care Unit," *Qualitative Sociology* 17: 383–395.
Robillard, Albert B. and Christopher Pack (1976–1982). *Research and Didactic Videotapes, Occasional Papers, In-house Memoranda, Tape and Video Recorded Rounds and Medical Clinic Conferences, and Lectures*. East Lansing, MI: Department of Human Development, Michigan State University.
Robillard, Albert B., et al. (1987) "Pacific Islander Mental Health Research Center." Grant Application Department of Mental and Human Services, Public Health Service (September).
Sacks, Harvey (1992) *Lectures on Conversation, Volumes 1 & 2*, edited by G. Jefferson. Oxford: Blackwell.
Sacks, Harvey, Emanuel A. Schegloff and Gail Jefferson (1974) "A Simplest Systematics for the Organization of Turn-Taking in Conversation," *Language* 50: 696–735.
Schrecker, Friedrich (1980) "Doing a Chemical Experiment: The Practices of Chemistry Students in a Student Laboratory in Quantitative Analysis." Unpublished paper, Department of Sociology, University of California, Los Angeles.
Schutz, Alfred (1962) "Symbol, Reality, and Society", in Alfred Schutz, *Collected Papers, Volume 1, The Problem of Social Reality*. Martinus Nijhoff, 294–356.
Senior, James K. (1958) "The Vernacular of the Laboratory," *Philosophy of Science* 25: 163–168.
Suchman, Lucy A. (1987) *Plans and Situated Actions: The Problem of Human-Machine Communication*. New York: Cambridge University Press.
Suchman, Lucy, Randall Trigg, and Jeanette Blomberg (2002) "Working Artefacts: Ethnomethods and the Prototype," *British Journal of Sociology* 53(2): 163–179.

Sudnow, David (1978/2001) *Ways of the Hand*. Cambridge, MA: Harvard University Press; Revised & Rewritten, MIT Press.

Wieder, D. Lawrence (1974) *Language and Social Reality*. The Hague: Mouton.

Wieder, D. Lawrence (1989) "The Production and Recognition of Obvious, Ordinary, Orderly Practical Action: Clues from the Study of Magic," American Sociological Association Annual Meeting, San Francisco, CA (August).

Zimmerman, Don, and Jack Whalen (1987) "Multi-party Management of Single Telephone Calls: The Verbal and Gestural Organization of Work in an Emergency Dispatch Center." Presented at the Surrey Conference on Video. University of Surrey, Guildford, England (7–9 July).

PART II

Discovering work of the sciences

Five seminars on the work of the discovering sciences, Department of Sociology, UCLA (May–July 1980)

Harold Garfinkel

EDITOR'S INTRODUCTION TO PART II

Michael Lynch

In the spring and early summer of 1980, Harold Garfinkel devoted a series of seminars to the topic of discovering work in the sciences. The seminars were part of a graduate course at UCLA, Sociology 292: "Special Topics," although many of the persons in attendance were either advanced PhD students, who had completed their course-work requirements, or visiting faculty members and postdoctoral fellows. At the time, Garfinkel was preparing a presentation for a plenary session for a large symposium to be held later that year in Toronto: "The Present State of Social Studies of Science." The meeting was sponsored by the journal *Philosophy of the Social Sciences* and four professional societies: the History of Science Society, the Philosophy of Science Association, Society for the History of Technology, and the Society for Social Studies of Science. Gerald Holton, a leading historian of science, had agreed to comment on the presentation. A selection of articles from the symposium was published in *Philosophy of the Social Sciences*.

Five seminars are presented here in the order in which they occurred in the spring and summer of 1980: May 22, May 27, June 3, June 19, and July 1. The July 1 seminar was attended by a notable visitor, Professor Robert Westman of the UCLA History Department, who later joined the History Department and was a founding member of the Science Studies Program at UC, San Diego. That session also was attended by Eric Livingston, who was working on a dissertation at UCLA under Garfinkel's supervision, and at least two former PhDs who worked with Garfinkel (Ken Liberman and Michael Lynch). At the time, Lynch was a postdoctoral fellow in the Sociology Department at UCLA, and he and Livingston were collaborating with Garfinkel on his presentation for Toronto. Years later, Liberman collaborated with Garfinkel on the special issue "The Lebenswelt Organization of the Sciences" (*Human Studies* 30(1): 1–56).

Garfinkel recorded the seminars on audio cassette tape and arranged to have them transcribed. Copies of the transcripts were available in the Garfinkel archive in Newburyport, Massachusetts. The unknown transcriber, whose name was not included on the transcripts, did an admirable job, although there were some phonetic spellings of names and guessed-at words and phrases. Anne Rawls and Jason Turowetz, through an arrangement with the University of Siegen, Germany also furnished digital copies of the tapes, and these were invaluable for checking, correcting, and filling in blanks in the original transcripts. I also received invaluable help with locating and preparing materials for this volume from Clemens Eisenmann and Jakub Mlynář during a visit to the Newburyport archive in October 2021.

The plenary presentation that Garfinkel was preparing for the symposium in Toronto focused on the first discovery of an optical pulsar by a group of astronomers at Steward Observatory on Kitt Peak in Arizona. The discovery was announced in 1969, only a few years after radio pulsars were first identified and characterized by Anthony Hewish's group at Cambridge. Simply put, pulsars were discrete sources of rapidly pulsating energy, which Hewish's group and other astrophysicists had begun to attribute to highly compacted "neutron stars" that are so dense that they spin at an incredible speed of many times a second and emit energy that pulsates with each rotation. Supernova remnants – resulting from the collapse of a red-giant star – were deemed to be possible candidates of sufficient density to produce radio pulsars, though there was debate about whether they would emit energy that would be visible from earth in the optical range. Due to the relatively low resolution of radio surveys, the approximately two dozen pulsars thus far documented had not been correlated with visible stars. Three astronomers affiliated with Steward Observatory, University of Arizona – John Cocke, Michael Disney, and Donald Taylor – collaborated in an effort to discover whether an already documented radio pulsar in the vicinity of the Crab Nebula could be correlated with a star that was visible with the aid of a telescope in the optical range. Cocke and his colleagues surmised that a source that might be sufficiently dense to produce a pulsar would be NP 0532, a faint star that was part of a double-star system and was considered a possible remnant of the supernova explosion that was visible on earth a millennium earlier. Taylor, who did not join Cocke and Disney during a three-night series of observations on Kitt Peak, designed an electronic device called a computer of average transients to collect photons from an optical telescope and display the cumulative pattern on the screen of an oscilloscope. By setting the frequency to the measured period of the particular radio pulsar (approximately 30 times a second) and setting the 36-inch telescope on NP 0532, they hoped to identify the pulsar with the star. Aided by the "night assistant" at Steward Observatory, John McCallister, they spent three nights at the observatory. They failed to observe the pulsar on the first two nights, but after making adjustments on the third night, Cocke and Disney set up their equipment for a series of observations. According to their account afterwards, they inadvertently recorded their voices on a track of the same tape on which they recorded data from the equipment. The roughly half-hour recording documented a series of observations in which they initially observed evidence of a "pulse" on the oscillograph screen, and then made further checks to eliminate sources of possible noise or artifact. As he elaborates during the seminars, Garfinkel received a copy of the tape from the American Institute of Physics and undertook a study of the recording, which also included interviews with Cocke and Taylor and reading relevant publications about pulsars.

In the seminar series, Garfinkel discusses the pulsar study and also developed a distinctive praxiological analysis using themes associated with gestalt theories of perception. Large portions of these seminars were made up of prepared lectures and extemporaneous remarks by Garfinkel. The edited and abridged versions of the seminar transcripts presented here preserve Garfinkel's "lectures" along with a selection of his exchanges with students and visitors. Student presentations and many of the exchanges between Garfinkel and other participants were deleted from the present version of the transcripts in the interest of length, coherence, and continuity. However, some exchanges with students and visitors open up relevant issues and are preserved, especially the exchanges with Professor Westman in the July 1 seminar. In the interest of maintaining a continuous and coherent text, I also deleted portions of each seminar devoted to "house-keeping." Note that all footnotes to the text are editor's footnotes that supply references to mentioned authors or sources. The footnotes also include remarks about unclear words and passages, and occasional comments on particular issues that were discussed and debated in the seminars. Editorial remarks within the body of the text are placed in square brackets.

The original transcripts identified most speakers other than Garfinkel as "SPEAKER." Although, with the aid of digital copies of the audio recordings, I was able to identify some of these speakers, I was not always able to do so, and even with familiar voices (including my own, at times – this was more than 40 years ago, after all) some guesswork was involved. Given the focus on Garfinkel's presentations, with some exceptions (such as Westman, and other cases where speakers are identified in the transcript), I denote speakers anonymously.

Although the seminars are specifically focused on the optical pulsar discovery, other topics are woven through the five seminars. Perhaps the most sustained theme throughout is Garfinkel's "respecification" of the natural sciences as discovering sciences of practical action. This, of course, was the titular theme for the manuscript in Part I of this volume. The seminars not only provide earlier versions on the topic of that manuscript and the pulsar study, they also elaborate upon and provide insight into what those texts present in densely written prose. Moreover, they elaborate upon many other topics. The first seminar discusses alchemy as a reflexive examination of laboratory practice and a precursor for chemistry. The second seminar elaborates upon the material and practical differences between the "discovering sciences," as Garfinkel conceived of them, and the social sciences, and it also provides a reading of Thomas S. Kuhn's treatment of the Galilean law of free fall as (in Garfinkel's terms) an indexical expression that is adapted to specific material realizations in connection with the pendulum and inclined plane. The third seminar (June 3) develops a distinctive, praxiological conception of Gestalt theory in reference to embodied work, and the fourth and fifth seminars (June 19, July 1) further elaborate upon his ethnomethodological treatment of themes such as figure-ground, the adumbrated object, and finding the "animal in the foliage." In addition to including a lively dialogue with Professor Westman, the July 1 seminar includes some of Garfinkel's extemporaneous remarks about "the demonic order" of contingencies evidenced in and through scientific practice. Many more topics and examples also appear throughout the series of seminars.

SEMINAR 1

Discovering work of the sciences (May 22, 1980)

Harold Garfinkel

Alchemy, Chemistry, and the Work of a Discovering Science; Introduction to the Case of the Optical Pulsar Discovery; "Curious Absurdities" in Sociological Studies of Work; "The Animal in the Foliage" and other Gestalt Themes; Gerald Holton's Account of the Millikan-Ehrenhaft Dispute

GARFINKEL: We will be going over materials tonight on the problem of what makes up the work of a discovering science, with such constraints as might exist on our theorizing. We found some materials that are available to us on the optical pulsar. I'll tell you a little bit more about those materials, but first let me introduce it by telling you of a very nifty speculation by Trent Eglin, who was a student here in the early 1960s and who introduced the crowd of us who were here at the time to the importance of our coming to terms with what it was to be doing scientific discovery. But he did it out of an interest – a really serious, committed, detailed interest – in laboratory alchemy.[1] And he had a lovely way of posing it.

He posed the issue by asking two questions. First of all, Newton, according to Merton [1965], is supposed to have engaged in a gorgeous bit of modesty by saying, as Merton puts it, that if he was able to see further than anyone else, it was by standing on the shoulders of giants. Question: Whose shoulders was he talking about? He could have been talking about, as Merton made him talk about, the proto-physicists. But Eglin had an argument to make, and his argument was, no, Newton was not talking about proto-physicists. So that's one thing I'm going to tell you about Eglin's argument.

The other thing that Eglin started with was pointing out that between the sixteenth and seventeenth centuries, laboratory alchemy disappeared from the

---

1 In the 1970s and '80s, Garfinkel circulated a draft of Eglin's paper that later was published as a chapter in a volume that Garfinkel edited (Eglin 1986).

earth. It had been prevalent in Europe just without question. In fact, laboratory alchemy has been prevalent and has had a history in every literate society. So it is all the more interesting, then, that in one hundred years, this immensely elaborate development disappeared. That is to say, its practitioners were no longer to be found.

Question: What happened to laboratory alchemy – did it go into the grave? Eglin makes the argument: no, it did not go into the grave, and also it's not true that Newton was talking about proto-physicists.

His argument goes like this. He said the history of physics and chemistry, for example – more particularly he talks about the history of chemistry because elaborate histories have been written of chemistry by chemists, and the argument that he's making comes out very clearly when he addresses the histories that chemists have written of their own discipline. He says that a chemist writing a history of his discipline is apt to start with the victories in hand of analytic chemistry. He starts with a point of view of the achievements in hand of twentieth century analytic chemistry. With those achievements in hand, he then constructs a chronology, building back the chain of events that stood in precedence for each one that came before it. Building that chronology back, the chemist then finds a beginning place, which is apt to be someplace in about the fifteenth century. In that beginning place he finds there a laboratory alchemy and with it the beginnings of analytic chemistry, as a very young, newborn, but immensely potent rival; that is to say that young analytic chemistry, being right and effective and factually correct and respectful of worldly matters, was able to reveal thereby the corruption and the shortcomings and the rosy trail (or worse) that the rival alchemy posed. In summary then, what Eglin argued was that it's the analytic chemist writing a history who finds that alchemy and finds that chemistry in the beginning. So if it lost out –

[Brief interruption – apparently someone entered the seminar room, inquiring about whether it was open to visitors.]

GARFINKEL: That's called turning away the zoo visitor, or worse.

In any case, what he [Eglin] points out is that the analytic chemist would have found them together by reason of this method of building that history and that chronology, and then re-reading it from the beginning to provide for the way in which an effective rival failed.

Now, what Eglin proposes is that he doubts that anything of the sort happened. He thinks it's a misreading not only of alchemy but also of that chronology. . . . What he proposes is that the laboratory alchemists were not doing a poor version of chemistry; they were not studying the world for the existence of chemical events. It doesn't mean that they were ignorant of chemistry. But their practices in the lab were not directed then to learning what from the point of view of twentieth-century chemistry would have been a version of chemistry's facts of life. So they were not in this sense rivals of a proto-chemistry, they were not proto-chemists, but they were instead investigators into the character of practical action, and they were using laboratory materials with which to study *in situ* what a structure of effective practices, chained to the materials with which to learn its ways, indeed looked like. And the laboratory exercises then were required, since the reasoning was, in fact, attached to and not separable from the moral structure, practices and instruments that made up their lessons. So, in fact, he speaks of them as proto-phenomenologists of practical action. And they were using their laboratory exercises to get across to the structures of their own embodied reasoning.

Now the interest, he said, was the interest in discovering. What was it, as worldly practice, to be discovering the world as a domain of practical activities?

His idea is that in the sixteenth century, you had the beginnings of the factory system. And with the beginnings of the factory system, what had prior to that been a craft that knew of its effectiveness in, say, the situated character of materials and practice, and the rest, now became – he speaks of it as it becoming societalized. That is to say, it's turning into, above all, an accountable practice. It makes now a serious, accountable difference that you know how to combine metals, for example, so as to produce a given alloy. And this kind of practice became subject increasingly to its recorded and transmissible accountability. So that the rise then of an industrial practice of chemistry that became increasingly cost-accountable drove out of sensibility the esoteric telling and demonstration that made up the pursuit of discovering practices. However, Eglin said, though there was now increasingly no suitable publicly available way of making laboratory practice accountable – that is, making it subject to standard reporting – the preoccupation of the practitioners with the effectiveness of their discovering practices nevertheless remained. But it lost the singularity or, say, the availability of its voice. In fact, it didn't have a voice that was comparable to the standard voices that were being demanded now of this way of carrying on industrial, chemical investigations, let's say, with respect to a plant and the conditions of its existence then tied to the operations of a market.

So it's Eglin's speculation, then, that laboratory chemistry[2] didn't go into the grave, it went into the laboratories; that it remained a standing preoccupation, say, of industrial chemical practitioners (that is, of investigators), but that things that mattered, one's local practices, the constituent practices, came increasingly under formal and transmissible accountability.

So he proposes that if you're going to get a look at where alchemy is to be found these days, then you don't want to look in the graves because the alchemists are not in the graves. It's true that the early ones died off like anyone else. But the life of alchemy is found in the laboratories, available to whosoever, indeed, takes on the tasks of a discovering science such as chemistry, mathematics, and whose reflections are hopelessly (that is to say, without the possibility that they could be otherwise) chained to the effectiveness of discovering practices as the day's work. So if you want to say, "Well, where are the practices of alchemy to be found?," they are to be found, then, in the case of a mathematician at work with other mathematicians at the board where he must be preoccupied with the effectiveness of mathematics' own identifying,

---

2 Garfinkel clearly says "chemistry" here, but from the context of the argument it seems that "alchemy" was what he meant to say.

detailed work as local embodied work found *in situ*, for which the official accounts of his discoveries must read those practices out of relevance, even while he must be committed not only to knowing but also to deepening his craft, to reflecting on his craft in order that he be a better person in the world, which is exactly the alchemists' insistence.

Now then, Newton was himself a practicing alchemist, and the historians of science are embarrassed by the vast preoccupation that he had with esoteric writings.[3] What they figure is, "Well, look, he was so smart in other respects that he can be forgiven his lunacies." There is some reason to think that, no, it's a different thing we're dealing with. Eglin's conjecture is that when Newton said if he saw further, he was standing on the shoulders of giants, he was talking here about the alchemists since it was from them and as one of them that he was indeed a student of discovering practice.

Now, it doesn't make any difference that Eglin's conjecture might be counted right or wrong, that he isn't a member of the Warburg Institute and its high-priced personnel who know all about the social structure of Medieval science. What I propose to you is that the conjecture is very interesting, which is to say it leads us to entertain some questions and some phenomena that otherwise don't really offer themselves. So, let's say the conjecture is to be prized for the consequentiality of it. It doesn't take us away from the study of science, even as the practitioners of the sociology and history of science and social study of science know it. So, I recommend that this conjecture is something to start with.

[ERIC LIVINGSTON PRESENTATION – Deleted][4]

GARFINKEL: I want to tell you a little story about how we come to be together tonight, with an interest in the question of how do scientists do their work actually, not imaginarily; actually not according to a construction; actually as a matter of discovery rather than by playing the usual no-lose/no-news game of explicating a definition.

In 1975, I had the immense good fortune to spend a year at the Center for Advanced Study [in the Behavioral Sciences at Stanford University]. Gerald Holton, who is a distinguished physicist and historian of physics, as well as a historian more generally of the sciences, was there. He and I spent a lot of time talking about our mutual dissatisfactions with the current state of materials that bear directly on the question: What is it that scientists do that makes up as the day's work the discovering practices that they're engaged in? So, if they're physicists . . . then the day's work has to consist in this: they're going to be

---

3 Garfinkel was very likely aware of Dobbs' (1975) historical account of Newton's alchemy that was an exception to what he says here.

4 Garfinkel introduces Eric Livingston (an advanced PhD student at the time), who presents a historical case of an experiment at the end of the 19th century by J.J. Thompson, which at the time was taken as a demonstration of the existence of an elementary particle smaller than the atom. I deleted this portion of the seminar in order to retain focus on the continuity of Garfinkel's lecture in the abridged version here. Also, aside from a brief comment later in the seminar, and a few others later in the series of seminars, Garfinkel did not incorporate Livingston's presentation into his discussion.

making discoveries in physics – not in something like physics, not in-principle physics, *et cetera*, but *just this* and not something else.

In any case, Holton at the time said that there were not more than six collections of materials that could be taken seriously in order to address that question. That was in 1975. For example, the collection of interviews. To give you an example of how impoverished that stuff could be, there was a collection of interviews carried on by distinguished physicists with other distinguished physicists, in which they were asked about the distinguished work that they had done. They were asked to give some kind of biography to these. They were closely reasoned, closely attended, intellectual biographies – technical biographies of these men, being interrogated by someone who knew the business, so to speak. So that's one collection of materials. Kuhn's interviews with Heisenberg, for example, are now known to be of that sort. If you want to read super-gorgeous stuff for social science interviewing, then you want to look at some of that.[5] These are to be compared, let's say then, with Harriet Zuckerman's [1977] interviews with Nobel Prize winners. We have several documents around of that sort. It is not putting Harriet Zuckerman down; it is saying, though, that when you examine her interviews, what you will see is that they are content-free. Or when they are not content-free, she doesn't do better than make mention of the man's work. That's because she is not herself a physicist and didn't have to be in order to carry on that work.

So here are the six collections of materials. That was the source of Holton's dissatisfactions. He had had for a long time this insistence on a need for studies and the need, as he spoke of it, for material on what was problematic about it. He spoke of them as problematics of the availability of adequate documentation for the issue that was prominent and that stood unresolved. The issue is how actually do scientists do their work? His favorite way, then, of replying to his own question was to insist that what was needed was that we put our eyes to the keyhole, by which he didn't mean thereby that we preserve the anonymity of the observer but rather that we go to places and look into those places that otherwise are hidden, secretive, out of the way, and not ordinarily come upon.

In voicing that dissatisfaction, he was talking, in dissatisfaction, on behalf of, even at that time, a swiftly elaborating set of studies that claimed to be concerned with the work of a discovering science. So, for example, Polanyi's [1958] *Personal Knowledge* is concerned with exactly that issue. During that year Merton and Zuckerman collaborated with Joshua Lederberg, a distinguished microbiologist, in fact one of the founders of microbiology. His discovery was . . . of the sexuality of bacteria, for which he won the Nobel Prize. They had already spent time before they got to the Center and now were continuing at the Center. The three were collaborating to turn Lederberg's discovery into the autobiography of that discovery, in the search for what he could say or what

---

5 Garfinkel is referring here to oral histories in the Archive for History of Quantum Physics at The Bancroft Library, University of California, Berkeley. Among the materials in that archive is a lengthy interview of Werner Heisenberg by Thomas Kuhn.

they could collaboratively come to in agreement were the effective strategies of which the discovery consisted. So that's what their search was about.[6]

Well, other studies are those of Herbert Simon and Alan Newell, who have published materials on what kinds of work mathematicians are doing when they are doing mathematics.[7] There is, of course, Kuhn's work and so on. I won't take up your time with going through that roster.[8]

I do, however, want to make the principal point, and that is that there is widespread interest in the issue of what specifically is the work of a discovering science. Accompanying that widespread interest is a dissatisfaction not only on the part of the practitioners (that is to say, on the part of the scientists whose work might be the object of such interest), but the inquirers themselves (like Merton, Lederberg and Zuckerman) are by no means thrilled with their inquiry even though it's incredibly rich.

You could ask: well, what is it, then, that falls short? The thing that falls short is that they know and needn't be reminded, although there is everyone around to remind them, including me or us, that their procedures are such as to circle back on the same old entanglements with which we are all familiar: i.e., you want to know what the work of discovering could be? Well, then there are the resources of ethnography with which then to propose some stories of how the work was done. Trouble? You have the story, though it will not respond under any interrogation that you can imagine to the task of formulating and solving as a matter of structure what the discovering practice consisted of as a production. That is to say, what was it as a production to have come upon whatever, say, the discovery of the sexuality of bacteria, or the optical pulsar, or whatever.

So, there were other entanglements. They could then settle for analytic, just-so stories. We are all familiar with how that's done. They could start with a definitional account of discovery. Or they could start with the notion of a discovery generally speaking, and so on, and so on. In each of those cases the dissatisfaction remains, because what is wanted is not to come then upon the same old difficulties and the same invocations in the end that what we have will be adequate for practical purposes, since it turns out that what they are in the end as adequate for practical purposes is, in fact, what all practical purposes look like and consist of, and there's no way of breaking out of that without finding a radical way to start again.

Okay. Now, it was in the course of one of our conversations that I proposed to Holton that the thing that was curious in such studies as he told me about,

---

6 See Zuckerman and Lederberg (1986).
7 Garfinkel does not supply a reference, but he appears to be referring to Simon and Newell's efforts to develop computational models of problem solving, such as Simon and Newell (1958).
8 By 1980, Garfinkel had become aware of the work in social studies of science that criticized the lack of attention to the "content" of science by sociologists; for example, Bloor (1976), and Latour and Woolgar (1979). Apparently, Garfinkel was not aware of such work during his time at the Center in 1975, and with few exceptions constructivist work on science treated the concept of "discovery" with skepticism, without addressing what Garfinkel calls "discovering *work*" as an identifying feature scientific practice. For interesting constructivist treatments of discovery, informed by ethnomethodology, see Brannigan (1981) and Woolgar (1976).

and such studies as his own – absolutely distinguished – studies, is that they seemed invariably to make use of a curious subjectivity of the analysts and thereby of the scientists whose work they were studying. That subjectivity is so-called "disembodied" subjectivity. That is to say, the subjectivity of the prevailing studies of scientists' practices provides for an intentionality, for example, to the activities that make up that work. But that intentionality is entirely a mindful category, or it is mindful stuff. And the notion of the subjective relevance, let us say, of the intention or of the purpose of the aimful, or originating, or grounded character of a course of action that makes up knowing what you're doing, or knowing what you're after, or knowing what you're searching for – that this subjectivity was such as to provide for the analyst the standing excuse and a standing way in which the analyst's entire inquiry could be brought up without giving embodied action a second thought. So that subjectivity, then, in the analyst's hands has the function of excusing all relevance of embodied action, while maintaining the claim-ability on the analyst's part that indeed he was getting at the structure of practices that made up the work of a scientist.

So when I pointed then out to Holton that Merleau-Ponty put in our hands a philosophy of embodied action; put in our hands a way of speaking about and of seeing activities for the exhibited relevance of embodied practice, that the import of this would be to make of shop work and of shop talk a phenomenon that had hitherto not in fact been examined, though it had to be the preoccupation of every practitioner – which is to say there is no way of doing chemistry in the lab unless you are at the bench. It turns out those are bodies that are oriented to material at the bench. Question: it could be that that makes one hell of a lot of difference. I became really fascinated with that possibility.

Then I proposed to Holton that what would be needed would be that we would bug the world. That is, we would get one hell of a lot of video machinery; we would put it into every lab around. We would turn the machinery on, and we would never turn it off. Then we would haul all this stuff away and look at it for a change. The reason we would have to bug the world is that you would have to turn it on and wait because you couldn't tell when the goddamn discovery would turn up. All right? That's why you would need so much machinery, such a tremendous staff, *et cetera*.

He said that he thought that was perfectly reasonable. [Students laugh.] We would have to simply go in as "anthropologists." We would have to be on the scene. And we agreed that we should have to become competent to the practices that we were studying. Otherwise, what was visibly there would escape us into stories again of what's going on that were inventions of practice, and so on.

Then he said, "All right, you can't bug the world. But you'll be interested to know that the optical pulsar when it was discovered was discovered by two novices who happened to come together at the University of Arizona one summer." They were treated by the local company of astronomers, since both of them were theoretical astrophysicists and professedly knew nothing about the actual work of observing through a telescope, as *pishers* – that is to say, as youngsters who were wetting their pants, that you couldn't expect from them that they would have anything more to turn up then you simply would pat them on the diaper and say, "Good going." It wouldn't be worth anything. [Students laugh.] Okay?[9]

So these two novices then got three nights of viewing on a second-rate, 36-inch telescope, and figured out beforehand just where in the Milky Way – that is, in the so-called Crab Nebula – they were going to aim their little itsy-bitsy telescope, after having figured out which pair of stars in the center of that nebula were apt to have been the source of a hitherto registered radio pulse. So there had been these radio pulses that finally had been established in the discovery the year before by [Anthony] Hewish and his company. And here they were, then, along with everybody else in the company (that is, among the astronomers and the astrophysicists). Whoever could get to a telescope, in fact, was out in the search for whether accompanying these 15 radio pulsars, which at that time [1969] had been established, one of them might have an optical component. so here are these two novices, literally these two novices, that were given three nights on the machine with the idea, "Well, okay, they'll learn at least how to operate the telescope."[10] And that in itself was an achievement because theoretical astrophysicists, according to local prejudices, don't really do observation. They don't know how, they don't get their hands dirty, and all the rest of the stuff; we're all familiar with those charges.

So, these two birds went through this little calculation. They figured they would put it on something called "Baade's Star," which is something called a "south proceeding star." It doesn't make a damn bit of difference. I'll make these materials available to you. You can read it. It's very interesting to read the original reports, as well as the reports about them.[11]

The first night of their observations, they got nothing. Just zero. Then during the following day, they were going over their results, and they found that they had made an error in calculating the distance across the star that the light would have to travel. Not incorporating that into their calculations, they had positioned the telescope incorrectly, meaning it was just a faint hair off. But given the vast distances, et cetera, it was enough so that they got zilch. So, they spent the day making the recalculations. And that second night they positioned the telescope to make up for that error. They

---

9   As Garfinkel et al. (1981: 131) make clear in their subsequently published article on the optical pulsar discovery, the two astrophysicists (John Cocke and Michael Disney) were accompanied by a "night assistant" (Robert McCallister) who assisted in setting up and running the equipment. Garfinkel jokingly exaggerates their naivety here, but by their own account, Cocke and Disney were theorists who were not experienced with operating observatory equipment. A third astrophysicist, Don Taylor, was not present at the observatory at the time, but had built the electronic apparatus that collected photons from the telescope and analyzed them for a possible pulsed frequency corresponding to the frequency of a radio pulsar that was possibly the supernova remnant in the Crab Nebula. Radio telescopes provide less precise resolution of the sources of signals than an optical telescope does for visible light.

10 These inexperienced observers nevertheless began the exercise with what turned out to be a successful rationale for focusing on a supernova remnant that might be the source of the rapid pulsation in electromagnetic radiation detected in the vicinity of the Crab Nebula.

11 Some of the documentary materials are included in appendices of Garfinkel et al. (1981).

had done 16 observations the night before. The 17th observation was the observation they started with, and the 17th observation has the pulsar in it. They make 17, 18, 19, et cetera, through 34 observations; and now, said Holton, these bozos were so little adept with the use of that equipment that they didn't realize that they had turned on the tape recorder and left it on, into which they otherwise would have recorded separately the results of each observation.[12] But no, they didn't do that. They got the full recording for the 17th through the 34th observations of the discovery of the optical pulsar.

Holton said, "You need material like that, don't you?" [Student laughter.]

Yes. "It's available on a quarter-inch tape at the American Institute of Physics in New York City on 45th Street. I'm one of the founders of that Institute. I would be very happy to write to the two people there who are very decent, and they will be very happy to talk to you and give you access to the tape."

So in the spring of 1976, I went to New York City and, sure enough, met the two, the Director and the Assistant Director or Executive Director, a man and a woman.[13] They, in fact, were very interested in a few sketched notions I had about it. Sure enough, not only could I listen to the tape, but they were very happy to make a copy when and if it appeared that I was in fact going to dig in and do something with the tape.

So I won't go through the rest of the history. But the fact is that we now have the tapes in these cassettes, together with a 34-page transcription of the tape that Mike Lynch made.

Now, with those resources the question is: well, what the hell kind of resources are they? Is it that we have something good, or is it that we have something to start with that could lead us up an initially promising trail and finally out into Cloud Cuckooland? The issue is very serious. It could, in fact, go either way.

Here's what's good about it. We have an unprecedented record of shop talk that makes up the talk, in the course of which whatever we would say a discovery would have to sound like, as shop talk, it is surely then to be compatible with what's on that tape, which is to say we might learn then from the tape.

At the same time, we are armed with what? With the resources of conversational analysis.[14] Yes? No. What we're talking about is shop talk. What conversational analysis puts in our hands would be what we could call claims and

---

12 Later in 1980, Garfinkel and Lynch interviewed Taylor and Cocke and were told that the voices were recorded on a channel of the same tape used to record electronic data from the source, and that the night assistant did not fully disconnect the jack for the microphone during the series of observations, thus recording the voices and data on different channels.

13 Spencer Weart and Joan Warnow.

14 Garfinkel, as well as many other ethnomethodologists at the time, preferred to speak of "conversational analysis," which was widely used among practitioners before Conversation Analysis (CA) become established as a name for the professional field. A reason for holding on to the term "conversational" was that it was more clearly associated with an emphasis on 'analysis' as primary feature of the endogenous production of conversation, and only secondarily an academic undertaking.

assessments as a conditionally relevant pair, which are such, however, that the features that they would have are taken from the kind of talk that anybody can do, what it is then that persons might be agreeing to. These two birds, one is called Michael Disney and the other is called John Cocke. Cocke and Disney are into a Mutt-and-Jeff routine. One is saying, "We've got a bloody pulsar." And the other is saying, "now, now. Now, now." Well, this repeating structure is one, where one is claiming and the other is withholding agreement. So that would look like – you get that in the world as a massive, recurrent phenomenon everybody does. You can see that. I'll give you copies of that transcript. When you hear it, you'll understand that what they're agreeing to has nothing whatsoever to do with agreement generally speaking or agreement as slobs agree. That is to say, it isn't the agreement that you find, generally speaking. The last thing we want to do is to speak of that agreement or to analyze that agreement as agreeing generally speaking. What we really would like to do is to find in what way did the things that were being agreed upon or being offered as agreeables; did they have a technical content that could not be put aside without our losing just what was identifying in the way they were talking as the shop talk of theoretical physicists who, as part of a community of other physicists, had come upon a display and now had to find their way through the presence of that apparatus, and their own talk in the presence of that apparatus, to arrive finally as the achievement, at a naturally theoretic account of the practices that made up the appearance and progressive elaboration and availability of a just-this that's the pulsar after all.

Now then, the problem is this. If you take just the conversational analytic version of that interaction, or that transcript, then you have to lose something that is really critical and essential, and that is that there was this machinery in that dome. This machinery was technical stuff that displayed, that accumulated these photons, accumulated them in the certain technical way for which they had ways themselves of calculating to see. . . . .[15]

So that means, okay, we have a perfectly good transcript. The question is, are we now going to learn what our lunacies would be if we attend to the transcript and disregard the fact that as shop talk, the talk is hopelessly chained, as embodied talk, to the looks of the things that the talk then is revealing of. But then you could say in the same way that it's chained to the looks of that display that is such as to be, in attending it, revealing of what the talk is talk of. This is to say that it's not that the talk maps onto the display, the talk and the display indeed are mutually revealing of their technical content for each other, and this as something that these two bozos are in fact doing and engaged in and that make up the night's work. If there's a discovery we're going to be talking about and we want to pin it to the character of practice, if it's going to have to consist of practice, then we're going to have to respect *that* feature and

---

15 A gap in the tape of the seminar occurred at this point.

we're going to have somehow come upon what the discovering practice could consist of, where the discovering practice would itself be all of what a physical phenomenon could consist of.[16] Now that claim is perhaps jumping the gun. So, now let me review what we're going to be doing.

I proposed earlier in our seminar meetings [see p. 21, this volume] that there were some curious absurdities, some standing absurdities, in studies of work. I think I might have spent some time in the evening saying: look, if you talk about the absurdities of the work of professionals, you don't know anything until you've seen the absurdities of scientists' work. So we have, then, that list of absurdities and it included as well the so-called absurdity that turned them into a kind of coherent phenomenon. We spoke of the irrelevance to the practitioner's interest in the practices that compose the quiddity, the just-here/just-this of the practice as in-place, on-site, *in situ* effectiveness of the day's work.

So, we've been talking about astrophysicists who now pose for us as a possible discoverable that their practices are going to have to be such that the irrelevance of that quiddity will have been overcome in our own inquiries. Well, now, here's where the absurdities betray us. They make perfectly good sense to go through them, that is to say to see where scientists are concerned, where their work is concerned, the absurdities furnish aims and constraints on our inquiry. And that's very nice and very high-flown talk. But it's not better than high-flown talk, because the absurdities are absolutely silent on just how such inquiries get done. So nothing about the absurdities is going to serve us. But instead, we're going to have to do something else. We can't now simply engage in deep breathing about the irrelevance to practice. We're going to need something else.

Well, I would like to sketch the prize we're going for. Okay? So we won't get too lost in the detail. We are going to be looking at the work of Cocke and Disney as the lived-orderliness of the work of theoretical physicists. This is to say we want to be speaking of a science in and as the *Lebenswelt*. We want to be looking at a science in and as praxis – and not praxis generally speaking. [Pause]

We want, in fact, access to the *just*-what, *just*-this; not the "somehow" of that night's work, but the *just-what*-how of that night's work, insofar as the work itself is not different than the lived orderliness of theoretical physicists' own topics of order, now available as practical achievements.[17] That phenomenon, okay? Let me play with that in several ways just to put it into your hands, so that the full *mishigas* of it, the full lunacy, is at least out on the table.

---

16 Garfinkel later explored the possibility of reconstructing the developing record of the pulse in coordination with the developing interaction between Cocke and Disney, but during a phone call with Garfinkel, Taylor (who assembled the electronic equipment) informed him that the equipment had long ago been disassembled.
17 Garfinkel's characterization here of Cocke and Disney's work at Kitt Peak Observatory as the work of "theoretical physicists" is puzzling. The contrast between the series of observations recorded on the tape is unlikely to look anything like the work of the theoretical physicist Stephen Hawking (cf. Mialet 2012). However, there is a sense in which Cocke and Disney were working out a theoretical possibility about the origins of pulsar radiation when they focused on a supernova remnant. It also seems that Garfinkel may be speaking broadly here about physical scientists.

There is available for all of us – not just ethnomethodologists or anyone else – there is the omniprevalent difference that is made between the natural sciences and the humanistic sciences. That omniprevalent difference that's made, I'm going to propose to us, is a conventional difference. We have a comparison that we're asserting thereby to be a research for the adequacy of the claimed comparison. The comparison is that what we want to do is to recover a science in the entirety of its technical, substantive contents. We want to recover that science as a humanistic science. That is, the thing that's being said is that the concern for the science as *praxis* offers as a possibility that, let's say, physics is going to be a curious kind of science. In fact, it's a problematic science. Question: What kind of a science is physics? If we consider now with respect to its *entire technical content*, its entire technical content now is to be encountered as *topics* of order. And they are topics of order in this sense: that if physics is to be thought of with respect to these achieved topics of order, it's a science of practical action. Which is to say, it's not that physics is, but that physics, now encountered by us as the practical achievement of all technical contents as topics of order, is in fact a science of practical action. It's a *just-how*: the objects of physics in the company of other physicists, in the places of the shop, with just the equipment that there must be known in the fashion of its work, by those who by their embodied presence to their workings, in making them work are available then to what the work indeed, for consisting of, will look and sound like. And it won't be anything at all, but will be then available to the naturally theoretic version of that, since they talk of the naturally theoretic work that they do in the established terms that we found here in Eric [Livingston's] presentation of the experimental version of the objectivity of the electron.[18]

Now the question is: Is that proposal off the wall? The answer to that is *no*, it's not off the wall, it has some precedents. I will just mention names because we need to get into the content of the thing. Say, Holton and Kuhn are the names of scholars of physicists' practices whose stature is incredible – you only have to read these birds to see. I mean, it's just marvelous that the world can be that detailed and that somebody could know the kinds of things that these birds are capable of saying. Well, they are important for other reasons, much more serious reasons than that they write well or that they know so damned much. There's another set of precedents, and the precedents are available out of a company of students, principally students here that made up a local culture, beginning roughly in around 1972, and who as a developing culture in fact came upon, made explicit, worked out, sweated out, paid in blood for putting in our hands what I'll call the recurrent themes in the studies of work and the studies principally of the work of scientists. Tonight I'm simply going to mention their names.

---

18 The presentation by Eric Livingston on J.J. Thompson's demonstration of the electron occurred earlier in the session, but was deleted from the present version of the transcript. The reference to it that Garfinkel is making here to "established terms" is to the formal idioms used to characterize experimental procedures and their results.

. . .

Let me sketch, then who some of these people are. There is to begin with, and very early, David Sudnow, whose original suggestion was (but it wasn't available as stronger than a suggestion) that there exists this curious absurdity in the studies of work; namely, that you could learn all kinds of things about musicians except what it was they were doing in just the places where, in each other's company, with just the things at hand and the time they had, they were making, produceably, [understandably, learn-ably], they were making music together. He was the first one to point out the incongruous character of a literature that had everything having to do with studies *about* work and nothing of its identifying practices as the in-courseness of the *in situ* detail. That is to say, that concern with the detail was *dismissed* in the classic studies as a concern for the flooding, inundating, debilitating circumstantiality of endless stories to be told. Available at such detail, with such a notion of detail, that such studies handled, destroyed, or undermined the possibility of generalizability and, in fact, the availability to study of structures.

The studies of conversational analysis fairly demonstrated that there was something new in the world on that score, that the notion of detail now had to take into account that it was itself a curious feature of the world of embodied practice, and that the notion of detail had to provide as well not only that it was identifyingly organizational detail. A conversational greeting was a conversational greeting in and as a course of detail, and therein recognizably and understandably the conversational greeting *really*, not supposedly, not constructively. That was the big change.[19]

With the availability, then, of conversational studies, that was the strongest case in hand, or the studies were the strongest cases in hand that the claims of detail, and with them, the claims of just what structure could possibly be, had now to come in for revision, and a very radical revision, and a whole different conception of what in fact the ordinary society consisted of; where issues of the adequate analysis of the recurrent, comparable, standardized, typical practices consisted of.

In any case, the point that I want to make is that here is a community of persons. It begins, as I said, with Sudnow's suggestion. There were a series of people: [Albert B.] Robillard, Chris Pack, George Girton, Melinda Baccus, Mike Lynch, Eric [Livingston], Stacey Burns and, very early, years ago, Trent Eglin.[20] Those would be principal parties. I won't, for tonight, do the crediting. In a way, the crediting is perhaps the most arbitrary enterprise that one could imagine.

[. . .][21]

---

19 Garfinkel's comments about Conversation Analysis (CA) here contrast with what he says elsewhere (such as in Appendix 1 of Part I in this volume). That appendix was written eight years after this seminar met, and one could suppose that by then he had grown disenchanted with developments in CA. However, at that time and for many years later he also would uphold CA as an exemplary development, despite qualms about the increasingly formal-analytic tendencies in the field.

20 This list is former students of Garfinkel's, several of whom are included as authors of chapters in Garfinkel (1986).

21 I deleted around five minutes of the recorded seminar from the transcript at this point, as Garfinkel goes on to digress with some offhand comments about some of his students and former students, and

Let me review what the claiming is that's going on. [Pause] What we need to be examining is the discovery of the optical pulsar as the *lived* work of discovering the pulsar. It's being claimed, as well, that the work is adequately examined according to the interests, the methods and the recurrent themes of astrophysics as a science of practical action – that is to say, of astrophysics, of all things, as a humanistic science; of a science which, in the hands of our interest, is *hopelessly* concerned and directed to, as worldly achievements, the discovered optical pulsar as a producible, exhibitable, analyzable, exhibitedly analyzable topic of order. And that topic of order is itself a social achievement. So we're talking about astrophysics as human practice insofar, as we have encountered now its practices, that it consists in its technical content of the *production* of social order.

Now, the way to get free of the lunacies and the devils that start to float around or come into your life when you think of physics as a science of practical action is to remember that we're talking of their science as a lived science. Okay? (That is a –)[22] of the disengaged character of their science, of the fact that it has its products, it has its corpus of findings, it has its literature, and in that no mention is made, say, of embodied practice, let alone that its phenomena are anywhere available via the embodied practice, yet we know that it's *only* in the *vernacular* availability of those reports to the practitioners in the places where the inquiries must be done, that the report thereby, as a part of the lab setting in which it's consulted to get done what it speaks of, that the lab practice takes on as its life its character of sensible, and instructed, and instructable, and talk-aboutable methodic procedure. So that would mean then that their technical topics indeed are practical achievements. Yet that doesn't help us at all to simply speak about that, since there's nothing that's being said about practical action generally speaking; we're talking about *just that* practical action that makes up the encounterable optical pulsar. I mean, unless you have it for the technical detail of the seeable optical pulsar in the places and with the machinery with which, *as* a workable matter for bodies whose ways are that of making everything that *workable* means come true. Then, in those certain terms everything that the phenomenon could otherwise, in disengaged fashion, be claimed for or come to look like is now seen again in and as the achievement of practical action. So, indeed theoretical physics is to be spoken of as a science of practical action – and, quite seriously, as a *science* of practical action, unlike ethnomethodology which is not a *science* of practical action. It may be an artful way of getting some studies done, for the time being. And for sociology we have to say *for sure* it's an *art* of practical action, carrying about

---

projects the possibility that they will eventually come to teach mathematicians and physicists to more effectively conduct discovering practices in their respective fields. These possibilities are discussed in a more systematic way in Part I and elsewhere in this series of seminars.

22 The audio recording of the start of this sentence is unclear, but it should be evident that in the clauses that follow, Garfinkel is developing a contrast between disengaged treatments of science (e.g., in methods reports or erudite recollections) and the embodied, lived-work of the laboratory that provides for the practical sense of such disengaged accounts.

the trappings of and the demands for certain rigorous ways of carrying on its inquiries. It would be pointless – worse than pointless, it would be ignorance of the worst sort – to turn away from that as its features. It would also be distracting to then say that it's a science of practical action; whereas there's a good chance that physics is one science of practical action and biochemistry is altogether a different science of practical action. One of the interesting things may be the way in which finally these two sciences have to do with each other in just what practical action in fact for each could look like. What we're saying is that the optical pulsar is the achievement of a practice, that (includes) itself (as) a practice.

You might say: Jesus, this sounds like an operational definition with pepper and salt on its tail. Right? It's taking operational definition right to the end of the line. I wish you wouldn't, though, even though you'd want to.

The claiming now is proceeding, saying that all of the topical phenomena of astrophysics, or astronomy or of a science – you have to put into that notion of sciences, substitute for it, a *definite* science, not science generally – are order topics; and they are then to be discovered as topics of produced order of the streets, which is to say, they are to be discovered as the produced order with the use of the ethnomethodological policies: as, for example, that we remain indifferent to the methods of constructive analysis, that we are respectful of the use of the unique adequacy of methods, that we be following or finding these topics by following Sacks' example,[23] and so on.

More specifically: What is it that is being proposed, say, as the discoverable? Well, remember what we are proposing as the name of the discovery is the optical pulsar as a coherent phenomenon. Now let me show you some stuff on the board and then we'll have a notational way of saying just what the devil we're truly saying.

Let me use *OP* to mean the optical pulsar as a coherent phenomenon. Clearly, that's what we're looking for, which is to say, the in-course work *as of which* the optical pulsar as a coherent phenomenon is detectable, demonstrable, findable, . . . and so on.

Now, it's more than that. The discovery we are going to be talking about, by proposing – that is, we're going to be searching for what I'm going to call the *animal* in the foliage.[24] The animal in the foliage (pause) is the work of

---

[23] On Sacks' example, see Garfinkel (2002: 181–182), where he attributes a procedure for finding "perspicuous settings" to Harvey Sacks. The procedure involves the respecification of what otherwise might be called a theoretical concept, or in the case attributed to Sacks a legal distinction between "possessables" (a found object that "anyone" can take possession of) and "possessitives" (something that evidently belongs to somebody else). Sacks' gloss, as Garfinkel calls it, involves treating the use of the distinction in a real-worldly setting as a tutorial on what the distinction amounts to as somebody's lived-work. Sacks proposed that, instead of explicating the distinction through research in a law library, he could seek to learn of its use by members of a police department whose day's work involved identifying abandoned (rather than, say, stolen or legally owned) vehicles.

[24] The "animal in the foliage" is an allusion to a common type of picture puzzle that is sometimes used to illustrate the theme of figure-ground in gestalt theory. The puzzle consists in a line drawing in which objects are hidden in a dense array of lines depicting a scene (e.g., foliage), and the challenge is

finding the demonstrably coherent phenomenon and formulating it as a methodic procedure, given that if we're to formulate it as a methodic procedure, we are going to have to do something with the damned foliage. The foliage is nothing else than the laboratory embodied practices in the midst of which, as a part of which, over the course of our having to get the night's work done, those practices are extractable from the embodied presence to that display so as to find and formulate out of those practices, just those practices that can be formulated as a methodic procedure. That is to say, we want the naturally theoretic account of those embodied practices. That naturally theoretic account will be that the night's work is now taken account of in such established terms as to permit an extracted version of those practices with which, then, a practitioner, in reading that official version, can now on grounds of his competence to the embodied practice avoid being swamped by the foliage, and seeing through and disregarding those practices in favor of seeing and formulating just those that make up, over and over again, the way to (cite) just what it is that (this machinery . . .).[25]

So what we're saying is, look, the optical pulsar poses as the problematic phenomenon, poses as a discoverable, this: How do you find, say, given the hopeless presence of the (   ) to embodied work, to the material machinery display, the workings of things around – how do you then find your way to the formulated account of that practice, the formulation being such as to *render* that work in *established* terms, to put in your hands then an account that you know dignifies and lies on the face of it? It's only for the boobies who know nothing about lab practice that the account is disengaged from any thought to lab practice, and then be inspected and examined as a (process), as if it will yield up the secrets about how what it reports indeed is to be gotten again. Even the sociologists of science who know nothing about science are in entire agreement with the students of science.[26] They sing with one voice on that song; and that is that there is a world of difference between the scientific

---

to pick those objects out from the backgrounds in which they are hidden. A superficial understanding of the metaphor in this case would treat it as a reference to efforts to separate signal from noise, but Garfinkel (as he goes on to specify) is referring to the immediate task at hand of "extracting" (identifying, iterating, formulating) a procedure that (if all goes well) will later described in a report of the discovery as an effective procedure through which to find the pulsar again. The "foliage" would then be the immediate practical actions and circumstances that later drop out of relevance when the account of the formal procedure is deemed adequate in the community of astronomers.

25 Garfinkel's voice trails off at the end of the sentence and (ironically, given the topic) becomes lost in background noise.

26 For example, Robert K. Merton, who later was criticized by proponents of an ascendant sociology of scientific knowledge for giving an idealized treatment to the natural sciences, noted the following: "Typically, the scientific paper or monograph presents an immaculate appearance which reproduces little or nothing of the intuitive leaps, false starts, mistakes, loose ends, and happy accidents that actually cluttered up the inquiry. The public record fails to provide many of the source materials needed to reconstruct the actual course of scientific developments" (Merton 1968: 4). However, while noting this, Merton did not investigate the "shop floor" from which such accounts were disengaged.

report and the practices that the reports are to be read as accounts of. And *no* interrogation of those reports will recover, in fact, the practice as a structure of activities, as a structure of local appearances. On that they are absolutely in flat agreement. So, we're taking that, then, as a hint that what's going on. . . .

By the way, another name for the animal in the foliage would be a "figure-ground structure." Except that now that we see it as a figure-ground structure, instead of it being a function of perception, instead of it being a bit of structure with which we talk about it being a property of perceptual activity; instead of being an abstract function, it is instead a practical *achievement*. Cocke and Disney had in fact to *find* the figure-ground relationship out of the evening's work. And, the "animal in the foliage" is a metaphoric way of talking about what it seriously is.

Now I'm going to tell you something. If figure-ground structure is, as a Gestalt theme – if we understand it as a practical achievement – I think we understand that there are other Gestalt themes that also offer themselves as practical achievements. What we'll be doing in looking at Cocke and Disney's stuff is asking: Where in the scene do we find it evidentiary, let's say, in the account of what we could learn about the achieved figure-ground structure? I mean what kind of practical achievement is it? Obviously, saying, "My god, we've got a bloody pulsar!"[27] means just how that registering figure is separateable from everything else that can be going on in that lab to produce that oscilloscope display where, with whatever else can be going on in the lab, to see that pulse means that they are in deep trouble. "Yeah, oh my god, it's a pulsar" – unless it's those bastards down in the city have that radio station and we're picking up what they picked up in other places, and so on, "in which case, claiming that we found the optical pulsar portends of disaster in our careers." So the very fact that you see it already poses the issues that have this screwy name and that have to be worked out. So when Disney says, "Jesus, we've got a bloody pulsar," and the other one says, "Now, now," we figure they're on the way.[28] "Not yet in hand" opens up another Gestalt theme which is called the "adumbrated object."[29] The adumbrated object is the object which, over

---

27 See the transcript of Observation #18 in Garfinkel et al. (1981: 149):
  Disney: We've got a bleeding *pulse* here.
          (2.0)
  Cocke: W*a:::w!*
          (1.2)
  Cocke: You don't suppose it's really it, do you?
          (2.0)
  Cocke: Ca::n't be:.
  Disney: It's right *bang* in the middle of the period (Look), I mean right bang in the middle of the (sca::le).
28 Garfinkel is referring to lines 051–052 in the transcript of Observation No. 19 (see Garfinkel et al. 1981: 151):
  Disney: *By God! We got it!*
  Cocke: Naow, naow.
29 Compare to Gurwitsch (1964: 202ff.) on "perceptual adumbration."

a course of we'll call it human activity, shows itself in its developing aspects as the selfsame object throughout the changing appearances. The appearances are appearances of – given your perspective and point of view in its various aspects. So, to be addressed to *achieving* the adumbrated object is to *achieve* the object that remains the selfsame under the evident appearances at hand that they are not in fact the *same* appearances. They are different appearances, but they are the appearances of the object from the side, the object from the front. Haines Hall [location of the Sociology Department at UCLA] is always available and never otherwise available from the pavements, from the side. It is hopelessly, without possibility of being otherwise, achievable as an adumbrated object. The way you can see that effect is achievable is if you shut your eyes; now go about the business, in fact, of finding it as a blind man. With our eyes and our senses, it's the same old Haines Hall. You could put inverting lenses on to see what it is that you could be achieving. In fact, you might try it with the inverting lenses on to see all of a sudden: Holy Christ, it has a side; it goes from left to right and up and down; it starts in a place at a distance from the viewer. And, in fact, it's encountered via a path whereby its appearance comes from nothing to show itself as just that appearance. Hadley Cantril used to speak about a side of a building, except that he would preface it by speaking of that side of the building he came upon by walking in the way that he walked.[30] So it was the side of the building he came upon by walking up a path via a trip from the library and so on. So that's another theme.

Well, the adumbrated object is another; there's a super-gorgeous one that's called the Gestalt switch. There the achievement is that the *object in hand* is searched for as an anything-but-what's-in-hand. What else it could be but what's in hand is then posed and talked about in the Gestalt switch, because the switch is such that having encountered it, it's then seen in the encounter to be other than and different from what it was taken to be in the first place, and it stands there with utter contrast to what it was seen and witnessed and known for, and was achievably available as.

Very closely related to the Gestalt switch is something called the "incompatible alternative." . . . It's an alternative of the object. Now, here's what is being said. You know that figure. There's the black-and-white display: the cartoon presentation of the black faces on the white background or the white vase on a black background.[31] There's a duck that's seen until you see the rabbit.[32]

---

30 The recording is indistinct here, but Garfinkel may be referring here to Hadley Cantril (1906–1969), a Princeton psychologist and social psychologist.
31 This is a reference to Rubin's Vase, attributed to Danish psychologist and philosopher Edgar John Rubin (1886–1951). See Gurwitsch (1964: 118) for discussion of this alternating faces-vase figure.
32 Garfinkel is, of course, invoking the iconic example of the duck-rabbit, which originally appeared in a German satirical publication *Fliegender Blätter*. This and similar alternating figures were made famous in philosophy as well as psychology, initially by perceptual psychologist Joseph Jastrow at the end of the 19th century, and in Wittgenstein's (1958: §118) discussion of "seeing-as." N.R. Hanson (1965: 13) used a similar sketch of a bird-antelope figure to illustrate his account of concept-laden perception, and Kuhn (1962) used the theme of gestalt shift to set up his conception of paradigm shift. As is evident

FIGURE IIS1.1   Duck-rabbit

Source: From October 23, 1892, issue of *Fliegender Blätter* (http://diglit.ub.uni-heidelberg.de/diglit/fb9 7/0147?sid=8af6d821538a1926abf44c9a95c40951&zoomlevel=2). Public domain.

Now, it's not that you can't see both of them. You can see them. The thing that is interesting is that they're seen in alternation. In fact, perceptual psychologists tell us that you can rely on the speed with which the person can make them alternate as a mild test for the effects of being brainwashed. Imbibe alcohol, you can't do it.

Big point. The alternative speaks of this. If you're seeing it as the duck, that means then that in the in-coursesness of elucidating as a coherent ensemble of features, the duck can't be pursued simultaneously with elucidating as the in-coursesness of the ensemble of features of the rabbit. You can think of "rabbit" but can't see it. The attempt then to *elaborate* one thing while preserving as well the in-coursesness of the other as a task to be at work in doing – what happens is that the one will explode the other one; i.e., you can't do it without undermining the coherence of the effort that makes up in-coursesness . . . in the achievable. Remember, what I'm talking about is not seeing it in a glance but paying attention to the just-how it is composed in its functional characters as the features of the rabbit.

Now, I am proposing that that incompatible alternative is also a practical issue. There are some others. I'll just mention it and then I think we'll call it off for the time being.

Samuel Todes,[33] in an article that he wrote years ago on what he claimed were the phenomenologically demonstrable features of the "empirical object," claimed that the empirical object had, because of its peculiar temporal properties, the

---

in Garfinkel's discussion, his starting point is Gurwitsch's (1964: 112ff.) account of how the functional significance of details, such as the lines that make up the bill of the duck, become instantly respecified as the contexture of details that make up the ears of the rabbit. Garfinkel then transposes the "phenomenal field properties" from a contexture of details in a line drawing to the fields of technical action and developing visible data on an oscillograph screen at Kitt Peak Observatory from which the figure of the optical pulsar becomes tentatively resolved. Also see his discussion at the close of the seminar of getting the phenomenon out of the data in the case of Millikan's oil drop experiment.

33 Garfinkel is referring to philosopher Samuel Todes (1927–1994), who had studied Gestalt theory with Wolfgang Köhler and Aron Gurwitsch. Hubert Dreyfus promoted Todes' work (they were graduate students together at MIT), and introduced the posthumous publication of his major work, *Body and World* (Todes 2001).

character of a beginning, an in-course, and a terminal here [writing on blackboard]. His claim was that the object was given these specifics, its distinguishable structures. I'm throwing that into the pot, thinking that it might be of interest. I know damned well there's something to be done with this. I'm kind of hoping that that plays out because it will allow us a lot of ground.

I think I have the principal claims set out. The principal claim is that it's an order topic, to find that pulsar, how it's produced. That it's an order topic means that the production of it is nothing less than the production of social order.

[Garfinkel proposes to close the seminar at this point, and he and students in the seminar discuss the reading materials assigned for the next seminar. Before ending the present seminar, Garfinkel addresses a student's question and makes a brief foray into the Millikan-Ehrenhaft episode that he discusses in later seminars in this series:]

GARFINKEL: There's an article by Holton [1978] called "Subelectrons, presuppositions, and the Millikan-Ehrenhaft dispute." [It's on] the discovery of the charge on elections. . . . When Holton talked about how Millikan made [the oil drop experiment], he went through 160 drops. He threw out everything but 58 of them. He had good reasons for throwing them out, right? Which is to say, he didn't have good reasons for throwing them out. . . . [W]hat Holton did was to go to Millikan's literary remains (that is, his notebooks) and there examine, in the fashion of detective work, each page, what Millikan had given to each one of these drops, a page full of observations. [One notation] says "Beautiful. Publish it." Another, "There is something wrong here." So Holton goes through this and he tells how he came to that series of _____?_____. He talks at the Center [for Advanced Study in the Behavioral Sciences at Stanford] and several people say to him, "It seems to me that there's something wrong; that Millikan, after all, didn't use proper *procedure*. It wasn't really right; that he should have known better than anyone else or he should have known on his own behalf which drops he would preserve, and which drops he would rule out." And Holton said that that's the whole point. What he was doing is not different than what any investigator does. That's number one. Then the second thing – he said that if there are criticisms to be made, then the criticisms will go like this: he was using oddball procedures all the way through that experiment in order to find the drops he was looking for. That means, then, that there's something like this that has to be said: he knew what he was looking for, and with it then was able to find it; that is to say, he was able to get it out of his data.

Now, when Holton was criticized, he was told: well, Millikan, while he got the Nobel Prize, and though Ehrenhaft, his opponent, went crazy when Ehrenhaft used a contrasting procedure, the question was, "Isn't there a way, nevertheless, in which Ehrenhaft was right and Millikan was wrong? Isn't there a way in which, nevertheless, Millikan can be said to have used an incorrect procedure; that what he said, though it turned out to be true, wasn't in fact adequately, demonstrably true?"

When Holton replied to this he said, though it turned out to be true, wasn't it in fact adequately, demonstrably true? He said that Millikan – all these birds – have to be able to get what's true out of the data; and they have to do it on the site, they have to do it in the course of the inquiry. The thing that's interesting and that's problematic, and that we have to be concerned with if we're going to be studying the practices of discovery, is that somehow or other, these men know what they're doing. But we *don't know what it is for them to know*.

So the hints are that Millikan was *ad hocing*; or, in fact, Holton said, he was simply telling lies, meaning that he lied in the article [he published on the experiment] that these 58 are the entire course of the observations. You would have to say he's a liar, or he's ignorant, and so on. As a matter of fact, in that sense that he's lying, it's a very gorgeous sense of lie, because it's part of a family of charges that have to do with the character of acceptable work – that he's lying, that he's sloppy, that he's careless. All of these are charges.

Question: instead of their being now acceptable as extensive charges, what we would like to know is what, over the course of practice, that charge in fact might as well be the name for. When you say he's lying, what is it that he's doing when the pages of stuff are in front of him such that he reads out of eligibility for the writing of the article, that witnessed drop in that electric field; where he, for whatever reason, says, "It won't do," or "it's wrong," or "there's something wrong here," and so on?

So this machinery is kind of a hope to begin with that we really, in fact, could talk of a . . . proposal that the ground is being prepared to receive the figure that's still not in hand; but when it's in hand, it will fit the way the key fits the latch. So you're preparing a latch. If someone says, "Well, what's the key for?" you say, "I'll know when I see it."

But the problem is that we have to enlist the help of theoretical physicists – I mean astrophysicists. We have to have somebody, for example, just to give us the pictures that he takes to a lab, and give us a guided tour. . . . All this, but the way, is being done in preparation for a presentation of something like this at a meeting scheduled next October where we will present what ethno might say about the work of a discovering science.[34]

---

[34] Garfinkel is referring here to the scheduled presentation of "The work of a discovering science construed with materials from the optically discovered pulsar," a paper he delivered in October 1980 in a plenary session of The Present State of Social Studies of Science: A Symposium, sponsored by *Philosophy of Social Sciences*, History of Science Society, Philosophy of Science Association, Society for the History of Technology, and Society for Social Studies of Science, Toronto. This presentation was later revised for publication as Garfinkel et al. (1981).

SEMINAR 2

Discovering work of the sciences (May 27, 1980)

Harold Garfinkel

Thomas Kuhn on the Lack of Paradigms in the Social Sciences; Reading Kuhn's Notion of "Law Sketch" in the Postscript to The Structure of Scientific Revolutions; Occasional Expressions and Occasion Maps; "Wild contingencies" and bricolage expertise in laboratory practice; The Gestalt Switch as a Practical Achievement; Attaching Expressions to Nature; Bricolage Expertise in the Laboratory

GARFINKEL: It wouldn't be a bad topic for us to consider [Thomas S.] Kuhn's dissatisfaction with the use of paradigms in the social sciences. . . . Sociologists, and I assume the other social sciences as well, are just thrilled to be able to speak of paradigms in sociology. There are a number of hints to be taken – not just hints, but straightforward things – that Kuhn is looking, at least at the sociologists, with a very baleful glance and saying, "Look, I'm not talking about you guys." [Laughter.] There are a number of other reasons that that is so. For one thing, I guess it's in the Postscript [Kuhn 1970a: 174–210] or it's in the collection by Lakatos and Musgrave [Kuhn 1970b] – he comments on the year that he spent at the Center for Advanced Study when, altogether in contrast to, as he says, the situation in what we call the "sciences," he never saw it happen with sociologists that an issue would be brought up and then, on the grounds of an exemplary study, the issue would get settled.[1] So whereas . . . you get this curious phenomenon in the sciences, particularly in physics, where prior to some study you get this great conflict going on. Then

---

1 Garfinkel may be referring here to remarks Kuhn makes on pp. vii–viii of the "Preface" to *The Structure of Scientific Revolutions* about his year (1958–1959) at the Center for Advanced Studies in the Behavioral Sciences. For later reflections by Kuhn on the "line" he draws between the social and natural sciences (as well as the tentative way he draws it and the difference between other such lines of demarcation in the philosophy of science), see Kuhn (2000b: 221–223).

comes the study. The issue gets settled; and after that, you can't bring up that conflict again in the way in which it was available before. Kuhn apparently believes (and I'm sure Holton points to the fact that it's a curiosity) that it's in the sciences that you get such a phenomenon, but that in social sciences you don't have anything of the sort. Kuhn says the same thing.

So that's the first thing to consider; that, okay, Kuhn is talking about when he speaks about a paradigm, it being misunderstood when the social sciences speak of their work as in any fashion paradigmatic.

But there are other things that he speaks of that . . . drive that argument even further. Kuhn talks about the essential tie between what he speaks of as a law sketch or a law scheme (such as the law of falling bodies) and a physicist's grasp of a certain method of laboratory practice that furnishes, as an exemplary set of practices, a way of solving a problem *in situ*.[2] And the tie of the two is such that though you can disengage what he calls the law sketch (again, with the law of falling bodies) and attempt its interpretation without respect to the practices, when you do that, he proposes – and he emphasizes that particularly in the case, of say, of students who are learning physics – when you disengage it you get a version of science, you get a cogent interpretation of that law sketch, but it will not reflect, in fact, what the practicing physicist needs to have as that version of the law sketch that bears on the particular problems in the area in which he is dealing.

So, for example, if he is concerned with the motion of planetary bodies, then the law of falling bodies has to be rewritten to make it available for the definiteness of just what the expression overall means as well as what its specific terms have as their definiteness of sense. So if you deal with . . . planetary motion, then the facts of the matter (that is to say, the actual practices that are involved in the exemplary case of formulating and solving the problem) then it gives you what you are talking about. Whereas, if you are dealing with the motions of pendulums, then you have altogether a different version of what that law sketch would look like.[3]

So the whole point is that it's from the point of view of lab practice that the law sketch takes on its definiteness of sense and reference, which is to say that if you disengage it, then you get something like a concern for science, such as you would find, for example, in the endless philosophies of science, which can go on interminably, let's say, finding what the dilemmas could be that make up the investigation of the issues of science, even the issues of science as a practice. But it would lose essentially the grounded character of physics, say . . . what he calls their symbolic generalizations, or their law sketches, or their physical laws, found as they are, let's say, in these very tight expressions.

Now, where sociology is concerned, that would have to be another thing that's curious about sociology. [Pause] When sociology provides for itself as a science in the Galilean mode – that is to say, when it provides for itself as a

---

2 Kuhn (1970a: 187ff.).
3 For a discussion of how the law of free fall is locally (re)organized in demonstrations with pendulums, see Livingston (2008) "Praxiological Objects," chap. 27, pp. 227–241.

disciplined way of using the methods that are appropriate to the natural sciences in detecting, collecting, assembling, describing, analyzing, exhibiting, all the way through the natural analytic properties of practical action – in doing so, rather than it satisfying what Kuhn is talking about as paradigmatic ways of working, it doesn't do that but instead turns curiously into an endless interpretation of exemplary texts which are then exhibited as documented arguments about the character of the actions that it speaks of. So, if you look for the existence in social sciences of a practice (which would have to be then a lab practice), to know the practices of sociological inquiry that are at all comparable to the discovering sciences, then it's nowhere to be found. Instead, you get this exquisite insistence on literacy, on being able to talk science.

So when I read Kuhn on paradigms, I'm inclined to think that he is not yet talking about sociology. He has kind of a curious way of dignifying the work of sociological inquiry. One thing that is really interesting about Kuhn's talk of the work of physicists is that these lab practices that he is talking about involve bodies. I mean, you don't have a lucid thought that gets the work of a physical inquiry done, but you have instead a practitioner who has available the local set of practices that make up *in situ* the craft of inquiry. It is that craft of inquiry whereby it has put in his hands a promising method of solving problems, such that in a new situation he can find what about that situation is comparable, or is similar, to what his problem-solving procedure makes available to him. As *compared* with, say, that version that would say of his discovering procedures, or his effective practice in the lab, that he's a very bright fellow, for example; or that he's properly trained; or, better than that, that his results are guaranteed in that he can find the law of falling bodies again; or that the law of falling bodies is cogent with respect to his particular experimental situation; or that the experimental situation as a structure of proof, as a strong scheme of inference, guarantees then that the inferences that are drawn with its use are warranted inferences. This is an entirely different way of speaking about experiments than, say, Kuhn would speak about them. For Kuhn, the paradigm would look like: you have to have learned it in the way in which your fingers, arms and hands are positioned, and so on. They are not just waving around and picking up things in the lab. They are making an experiment work. That's what you have as a practice. The law of falling bodies is given its sense in that we have that as a local craft.

[Brief break, some interchanges with students.]

There's a section in that Postscript that is really worth reading for your interest. [Pause while pages are turning.] The Postscript to [the Second Edition of] *The Structure of Scientific Revolutions* (Kuhn 1970a: 174–210) . . . was written without his revising the original text (Kuhn 1962) in response to the . . . great amount of criticism that had been directed to him. In any case, he writes this:

> The paradigm as shared example is an essential element of what I now take to be the most novel and least understood aspect of this book. Exemplars will therefore require more attention than the other sorts of components of the disciplinary matrix.
>
> *(Kuhn 1970a: 187)*

He is concerned in the Postscript to set up four distinct features of what he means by "paradigm."[4]

> Philosophers of science have not ordinarily discussed the problems encountered by a student in laboratories or in science texts, for these are thought to supply only practice in the application of what the student already knows. He cannot, it is said, solve problems at all unless he has first learned the theory and some rules for applying it. Scientific knowledge is embedded in theory and rules; problems are supplied to gain facility in their application.
>
> *(Ibid.)*

Here he is talking on behalf of his critics:

> I have tried to argue, however, that this localization of the cognitive content of science is wrong. After the student has done many problems, he may gain only added facility by solving more. But at the start and for some time after, doing problems is learning consequential things about nature. In the absence of such exemplars, the laws and theories he has previously learned would have little empirical content.
>
> *(Pp. 187–188)*

[Garfinkel continues to recite the remainder of section 3 of the postscript, while exclaiming high praise for the claims that Kuhn makes about how scientists attach "symbolic generalizations" to "nature" such that a "law-sketch, say $f = ma$, has functioned as a tool, informing the student what similarities to look for, signaling the gestalt in which the situation is to be seen" (p. 189).]

. . .

GARFINKEL: I find that all of us are being elevated by his remarks. How to learn, faced with a given experimental situation. That given experimental situation is what we're talking about as the in situ occasion on which the experiment or this inquiry is to be done.

[After reading passages in which Kuhn gives historical examples of how the "law-sketch" or "symbolic generalization" $f = ma$ was applied and respecified in relation to different situations – including the inclined plane and the pendulum – Garfinkel reads:]

---

4 In his response to critics who argued that his use of "paradigm" was indiscriminate, Kuhn distinguishes three senses of "paradigm" in subsections of the postscript: (1) paradigms as community structure; (2) paradigms as the constellation of group commitments; and (3) paradigms as shared examples. The fourth "feature" that Garfinkel mentions is perhaps what Kuhn discusses in subsection (4): tacit knowledge and intuition. Garfinkel is most interested in subsection (3) and reads aloud for the seminar almost the entire subsection from pp. 187–191. Readers of *this* text would do well to consult those pages in Kuhn to follow Garfinkel's remarks here, as only a selection of his oral recitations of consecutive passages is preserved in this transcript.

... Yet the verbal statement of the law, taken by itself, is virtually impotent. Present it to a contemporary student of physics who knows the words and can do all the problems but now employs different means. Then imagine what the words, though all are well known, can have said to a man who did not even know the problems. For him the generalization could begin to function only when he learned to recognize "actual descents" and "potential ascents" as ingredients of nature, and that is to learn something, prior to the law, about the situations that nature does and does not present. That sort of learning is not acquired by exclusively verbal means. Rather it comes as one is given words together with concrete examples of how they function in use; nature and words are learned together.

(p. 191)

GARFINKEL: Now, it seems to me that's a kind of a statement in our own studies of what the discovering work of the science could be. We need to take it seriously. At least, I'm going to take it very seriously.

Let me give you an example. By comparison, let's say, to the sheer strength of that proposal that Kuhn is making, we could think that we have examples of our own, of something like that. For example, suppose you want to start with what would seem to be something like what Kuhn is talking about as the law-sketch. We won't go to that law-sketch. We'll just say, here is a recitation of properties of so-called indexical expressions. So we could lay out what those properties are, as, for example: indexical expressions are expressions that acquire definiteness of sense and reference at the time of their expression; or they are expressions that take on definiteness of sense and reference in accordance with the place that they are uttered; or they acquire the definiteness of sense and reference with respect to the biography of interaction in which they have been spoken . . .; or they are expressions which, though they have their definiteness of sense and reference on [an] occasion, can change that sense of definiteness as the occasion changes; and so on. In the article and, say, in *Studies in Ethnomethodology* there's a place there where I recited a list of such properties.[5] Let's take these properties and say: as ways of speaking about occasional expressions, if we attempt to elucidate their meaning by finding the sense for which those properties of expressions would be appropriate, then in that case we are bound to lose. Let's say it's a no-lose enterprise.

For example, we could say that if you want to see the case where occasional expressions are found, then a so-called sketch map would be the occasion par excellence.[6] Here's a map, here's the ocean, and here are the instructions on how to get to Garfinkel's house.[7] This is Sunset, and this is the light before

---

5 Garfinkel evidently is referring to Garfinkel and Sacks (1970: 348–349) and Garfinkel (1967: 5–6).
6 Garfinkel and others had a long-standing interest in the use of directions and sketch maps (or "occasion maps" as he called them) in the course of a journey. He discusses this topic in Garfinkel (2002: 179–183). Other relevant sources include Psathas (1979); Brown and Laurier (2005); and Liberman (2013: 45–82).
7 Garfinkel here is speaking of what, to him, would be a highly familiar route from UCLA to his residence in Pacific Palisades in Los Angeles: the route passes from Westwood, via Sunset Boulevard, and borders the Bel Air neighborhood. He is, of course, *not* describing what can be read off of a

Sunset, and this is nine miles approximately after the UCLA-Sunset intersection. Okay? And now that list of properties would be the inspiration that we would use in order to ask: What is there about an occasion map that makes it interesting and makes it analyzable for the events of it as an occasion map?

We would say, well, to begin with, here's Sunset. And in order to understand "Sunset," you probably would have to use [a recorder to track] the way you see that its character is such that it doesn't have a sense that is independent of the situation in which it would be used, the time at which you consult [with it provides it with . . . clearly]. And so on. In that way, though, we would have this list of properties.

But the thing about it is that that has to be crazy. I mean, that has to do exactly with what Kuhn is saying. If you do that, then what happens is that these terms have the character of an *empty sense*. Sure, you can now find examples endlessly in this map of just how the terms and expressions [how the surface is used, and so on] can be spoken of as occasional expressions. Fair enough? So that would be a matter of mapping the properties of occasional expressions as the philosophers have put them in our hands,[8] by consulting occasion maps in order to make the listed properties come true, or to make them come relevant, or to make them into good examples of what occasional expressions could be.

My understanding is, *that's* exactly what we don't want to do. What we'd like to say about that list of occasional expressions is that we have that as a list of expressions to begin with in the way in which Sacks put in our hands an exemplary procedure of this sort.[9] So I ask where in the world we would find a setting of practical action that would be such that what we're really talking about is there to be found as an ethnomethodological model, so to speak, of occasional expressions. What is it that we *could* possibly mean? What we want to do is to find a setting that would be such that we would there learn what this list might as well have been talking about. But it would be such that we should disengage the list. It would only be a point of departure. It would be a weak way. In other words, we are looking for a setting that would be such that it would stand to that list of properties in the way in which Kuhn's exemplary practice stands to the law-sketch. All right?

Well, in that case, it's not that the sketch map is the thing that we're looking for. What we're looking for is a sketch map used as a part of the *journey* that it speaks of. In that setting, then, you will find that this list of properties is now no longer of any use to us. It led us to examine the way in which the *journey* – the way-finding journey – is made up of work that consists of consulting the map *with respect to* the territory *as of which* the map by the user is set into correspondence or is found to be speaking of. So, it is in the way in which one is on the way to the destination that is readable in the map that provides for a place in which the journey would use a course of traveling and a destination. But it is readable

---

city map of the Los Angeles metropolitan region, but is suggesting how the directions provided by a sketch map make sense (or not) over the course of a singular effort to follow the route.
8 For a philosophical discussion of "occasional expressions," a version that Garfinkel had read, see Gurwitsch (2010).
9 Garfinkel discusses Sacks' procedure in the May 22 Seminar.

in the map in the way in which one finds that one is, indeed, on Sunset. So you are all ready, with respect to the map, to find the map's own significant territory. Right? Then how are you at any point in the course of the journey assured that in fact the map can be trusted for what it speaks of? Well, surely in the course of traveling on Sunset, you are assured that you haven't left Sunset. Well, Sunset may be not problematic for you. But if you turn off Sunset and you get into some of these branchings in Bel Air (where you can always tell what street you're crossing, but you never can tell what street you're on), in that case it is no longer clear-cut. Indeed, you are in the course of traveling, having to find the *just-how* to see the map's own significant territory, which would be seeing in the landscape the existence there of a landmark. It is not merely that you find a high school; it is the high school *on the way*. Well, then the just-how you are finding it now speaks of what these expressions offer as so-called "occasioned expressions."

It is not enough that you then say, "well, see, these are expressions that take on definiteness of sense," or "these are the times in which they're symbolic." That turns out to be a very misleading exercise, just a gloss. It's a way of speaking in passing. In fact, it's a way of collecting the properties of these expressions, disengaged from their map, and treating them as if they could be examined as expressions in their own right, in which case they are given the name "indexical expressions." And they're compared then with so-called "objective expressions." But you would have no motive to make that comparison here. That is, it wouldn't be interesting that you could compare an occasion map, let's say, with a map where the expressions would no longer be occasioned. It wouldn't be that the map compares with an analytic cartographic map. That is because your cartographic map itself could also be used as part of a way-finding journey, in which case it must take on the properties of this (   ).

So that means we are finding out something about practical *action*, and the expressions that are themselves revealing of the detailed ways of practical reasoning.

So, okay, then we'll say the use of an occasion map as a part of the way-finding journey would be an ethnomethodological model that is revealing of the definitive properties of occasioned expressions. Well, then there are other models as well, like the so-called Mooersian catalogue that is also an ethnomethodological model of occasioned expressions.[10] We don't even have to go through that; you could say, "Well, look, in our seminar meetings last quarter we began to get on to the possibility that there are ways in which formatted queues are models of occasioned expressions." We came on the account that parties give of the occasioned queue: "We are together." And then we get in to see how it could be that the existence of a formatted line would put in the hands of a member of the line a way of examining the line to find, then, in a way of speaking about the features of

---

10 Garfinkel is referring to the "Zatocoding" system developed by Calvin Mooers to catalog sources in engineering libraries. He discusses this in Garfinkel (2002: 128–129). For a concise account of Mooers' system, see also Ceruzzi (2019).

the line that it was, in fact, a grounded way of speaking, which is to say, that it is appropriate to the circumstances in which it was being said.[11] The circumstantiality of it was not a circumstantiality generally speaking. [It's borrowed] from the way in which the party himself, competently present to, and competently a practitioner in, a line and, with respect to joining one, has there a question: "Where is the next place in line?" "Are you in line?" . . . And so on, and so on. All those, then, would be revealing again of those properties of speaking and being understood, with definiteness of speech; ways [that] could be summarily put together by speaking of them as "occasioned expressions." But that would be another gloss.

Now, I'll make the "Garfinkelian Leap," which is: what we're proposing about . . . the optical pulsar is that we think to learn from that night's work – we think to ask a question on the basis of that night's work, where the question would be: What kind of science is theoretical physics, if with respect to its *every* possible technical matter that it could be concerned with, with respect to the *full* array of technical order topics, it is done as practical action? The idea is, okay, we'll take *its topics* and ask, what would be the character of laboratory practices that would be such as to turn its topics into situated expressions; that is, situated phenomena? Those situated phenomena would be the phenomena of interactional, embodied practices. They would consist of the looks of persons at work doing their work; that is, they're at the work of talking and exhibiting the events of theoretical physics and lab physics. So that's the ethnomethodological leap. Which is to say . . ., well, treat it as if we know that, in order that knowing it, you can go about the work of finding [it again]. . . . It's only that we're in hopes that we can make it come true [with evidence].[12] We are only claiming at the outset that it's true in order, then, that we could be in the pursuit of that order. So we only have to take it seriously then to. . . . That's the big proposal that's being made.[13]

Last week when I talked about the gestalt switch, . . . instead of treating it as a *feature* of perception, treating it . . . as an *achievement* of practical action, when you come to see [the phenomenon as having an] other and different sense than it was taken to be in the first place, and different than it was thereby *all along*. It wasn't that in the first place, but was a what-it-is, for making it as a structure of appearances *now*.

Now, a good way to see what could be involved *there* was called to my attention once by Judy Davidson, who was editing conversational transcripts.[14] She was

---

11 On "formatted queues," see Garfinkel (2002: chap. 8) and Garfinkel and Livingston (2003).
12 As indicated by ellipses and bracketed phrases, Garfinkel's voice on the recording is poorly audible here, requiring considerable guesswork to piece together what he might be saying.
13 At this point in the seminar, Garfinkel engages in exchanges with students about the necessity to "have a science" in order to pursue the "big proposal" he had just outlined. He mentions the unique adequacy requirement of methods. The recording is unclear through some of the discussion, and Part I of this volume provides a more coherent elaboration on Garfinkel's conception of that requirement. One student in the class goes on at length about his ethnographic project on a religious group. In the interest of retaining focus on Garfinkel's presentation, we are skipping over this discussion with students.
14 Judy Davidson was a PhD student in the School of Social Sciences, at the University of California, Irvine in the 1970s. She was one of Harvey Sacks' students and conducted research on invitation, offer, and request sequences (e.g., Davidson 1984).

editing them for mistakes; that was her job. Someone had made a transcript. Her job, then, in going through it was to find errors. What kind of a thing was it to find errors? What was it that, in finding an error, you were finding? One of the things she pointed out was, let's say, here would be a notational matter on the page. You're listening to the tape. You hear on the tape that the notational version of it doesn't read as the thing that hearably is there. So the first thing you do is to mark it in the tape as something that can be heard in the place. So that means you're going back to hear it again. You are now into the work of successive hearings, which is to say successive meanings – it's not that it's again and again and again that you hear it, then you hear it once more, then you hear it once more. Each time you hear it, you're listening for what it was, in the first place, to have heard it, just that, without its having the history that it now has. So you're into the work then, though of the successive listening or hearing, of finding what it was that was, through such a hearing, of coming to the thing that it was as a hearable in the first place as a single-and-only, and having *its* horizons, so to speak; its thing that it was headed to – which is to say, it has a local [bit] of context that is represented in the script, but in the hearing it is now being heard on the way it doesn't offer itself.

So marking it off, she can thereby come to see that it wasn't *this* as it was originally provided for. It was something *other* than and *different* from what it was in the first place, and was there in the first place to have been heard for that thing that is now represented as having been all along. So you are getting all that.

That is then to be compared with another kind of correction where, yes, it's like that, but not quite. There is more to be said about it. And the more-to-be-said adds to the thing that was there and hearably that, but doesn't *change* it for what it was in the first place. Okay? Yeah, it was an interruption; and the interruption, in fact, had a duration of such and such. *Et cetera.*

If that's the kind of thing that we could be paying attention to, then, for the first part, then we do have this gestalt switch; i.e., what we might encounter that our discovering scientists are doing is dreading the places at which they become convinced that they have hold of the phenomenon. Let's take an excerpt from the pulsar tape when Disney says, "We've got a bloody pulsar," and Cocke says, "Now, now." The two of them, indeed, may be collaborating to make it possible to *hold off* on too sanguine a recognition.[15]

You can imagine giving the student of physics advice: "Look, spend your time in the lab. Don't try to puzzle out the [finer sense of] these expressions, simply do the problems, but do what your instructor asks of you; spend your time in the lab doing those *experiments*. And when you've been doing the experiments, you will find that expressions will attach themselves to *nature*."

If he's like the kids in Sociology 1, he'll say, "Well, I'm perfectly happy if that should happen to me. Please give me a guarantee that if I spend four hours a week in that awful place, that I will come out with a grasp of what the structure of that experiment was and I will in fact have seen how the manual of instructions is a description of the work that I did there and furnishes me the

---

15 Again, student comments and exchanges are deleted from the transcript here.

point as well of what I did there, all of that being such that I will satisfy *you*, because when you ask me the questions you have just asked me about what I will have learned, I will be prepared to answer."

I guess it's part of Kuhn's genius that he knows damned well that in that matter of *attaching* those expressions to nature, that the mystery that Holton, Kuhn, and Polanyi are posing as the big prize that could be won by saying it's not that the discovering work of a science is *somehow* done and we would like to know just how it is done, but they know that if it's only at first hand that it's going to have to do somehow or other with a theory of practices that "somehow" gets translated into *a just-which-way how* – a just and only, and exactly, and definitely, and specifically, and in-no-other-place-but-here how. And how is that conducted while preserving the big issue of generalizability?[16]

GARFINKEL: I keep going back to my very favorite story on that score.[17] It's the story of [James] *Olds*, who comes into the lab to find his research assistant dusting off and rearranging equipment on the shelf, and then going into a fury and telling him, "Get the hell [out] of here. I don't ever want to see you again."[18]

I keep thinking, okay what Olds had in a naturally theoretic account of his lab practices, he had a naturally accountable version of the work of getting that phenomenon again, which is to say a naturally theoretic account of that phenomenon. All right? Let's say, a just-how you get an implanted rat to move toward an object when you have implanted it in a certain place and have jolted the rat. That means he can get that again.

I understand that to mean that in the actual case when it's to be done again, he has available in that naturally theoretic version of the work of that phenomenon the workings that get that blip again. He has an accountable version, as well, of the contingencies of doing it. Meaning, in that sense he is chained to the world. So in that sense it's a real-worldly thing. He can tell you not only the phenomenon but the how it can go wrong. Meaning, for the things that go wrong, he has an agenda, so to speak, of things that can come under examination. In that sense he has it *thematized*. He has the phenomenon topicalized with respect to the just-how it is being brought about. Well, if he has *those* kinds of contingencies, then also he has wild contingencies. And the *wild* contingencies would be the *wildness* not of the world but of his embodied practices in that place that make up handling machinery, picking it up, turning it around, not looking where he should be looking, tripping over . . ., et cetera, et cetera.

---

16 Student comments and exchanges are deleted here, and throughout the remainder of this seminar, where breaks in the transcript are noted.

17 Garfinkel's reference to "that score" picks up on a point made by a student's comment about the tentative way "attachment to nature" is forged, and its vulnerability to competitive claims in the scientific community.

18 See pages 33–35 of this volume, where Garfinkel discusses the incident where Olds berates an assistant who was moving laboratory equipment in order to clean shelves. In that discussion, Garfinkel mentions that he and Olds were graduate students together at Harvard. Both of them worked with Talcott Parsons, although Olds went on to establish a career in psychology, and became famous for experiments with mice on self-stimulation of the pleasure center.

It may be, then, that when you're into a discovering of a phenomenon that –
SPEAKER: It's a fragile attachment.
GARFINKEL: It's a fragile attachment in the sense that you'd give your eye teeth to settle once and for all: Well, we have the natural contingencies worked out. Right? "Oh god, give us a sign": which are the accountable contingencies and which in fact do we not have to pay any attention to? Like, say, if I bump against the lab bench, it's not worth anybody's second thought.

So it may be, then, that . . . if we say, here you have that figure-ground structure, and if the animal in the foliage is to be detected so that the foliage in fact are those practices, then those practices have to include, as well, wild contingencies. So the *wildness* of the world would have to be maybe something really in the way in which Merleau-Ponty speaks of the wildness of the world.

[Gap in recording, as the tape cassette switches to other side.]

I think there is something really to be done with the naturally accountable contingencies and the wild contingencies. I think I might have already told you of several other observations that my wife and one of her co-workers made.[19] One thing they pointed out – they were talking about how important it is to be doing lab chemistry, then you have to know how to make an experiment work. The problem is you can give some instruction on that up to the point where you would be admiring somebody's lab technique. And you say, "They have good technique." Then you would say someone else would have sloppy technique or bad technique. Even at that, you wouldn't have it sufficiently specified because, her partner pointed out, that there is always the case of graduate students in chemistry who have to give up careers in chemistry because they can't make the experiments work.

[A participant in the seminar asks if these are experiments that have assured results, in principle – i.e., experiments that are routinely used.]

GARFINKEL: Yes, that's right. It's not that they're doing discovering and can't make the discovery. It's that they can't make the experiment work in the way in which the manual – these instructions for the day's experiment say. . . . The idea is that these are not discovering experiments; these are pedagogic experiments. These are ways of learning in lab chemistry. Can't make it work. He was saying that there is a considerable – though he didn't know how large, but he thought it was large – percent of students who have to abandon careers in chemistry because they can't do it. That was one thing.

The second thing was Arlene [Garfinkel's] own observation. She said when someone comes to the lab to take up the job – not a novice; this is a graduate student, let's say, in biochemistry – who has a job in the lab and is going to be a research assistant in the lab, he does not know the vernacular practices of that lab; nor, for all the fact that he has had lab chemistry, does he in fact know how

---

19 Arlene Garfinkel worked as a lipid chemist in a laboratory at UCLA. She was one of the informants for his study of "contingencies" of laboratory work discussed in Part I of this volume, and he also formally interviewed her for that project. A transcript of a lengthy discussion between Arlene and Harold Garfinkel on "Scientists' Work" (April 8, 1976) is in the Garfinkel Archive in Newburyport, Massachusetts.

a lab works, does he know what in that lab is involved in fact gathering. So, she now has to spend a week or more *instructing* him in the practices of lipid chemistry in that place. And she said she *always dreads it*, that it's *an endless, endless* enterprise. She feels, when she's halfway into it, that she'll never stop ( ). Like, it just *wears her out* to have to introduce someone. And that's a someone who is coming into the place who already had a *preparation*.

Now, I really love those stories. I had thought: Well, okay, the way in which we get on to what I thought of as *unmotivated observables* of lab practice. We'd start to collect them by going to practitioners and offering them to begin with, "Here are some stories. Add to our collection. You know better than we do what we're talking about. Tell me another one like this one."[20]

GARFINKEL: I think I told you that Holton said that it was part of Fermi's reputation as a great physicist that he was a *bricolage* expert in the lab. Meaning, when others were stymied – there's a point in the local historicity of the work that they are doing when they are stumped. Though they know where they come from, it is of no use in telling them *just what* they need at this point to make that neutron display multiply. So there are the stories of Fermi who at the time of his great discovery reached over for the wax and put it in front of the beam, knowing exactly what was right; and it was improvisation. There was nothing that was available in the design or structure of that experiment with which to find it.[21]

When I was visiting the American Institute of Physics and talking with the director, Spencer Weart, [and saying,] "One of the things we would be looking for is the possible existence of the *bricolage* expert: either a person, or a function, or a skill." And it's this. I thought of it at the time as a big irony. You have this immense investment in exquisitely complicated costly machinery. Okay? And there's somebody who doesn't know of any of that kind of stuff but who produces a few shims and that levels the apparatus to *just* the exquisite level that's needed in order that everything works out.

[A participant in the seminar remarks that it is ironic that Levi-Strauss (1966) contrasts the *bricoleur* to the scientifically trained engineer, and yet his description of *bricolage* nicely characterizes engineering practice.]

GARFINKEL: *Bricolage* is in fact the heart of it. . . . I mean, if we're going to have to deal with those contingencies, then here is this miracle man and he's a mechanic.[22] And when I asked Weart, "Is that so?" he said, "Every lab has such a person." So that would be another source of the observable facts of life of the lab that are without adequate motivation in the theories of lab practice. That is, you have to go to the labs to know – there to see what it could consist of as local work, to find what these observables would be that everybody knows about but nobody gives a second thought to as not itself built into a theory of scientific practice.

---

20 See Part I of this volume on Garfinkel's pursuit of stories about recurrent contingencies of laboratory research, which he called "coat hangers": themes on which to "hang" stories.
21 This particular story was part of the lore of laboratory science. See for example, a popular essay by Price (1984) on "sealing wax and string" in laboratory practice.
22 "The local availability to 'our shop' of improvisational and bricolage expertise" is one of the "contingencies" of laboratory practice that Garfinkel elaborates in Part I of this volume (pp. 31–33).

[A participant in the seminar interjects, "They do give a second thought to it" and recounts how laboratory practitioners freely and "almost gleefully" describe such improvisational practices.]

GARFINKEL: . . . It may be that what we are talking about is the inherent wildness of a laboratory-available phenomenon in a discovering science. And the *wildness* is the potential threat that can occur from god knows what direction, where Dreyfus speaks about Pinter's play, *The Dumb Waiter*,[23] and speaks about the dumbwaiter that rattles into the scene; it comes down and intrudes. You get this sudden foreign intrusion into an island of order, where the intrusion itself reveals the fragility of the order. And maybe it is something like that, that we're talking about.

[Garfinkel refers to an "earlier conjecture" offered by one of the students in a seminar earlier in the year] . . . on the element of wildness that is found in the orderliness of daily life, that sociologists in their theorizing . . . haven't even developed a decent theory of the demonic component of ordinary action. But we might as well take it seriously because, at least talk-wise, it's not more seriously spoken of than we speak of wild contingencies, right? – those contingencies that escape the naturally theoretic version of what they are.

I mean, suppose that as a condition of the day's work, these birds in the discovering sciences are heading to beat off the demonic components in their own practice.

. . .

GARFINKEL: We need to find birds who could tell us of things like coincidence, luck, . . . romance – that is, they would have themselves a rhetoric with which to speak of that wildness. But then they would have as well the ire, the disdain, the recognition that some ways of providing for it are cuckoo, misleading, not to be trusted, talk of ignorance, the display of someone who doesn't know what it is to be doing such work, and so on.

It occurs to me too that when you get that collection of charges of failings: the investigator who lies . . . let's say for example, what Holton points out about Millikan, that he was lying, that he was *ad hocing*, that he was not considering all the alternatives he could have considered besides the ones that he selected to throw out the drops . . ., poor work, sloppy work, carelessness, fraud – what a *gorgeous* collection of moral charges. I guess these are moral charges directed to the hopelessly encountered [contingencies] of the lab's practices, of its machinery, its architecture, its surfaces.

. . .

GARFINKEL: I remember Holton saying that we have a standing thing that can happen, at least in physics, where a phenomenon is found in one lab and it can't be found in other labs. On that occasion the moral charges have to arise as

---

23 Garfinkel apparently is referring to Hubert and Patricia Dreyfus' discussion of Harold Pinter's play *The Dumb Waiter* in their "Translators' Introduction" to *Sense and Non-sense* by Merleau-Ponty. Dreyfus and Dreyfus (1964: xv) characterize the play as a contribution to the "theatre of the absurd" for the way it disrupts the organizational conventions of a traditional play as "something savage intrudes into an island of order."

possibilities. Not that they are thereby made, but that it has to – if it's not going to be fraud, then it's going to be something like: "Well, just what are you doing? So tell us!" There is now the insistence that it's going to have to reside in a methodic version of just how you're getting what you're *getting*.

The thing that's reminiscent about it is [Jean-Pierre] Rampal, the great flautist, was once asked, "What is it about the way you play the flute that makes you such a great flautist?" He was saying that instead of simply being capable of making beautiful flute sounds, that he had paid a great deal of attention in his own artistry to learning how to make flute-possible sounds, all flute-possible sounds. Whatever sound you could make on a flute, he wanted to know the just-how the sound was a make-able sound like that.

So what Holton is pointing out is that the pathological phenomena – he said, in fact, that there's a *name* for that. It's called a "pathological phenomenon." And there's an article he gave me . . . and it was an attempt to collect these cases and find an explanation (of sorts). . .[24] The fact that they're moral charges may in fact be the thing that goes along with the territory, let's say, of having to deal with a recalcitrant nature. "You son of a bitch, I wish you'd finally come clean! *I need that enzyme. Now, let's see it!*" No, he won't do it. So, there's an obligation. But the pathological phenomenon, then, is found in the fact that there's the insistence on a just-which-way it turns out to give you what you have. So one lab then will ask or require it of another.

. . . You can imagine what kind of hell on earth it must be for a local group to publish something and then comes the article in criticism: "I used so and so and used that kind of method, and (didn't get) anything like that. So, therefore, I've brought it under examination, and I can give you and explanation of why they got what they got, and why no other the lab can do it if they do what they do." And that has to be this side of hell.

---

24 This is a reference to a recorded talk delivered by Irving Langmuir to a colloquium on "pathological science," at The Knolls Research Laboratory in December 1953. The paper Holton gave to Garfinkel was a transcript of the talk published in 1968, as General Electric R&D Center Report no. 68-C-035, Schenectady, New York. The paper later was published in *Physics Today* (Langmuir 1989).

SEMINAR 3

Discovering work of the sciences (June 3, 1980)

Harold Garfinkel

Conversion, Discovery, and Respecifying the Gestalt Switch as an Account of Embodied Action

[A PhD student (Burke Rochford) begins the session with a presentation of his ethnographic project on religious conversion.[1] This part of the seminar is not included here, though Garfinkel uses the topic of conversation to transition to a reading of Kuhn on the gestalt shift (also called gestalt switch). Kuhn himself also likened a paradigm shift to a religious conversion.]

GARFINKEL: What we're looking to find is . . . what is the work [of a discovering science][2] . . . with Kuhn providing the first lead-in to what might stand as the initial way of thinking the work – thinking it as . . . materially grounded practices . . . that are themselves worldly stuff. They don't occur as long and uninterrupted thoughts. And it's not that it looks to a written document as a version of the inner state. . . . As Trent Eglin[3] used to say about the alchemists, there is nothing in the words, but you can't do it without the words. So that leaves us then looking to what the worldly stuff is, with [an] insistence on the discipline, on practices, on their interaction, . . . however they spend their time, wherever, with each other, soliciting funds. I mean, god knows where the work is to be found.

I take it, then, that the power of Kuhn's version of paradigm, the sense of it, is of a similar sort. He requires that if you're going to be doing science, you are going to have to be chained to the way in which physics looks as the lab's own

---

1 E. Burke Rochford was conducting an ethnographic study of the Hare Krishna movement, and later went on to teach sociology of religion at Middlebury College, Vermont.
2 Garfinkel here was addressing the student's presentation on religious conversion, but he soon transitioned to the seminar topic of "the work of a discovering science," and my ellipses and inserted phrases are aiding in that transition.
3 See the discussion of Eglin's (1986) version of alchemy in Seminar 1 (May 22, 1980) of this seminar series (pp. 104ff., this volume).

equipment. And that includes things like bodies, and positions, and places, and tubes that will hold the kinds of things that you're doing, the various chemicals that they're going to be made to contain.[4]

GARFINKEL: . . . Let me suggest a way to begin again on some version of the gestalt switch that came originally to be so motivating of this line of inquiry we are into now. . . . The scientist's object is that he has in hand a phenomenon that he is in the midst of discovering. But it's available, for all its coherence, as the *not-that*. So it's in the very way that he has available the coherence of his inquiry and the way of coming to the results he has, that he has as well the grounds for his suspicion that there's another animal entirely than the one he's looking at, and that other animal is the one he's looking for. *This* one he already knows too well, whatever else is to be said about it, it's not that. So, it's as if you're looking at an Escherian diagram or an Escherian painting.[5] No, never mind the Escherian painting; that's to be used for something else. Let's go back to the notions of . . . [end of sentence obscured by background noise].

The thing that my wife urges is that against your better sense and in the face of the fact that you would like to settle for what's at hand, you can't trust what's at hand because you know, even though you can't explicate fully that it's *not that* you are looking for.[6] So the question then is, in light of the fact that you have two – one in hand – that you are thereby motivated to find the thing that's being born.

Now, I understand the gestalt switch to consist of your coming into the thing, which you are in the presence of being born. But upon the occasion of its emergence, it is then available, trusted, there; and what it was in the first place that you were looking at, for which you have this *now*, from the point of view of the object of the world in hand, you see that it wasn't that in the first place, it was specifically other and different than that, and now it no longer exhibits in its arrangements, in its properties, the thing you have taken it to be. Indeed, you can't even *see* those things anymore. You might *remember* them, but you can't see them. Maybe you don't *want* to. It's a departure from your presence to the real world which is now being fashioned to the way you are now available to see it.

Now, I take it that it is *that* version of Kuhn on the gestalt switch that was initially appealing as the thing that conversion could be. The thing that I like about starting there is you get a very homely[7] version of that switch. In fact,

---

4 Garfinkel mentions here that he wishes Friedrich Schrecker were attending this seminar. Schrecker was a visiting student at UCLA from the University of Frankfurt, who had conducted and videotaped an exercise in which he assisted a paraplegic chemistry student to conduct laboratory experiments for his course requirements. Schrecker (1980) wrote a lengthy, unpublished report on the exercise, which is available in the Garfinkel archive. A brief summary of his project is described in Lynch et al. (1983: 225–229). Other participants in the seminar engage in discussion with Garfinkel and one another, and we pick up where Garfinkel resumes his monologue.
5 This is a reference to the illusionist art of M.C. Escher (1898–1972), whose work is discussed at greater length in Seminar 4 (June 19, 1980) in this series (pp. 165ff., this volume).
6 This is a reference to Arlene Garfinkel's comments on the lipid chemistry laboratory where she worked. See Seminar 2 (May 27, 1980) in this series (p. 135–6, this volume).
7 The exact word that Garfinkel used here is unclear, and "homely" is my guess.

Gurwitsch (1964: 117) comments on it in a gorgeous piece of passing talk. He proposes about a melody (which is the gestalt object *par excellence*) . . . that the melody is heard in and as the singing of it. So it's heard throughout the singing as its parts, but without isolating anything like its parts; you hear the melody in each of its notes, but not as an "eachness" of the notes. What he points out is that if you now take the melody apart by sounding its notes to make them appear separate, in the way that [John] Cage engages in just this kind of thing with his version of music, then what happens is that the sounds are taken (as you could imagine that the sounds are collected from the same population of sound), but they are not hearably the notes anymore. I mean, who would have thought that you were hearing that Middle-C? Now that you are reminded how, let's say, the prelude begins with this Middle-C, you are surprised. You are surprised to find it coming from there. So, the fact is you have to *stop* with the melody and *start* taking the melody apart, in order thereby to find that it could have a componental structure of sounds that, say, are made up of just sounds like this. (But you don't really recognize it as all of this.) Okay?

Well, then that has to say something very powerful about the availability of the world once the switch is made, because it is not that you *forget* the former world, it is that you don't have any more *truck* with it. It is that it is *pointless* to be in the presence of the world that you knew before. So you would expect, then, that for the science at least, what it was on the way to becoming what you finally see that it could have been is now of mere interest to antiquarians perhaps, or to historians, or to curious people who are preoccupied with furnishing a science now flush with victories – in giving that science the collection of its failures. Who needs it?

So you might find then, if you are going to be digging into the conversion, that you want to ask, for the persons who have undergone the change, what they can tell you about it and what they remember of it. You may find, then, that it becomes available to you via the strangeness with which they remember a former world. A former world would be a former life. In either case, you have a way of living; that's the thing that's so really powerful about Kuhn's recommendation. He is talking about living physics. When I say "living physics" I don't mean physics *alive*; I am talking about *living* like that. My wife is a biochemist; that's the way she lives. All right? It seems to me we might as well pick up that suggestion because we are hellbent to exploit the notion of practices. In fact, we want bodies in there, and we want presence, we want instruments, we want the material character of settings. If bodies can't be seen in chairs, they have nowhere else in the world to go. In that case, they are for sure between heaven and hell. I mean they are simply suspended somewhere in a goofy kind of transcendent air. Who knows where they are.

So what we're proposing is: well look, we're going to take them seriously. Either they are going to be chained to worldly things (and that's what practices would have to consist of), or else we're back to the same old Cartesian enchantment, which is that they are bodies, they are biological bodies, they have brains that register the world. . . . So the trick is always to specify the coupling.

[After an exchange with a participant in the seminar, Garfinkel elaborates further on the coherence of a melody.]

GARFINKEL: If you change your figure of speech and, instead of having just a melody that poses for us the question, "How are the notes linked?," we will change it and say never mind that disembodied kind of melody. Instead of our thinking of melody as "listened for," which would pose the problem there of hearing's body or listening's body, we want the body there in the first place, full-blown, no questions about it. So we'll talk not about hearing as they're playing it, in which case now we're talking about the melody. We're talking about *playing* the melody. We can start with the novice who has got the piano, and the teacher is saying, "You want to play Bach? You can't play Bach; you just began. You just started this afternoon. It'll take you years to learn to play Bach." The problem is thereby posed of how a body, how playing hands will find their way over that keyboard, to have then in the smooth playing proceeded through a course of note-possible places, to have arrived at a semblance of the Bach.

We can then provide: "Okay, here's what's peculiar about coming onto these objects." They take hopelessly – they are finally available only in that there is available a smooth skill, a proceeding literally from a beginning through a course of places that the fingers in fact are doing. And that comes then to a melody whose linkages consist of not the lucid thoughts that connect them, or not of principles that connect them, but of a course of sounded doings. All right?[8]

It seems to me that what we need to do is remember again that for the scientist, his discovery is this. He somehow or other is tormented again by the possibility in hand of a sounded doing that doesn't yet . . .

[Brief gap as tape ends]

It is that it sounds like an Abner Dean[9] version of the change in the looks of the world. And he [the scientist] would be very happy to settle for that, except that he doubts that it occurs in a sudden coming together of the world in its entirety, but that there's a curious working out that is being overlooked. And in this case, the body runs quickly through the world, insofar as the world is imagined; and then it has the awful business of having then to live it out. And that's where the conversion really lives. That's where the problems of conversion are apt to be found. It can occur to us in a flash, "Ah, see, that's what it's like after all." It wasn't that "I needn't despair of my drunkenness: I can be forgiven all that." And it's seeable in a flash. We all know the so-called "ah-hah" that is unmistakable, except that, Holy Christ, what are you going to do about that – you have to get up from the chair now and walk down the hall. And what about that?

[An exchange follows with a participant in the seminar about so-called "ah-hah" moments in the psychology of discovery.]

. . .

---

8 On "sounded doings" and related points about playing music, see Sudnow (1978/2001).
9 Abner Dean (1910–1982) was an American cartoonist known for depicting surreal scenes.

SPEAKER: But when we think of discoveries or those few discoveries that are looked at in detail, you see a temporal course of action.

GARFINKEL: Right, it has a career.

[A further exchange occurs with others in the seminar, after which Speaker proposes that Garfinkel "talk about the gestalt switch," and Garfinkel proposes, first, to follow up on an earlier remark.]

GARFINKEL: . . . It seems to me that there are two things to take into account here. One, about that moment [of discovery], that we might have a rendering of the work of the discovery that provides for it as the properties of a moment. And the discoverer might himself say, "I was sitting in my study" or "I was staring into the fire" or "I had been preoccupied with the problem for weeks on end. I happened to look out at the beauty of the landscape, and . . . ," and then provide in that version of the seen-in-a-glance the matter that the discovery consists of. Our suspicion about that rendering is that it slightly exaggerates head stuff.

. . .

Nevertheless, there's a nay-saying we want to introduce to our own enthusiasm. It comes from the story that Schutz tells of Mozart's telling of his own experience in composing.[10] And that is that he is supposed to have said things like this about the composition that occurs to him. He says: the most *delicious* thing about it is that when it occurs to me, it occurs to me from beginning to end, complete with its *full* sequential character, heard in every detail in a movement.

Question: *Just what is that man talking about?*

The story is told about Brahms, similarly, that he would say things like: "When I want to hear an *excellent* version, an excellent rendition, of Beethoven's Ninth, then I get myself a good cigar and stretch out on the couch."

Now, I take it that what these men are talking about is the two different versions of the composition heard in its entirety in a moment and available from beginning to end as that symphony. What the phenomenologists point out — what Husserl [1970], for example, points out about some objects — is that they are *essentially* polythetic, meaning that they can't be seen in the ground; that to hear the composition that I've been telling you about, I can't provide it for you in a gist — I can't give it to you in one penetrating way, but I now must take you through it in the same real-time steps for which it's available in just this way. It's essentially multi-thematic in terms of the way one hears it over the course, starting at the beginning, available at every present time in the course, and so on.

Mozart's claim runs counter to that description. The question is: How do you go about taking seriously that claim?

I take it that what we've been providing for is that a discovery can be in hand as more than a conviction. It's there as a conviction long before it is then available. And it's not that it's there in its conviction, the discovery is there, not

---

10 This is perhaps a reference to Alfred Schutz's essay, "Mozart and the Philosophers," in Schutz (1964: 179–200).

as a guide to the action but as the foretelling of the thing it will come to, as the condition under which one might possibly be in pursuit of the thing that – because you know – you are capable now of finding it out. In the discovery of the double-helix, it occurs to these bozos in one visual glance: "Christ, that helix – we had it inside out. It's to be the other way." Now comes a frenzy of activity while they find out the thing they know all along.[11]

So the notion of "embodied practice," it seems to me, has to be something that chains the head stuff to the world. Okay? And that's in order that we're not to be taken in by long thoughts, thinking that as long AS your thoughts are pure, the world will come aright because it never betrays adequate thoughts about it. And we clearly don't trust that version of scientific practice, or conversion in religious practice, or play, as far as that's concerned. But your big reservation is when you're talking about scientific practice.

So we don't trust that one, but neither do we trust the engineering version of methodic procedure: "As long as you train your body to know its way about the lab, you can count on it working. It will have a sequential order; it will have a sequential course. And you put the liquid in the flask before you put it on the Bunsen burner" – that kind of thing. Well, so it can't be, in that curious sense, an engineering version of sequential action.

But I take it that those are our suspicions. That doesn't yet give us our victories. The victory that we're looking for is that we will finally have set on its feet the prevalent concern to be able to say in literate discourse what the work of a discovering science consists of.

[A student raises the topic of play – which had come up earlier in the seminar.]

. . .

GARFINKEL: . . . There is a feature about doing something playfully that we might speak of as: "Oh, we're just doing it to see where it goes." Say, the contrast would be doing it for good reasons, or doing it with sober, serious purposes in mind, or doing it with there existing a lucid thought, and *that* available as an explicatable matter to which it is understood one's action is directed in conformity. Being a really Machiavellian playful fellow.

LYNCH: Or [Talcott] Parsons' actor.

GARFINKEL: Or Parsons' actor – exactly right – who has, in fact, better than a lucid thought. I mean, he is oriented to a legitimate order of possible ways in which the world in fact can be made again under his collaborative activities, *et cetera*.

---

11 Apparently, Garfinkel is referring to James D. Watson's (1968) dramatic account of his and Francis Crick's discovery of the double-helical structure of the DNA molecule, and specifically of the moment when Watson used cardboard cutouts to work out an arrangement of the nucleotide bases paired on the inside, with a sugar-phosphate "backbone" on the outside, which was the reverse of what he and Crick had devised earlier in a failed model. Garfinkel's brief and casual reference here would be unlikely to pass muster with historians of molecular biology: although Watson and Crick worked with a conviction that the molecule was helical, and having successfully demonstrated their model they *then* could say that they "knew it all along," even Watson's self-serving narrative acknowledges the uncertainty with which he and Crick proceeded until other key colleagues and rivals agreed that it looked right.

Now, where the playfulness is concerned – well, I'm struck by the way in which my life has been irresponsible; meaning by that, that I quickly caught on in graduate school that I could have a career as a sociological theorist.[12] And the thing that I caught on to was that I could be paid to play, meaning that I could put together these concoctions and take them wherever I figured I needed to go, and require of my colleagues that they be patient: "Well, we'll just . . . see where it leads." And nobody is obligated to like it from the beginning, or even like it in the end: Anytime you want to drop out, go ahead. But this thing's going to be my baby. And I'm not guaranteeing anything; if you want to come along, fine.

Now, there's a certain way we do theorizing, particularly when you have only the vision of what you're up to. But if anybody *holds* you to justify why you should be up to it, or wants you to guarantee in the beginning, "Look, it is all going to come out right in the end. It'll be read, it will be intact, it will be interesting, it will be consequential," and all the rest of it – but you don't have it for a guarantee. And you don't even say, "Look, it has happened in the past and it hasn't ever betrayed me." It's not even that. It's that, "Oh I know it will come out right." And that's a part of the thing that you're doing while you're doing it.

So it's really a goofy kind of – the way to talk about it, I guess, is that it is *playful*. Maybe it's like children, because it has among other things, it does have this . . . feature of its irresponsibility. For example, where conventional analytic theorizing is concerned – not ethnomethodological theorizing, right? – but let's say where theorizing is getting done, you are in fact playing with a developing structure of opportunities of where it's going to go next. Those opportunities in fact are chained pretty much, even to the way the stuff looks on paper, the way it looks on the paper you're writing. So there's that about it, let alone that somebody in a course set you an assignment – this is now graduate student days – and by Friday you are going to have to have that paper written. Maybe you have massive notes, and you have to find a coherent way through that mass. So you literally build an argument. And what you're seeking to do is to work off those papers, the stuff that's on those papers. So, in fact, you can forget the papers as the thing works out along this chain. It includes the use of *footnotes*, and *references* and so on.

I think I have told you about Harvey [Sacks]. Harvey had it as a standing joke that since we knew something about how arguments got done, we ought to put together collections of footnotes that we would *sell*: "You want three pages of footnotes? We can give you three pages of footnotes for any paper. . . . *These* footnotes will cost you five bucks a page. But I can give you some others for about 40 cents a page; but I won't guarantee anything."[13]

It sounds like it's foolishness. But think a moment: look, it's not so foolish. We could all do it as an exercise: would we know a footnote if we saw it, even

---

12 It is evident from the audio recording that Garfinkel not only is speaking about play, but that he also speaking playfully. Others in the seminar laugh after his mention of his own irresponsibility and after some of his further remarks about the permissive free play allowed with sociological theorizing.
13 Several students laugh throughout the story of Sacks' joke about selling footnotes.

though we don't have yet a topic in hand? And they don't come out of the blue; they come from a history that we are not using explicitly in order to do that recognition. So there is that kind, it seems to me, of textured, sensible, historicized account that we are talking about. And it may be that when you are into scientific discovery, if it's a discovering science, that the playfulness won't get you what you want more than anything in the world; and that is that you need finally to get a beast which can be a recalcitrant beast. It can be out of your control just because of the curious things that we started talking about last week as "wild contingencies" of an inquiry.

[Further talk among participants in the seminar about play and other topics.]

GARFINKEL: . . . Our concern to be studying the work of a discovering science gets us lots of mileage as long as we deal with *renderings* of that work, without knowing what that work is, because we know something of what its material contents are as renderings. Not knowing yet what the practices of discovery could be, we can be assured that if Escher gives us a way of speaking about Escherian models of practical action, and if we know then that we can put together coherent interpretations and demonstrations of what discovering practice is by the way in which we can operate with drawings, and material features of drawings, then there are lots of interesting things we can provide for what the renderings could be.[14] Particularly we will have to say, "Look, these renderings are such that they're going to bring home a version of a discovery and portray it as the properties of a Galilean science." Meaning, already the report that we've started, the scientific paper, renders the work of the discovery as the properties of a Galilean science; that we, for example, know that the voice of the transcendental analyst, as compared to the voice of the fictional narrator, and so on. So we can really lay out what these properties are.[15]

[Participants in the seminar raise some questions about what is different about the gestalt shift in science as opposed to art and other activities.]

GARFINKEL: Well, I'm thinking that there are some themes that we find ourselves returning to that are kind of recurrent in the work of a discovering science. At least there are some themes. The recalcitrance of the world is something we come on over and over again in the attempt to open up the recalcitrance of . . . a discoverable. We have been talking about the *contingencies* of lab practice. That is to

---

14 Garfinkel is referring to M.C. Escher's drawings of, for example, a complicated arrangement of staircases that, when inspected closely, could not possibly exist in three-dimensional space. In Seminar 4 (June 19, 1980), Garfinkel also references Escher's "tessellated" drawings of figures such as black and white ducks facing in opposite directions as "models" that demonstrate figure-ground relations through illusionist art. Such illusions exploit the properties of a two-dimensional rendering of three-dimensional space. By analogy, Garfinkel suggests, a theoretical or philosophical rendering of discovery can deploy the arts of description and modeling to make out the "process" of discovery in ways that are deeply at odds with what the embodied, material *work* of discovery might consist of.

15 Garfinkel et al. (1981: 238, n. 21) remark that their usage of "Galilean science" is informed by the "discussion of 'a science in the Galilean mode'" in Husserl (1970); commentaries such as "The Last Work of Edmund Husserl" in Gurwitsch (1956); and Carr (1974).

say, it's not merely that a chemist is doing chemistry but that we've been wanting to talk about the apt and familiar efficacy of the practices that make up the way he lives – meaning, the practices that make up the effectiveness of the day's work. He is out to be doing discoveries in chemistry, nothing else – I mean, nothing that would interest us, in any case. (I mean, they spend a long time washing dishware.)

Now, it was with that as the *reminder* that we have been given by various people, and that we've been reminding *ourselves*; namely, look, when it's all said and done, and all the program is in hand, and the bibliographies are there, there will be systematically the gap in that literature: just what is it that the physicist in fact had to have been doing, in the company of and under the examination of physicists, that made it specifically and embodiedly the looks of science – if you say "physics at work" you might as well say "the looks of physics' own identifying ways." When you have to make discoveries in physics, what the hell is it, for consisting of that, it would have to look like?

So when we took off with that as a favorite preconception, then . . . we found ourselves talking to each other about some possibly leading notions. One of these leading notions was that *if* we encounter in the vernacular account of something discovered – a discoverable – that it would come out of a background – it would appear as a phenomenon only on some kind of ground – literally, say in the case of the pulsar, where we imagine that these birds are looking at an electronically displayed pulse of photons that the machinery displayed oscillographically. . . . Without knowing *how* these two birds [Cocke and Disney] were witness to that, we were kind of confident that they either knew, or somewhere along the line they were going to have to be answerable to the claim of that pulse, that it was not a coincidence, wasn't an accident, wasn't a fraud, wasn't a trick; it wasn't sloppy work, it wasn't that it was seen but too soon claimed. This is to say we have yet to know . . . the way in which that machinery could be operated, meaning that they were themselves at work with that machinery to understand about the machinery that it would work in such a fashion that the pulse could be read definitely as *that*, given that it could read alternately to have been produced in different ways. So with that notion, then, that it's not only a figure on a ground, it's a figure that the one witnessing it can come to as a *claimable* figure on a ground. So in that sense it was the figurative animal in the foliage that was seen.[16] Question: What kind of foliage are we talking about? As soon as we talk about the foliage, we find ourselves returning over and over again to the local, mundane practices that make up the visible presence of the night's work.

So that led to the interesting conjecture that, rather than treating the gestalt theme of the figure-ground structure as an analytic explanation of perception by saying that the figure-ground structure is in fact something

---

16 Garfinkel also used "the animal in the foliage" analogy in other seminars in this series, and also in the 1988 manuscript reproduced in Part I of this volume.

that we'll use as analysts to *explain* what the work of perception is—[17] You want to know what perception is? It is specified by providing for a figure that's seen on its ground. And now when you look for the conditions under which the figure may be seeable, you *see* it as something on the ground. And what kind of thing could a ground be, given the history of experimental psych and its preoccupations with elucidating that kind of claimed way of seeing to find something seeable?

Our provision was to take that advisedly, because the notion was to use that figure-ground thing as an achievement rather than as an explanation of a perception of the scientist. So what we wanted to do then was to return to a version that figure-ground structure was a way of speaking about: a formulation of work for which it might as well stand for the while as a formulation of what the practices were then, whereby the beast was seen through the foliage now became exactly the problem when you say it was an *achievement*. And it was more than an achievement in the sense that it was a thought in Cocke's and Disney's heads. It had to be, as well, the way in which at work that night they had to *find* and *disengage*: they had to *find* in the embodied presence to that machinery, which was itself available for them as their practices; they had to disengage, they had to find, they had to render, they had to come upon their work and disengage it from that local practice. So they had to come upon what we speak of as a "naturally available account." They had to engage in *formulating* whatever it was that they were doing, "formulating" in the sense of the "Formal Structures" article about formulation (meaning that it was itself already a hopelessly, and essentially a situated, account of their work).[18]

So we thought: Well, if the figure-ground gestalt theme is a practical achievement, we might as well go whole hog. That is to say, let's assume that there's something to it. Then, let's assume we have a gold mine. Meaning, we have a list of names, and "figure-ground" is this kind of a name; it's a name

---

17 As I understand it, this sentence is unfinished, and that Garfinkel is *not* suggesting that his conjecture is to use the figure-ground structure in an *explanation* of "perception." Instead, this sentence and the remainder of the paragraph elaborates upon an analysis of perception that Garfinkel's conjecture *rejects* in favor of treating the "ground" as the praxiological context from which the "figure" is "achieved," and from which it is "disengaged" as an independent phenomenon. The first sentence of the following paragraph picks up the conjecture that Garfinkel alludes to here, and specifies how he treats figure-ground, not as a psychological explanation of perception, but as a practical achievement.

18 Garfinkel is referring to the paper "On Formal Structures of Practical Actions" (Garfinkel and Sacks 1970), which was an assigned reading for students in the seminar. The Formal Structures article argues that "formulations" – explicit references in a conversation to the actions in that conversation (e.g., "You didn't answer my question"; "Is that a request or a demand?") – are more and other than descriptive references to events in the conversation, as they are themselves situated within the ongoing conversation, and as such hold distinct interactional implications as objections, insults, ironic comments, and the like. Garfinkel and Sacks further argue that concerted actions in conversation for the most part are unremarkably produced and understood with only an occasional need to rely upon formulations to clarify, explicate, or repair the interactional sense and organization of the constituent actions (see Lynch [2019] for an explication of that article).

for work of an unknown sort. Since that would be a way of specifying what it could be to be at work in, say, *finding* the pulsar, then we encountered the possibility that there are other kinds of work as well that are going on in that lab; i.e., there was the idea of the gestalt switch, there was the proposal of relations of alternativity.

There are others that occurred that I will simply name for the time being (we will get to them; we need to): that the object that they provide for as the optical pulsar is an *adumbrated* object.[19] That is to say, it offers itself from the point of view of the developingly available aspects, or the facets, of it that make up its actual appearances. It looks like this on the *screen* [of the photomultiplier apparatus in the observatory] under these contemplated and [already] done operations; it looks differently when this condition or that condition is introduced into a coherent version of how it's going to change in its appearances as a condition for manipulating it. (. . . walking past it, seeing it. I'm not talking about the pulsar now – I'm talking about adumbration, other adumbrations).[20]

Now, they didn't have the world available for discovery as a guaranteed course of adumbration. They had to *discover* what adumbration could be. That doesn't mean that they didn't know *anything* about a pulsar. But they had to come to terms with that lab, that particular – just *that* lab's *way* in which a claimable pulsar would be obtainable and displayable, and so on.

I take it that the issue of the adumbration may throw light, then, on what they were up against when one of them says, "It's a pulsar," and the other holds off. Or, apart from what they're up against, they must provide for their work as having a career to it. It's not available just in the announcement, "Oh, we've got it!" But the very "we've got it" is itself a part of an adumbrated series of appearances. Therefore, if they say "we've got it," they're committed to the horizonal consequences of such a claim as "we've got it." That's why they're up against it.

LYNCH: Say you take the phenomenologists' accounts of the adumbrated character of appearances. There is an interesting difference, I think, between their accounts and the way in which we could reconstruct the Cocke and Disney situation. This has to do with when Gurwitsch or Husserl talks about the object (whether it's the chair, or the tree, or whatnot), it's an object that's unquestionably at hand. And the philosophical trick is then to open up the ways in which it's at hand –

GARFINKEL: Right.

---

19 The phenomenological theme of adumbrated object was introduced in the first seminar in the series (May 22, 1980; pp. 121–2, this volume).
20 The part of this sentence in parentheses marks that the recording was faint and obscured by background noise. Clearly, Garfinkel is speaking about the optical pulsar case earlier in the paragraph, but it seems that, toward the end, he reverts to the familiar example from the phenomenological literature of the appearance of the house-from-the-front as an adumbrated object that changes as one walks past it, goes around to the other side, or enters inside it, while retaining the sense of it as the same house seen in its different aspects.

LYNCH: — that it brings into play the succession of actual and possible views of the object, given Merleau-Ponty's account of the body's ways of synthesizing and inspecting the object as adumbrational appearances.

GARFINKEL: Well, just a footnote on that, the way in which they can be so confident is because they are using the exemplary instances, not —

LYNCH: Yeah, the secure object.

GARFINKEL: — number one. The secure object, is that what you said?

LYNCH: Yes.

GARFINKEL: Sure. And the other kind of secure object is that very frequently, at least in Gurwitsch's case, the properties of the gestalt figures are in fact the properties of *line* drawings.

LYNCH: That's right, which makes it demonstrable in a written inquiry. . . . In the discovering work, although the explication of the adumbrated object through phenomenology is very illuminating, it nonetheless doesn't account for the character of the object as itself in question. That is, throughout the ways it is approached, it itself stands as a provisional "it"; or it can stand as an "it," that in the next rendering of it, the next perspectival revelation of it, it can become something else, or it can become nothing, or it can become nothing but the actions which were taken to appropriate it. So that when you talk about the figure and the ground, where the ground is constituted by the very ways in which the object is approached, that itself becomes part of the inquiry, revealing what that might be, not as something initially disengaged from the object but as something that might be disengaged from whatever that object might be in the end, once it is revealed as *that*. So it's a very interesting setting — it's almost like a natural experimental setting — for a phenomenological inquiry, in that you no longer have to do a reduction on the already secure object to open up the practical ways in which the object is secured and made available; but that, *in* that the thing is yet to be a thing and has various manners of being a thing appropriate to the way in which it is revealed, it provides the possibility that the phenomenological account could be instructed by what is done in approaching the object.

And it goes deeper than that. Here its object*ness* is what's in question, the thingness of it is in question, and in a way that can't be recovered when the secure object, the one we already have as unquestionable, is taken at hand prior to the inquiry in order to motivate the inquiry of the phenomenologist. So it's a funny way of recreating the phenomena.

[Three-second gap in the recording.]

LYNCH: The curious character of the object, the discovered object or yet-to-be-discovered object, or an object in the course of discovery, they can't account for. They can only account for what a *worldly* object could be as already worldly, not as something brought into question or brought to a conclusion.

It has to do with recalcitrance too, in a sense. The chair can't be recalcitrant in the same way in which the pulsar can be recalcitrant. It can be recalcitrant in the sense that however you might want to wish it away, it's not going to go away. They could only *wish* that it had that recalcitrance, but it has a different sort.

GARFINKEL: You know, there is something really wild that your observations touched off. There is talk among the phenomenologists – Husserl and Merleau-Ponty, for example – about the reference to passivity and perceptual passiveness. What you are talking about here, that there is something different in the recalcitrance of a chair and the recalcitrance of a pulsar – the recalcitrance of the chair in a way is hardly recalcitrance at all. Which is to say, it offers itself as the *passivity* of the perceived chair. Meaning, I would like more than anything in the world to be able to see again what the chair offers itself as, let's say as a chair; I would like to see it as something other than the chair.

LYNCH: Eidetic variation?

GARFINKEL: Right. Well, I can do it by turning it into "the chair as meant," in which case I can turn away from the perceived chair. I am no longer in the presence of the just that chair, but I have now a chair that I can talk about; that's in the *first* case available as something to talk about. Better than that, it's available under the auspices of the doctrine of the ideality of meanings. Meaning, attending the chair, I can now address the chair *as meant*. So the chair in perception is the chair-as-perceived. With that, I can turn away from the way that the chair, in fact, is available as an *embodied* practice. Obviously, I can always go back to the chair that is now a meaningful chair. I can try to remember: Was this in fact available like this? Is this what I meant? The back was in fact with uniform blueness across it and turned in its form? Maybe I'm not remembering correctly; I'll turn away from remembering it, and *see* again the thing I'm looking at; and seeing it, I can then return to the thing in its status as meant.

Now, in *that* case I'm dealing with, as you say, a *very un*-recalcitrant object – the idea that I find myself defeated in the attempt to see it as anything else than the chair. Now, the thing about that optical pulsar is that they were first-time-through in coming on what it could in fact look like, given that it had to look the way it was going to look, given that they had the apparatus with which to come into its presence as the practice of disclosing it. So, it looks like the availability of the pulsar doesn't consist of anything else than a *coherent practical action*. And that's why I thought: Jesus, what would physics look like if it's going to have to consist of a theory of practical action?

Compared with chemistry, which would also be a theory of practical action, but it wouldn't at all be the same because the way you make enzyme chains available to the kind of thing that embodied practice would provide for, or there would consist, would have to be altogether different.

The big point in any case is that is that the pulsar has this *curious* feature of their coming upon it *first-time-through*. It's very much like a conversation. Wouldn't it be *great* if we could count on the fact that the talking that we're doing is after all available in God's head, as a prefigured course of talk that consists in its entirety of all of the features in God's mind.

Now who has access to God's ear? Any one of us? Possibly the *saint* among us? Who would that be? No one? Oh we're stuck. [Laughter by others in the seminar.] Now we're really up against it . . . we're *screwed* for sure. 'Cause *He's* the one who'd know about it. If that's not so, then we're *hopelessly* bound to the temporality of it. However the thing is going to look, it's going to have to look in just the way it is given to us over the course of time it takes as of which the thing is disclosed. Which led Gurwitsch, by the way, to say it didn't really make any difference *what* claims were being made by the great philosophers about the temporal organization in the development of the coherence of objects; that *God* himself would have to see things in a time that was hopelessly human in its characteristics.

Well, it may be that what we're doing is taking very seriously what we have to take seriously when we come to matters of discovery: that it is unavoidable about the discovery that you can't simply reach through, grab it by the throat, "Come on, you bastard, tell me. Which way is it now? True or false? There or not? Looks like this, or what?" But *instead*, we somehow have to hear the conversation in and as the course of our being ourselves the parties who are *doing* it. So whatever is then to be *made* of it as an object requires that we come to terms with it as those practices.

We used to think that, well, that's defeated, because as soon as we use a docile record,[21] then we lose it. But I don't think that that's so now. I think the thing that we're finding is that there *are* ways of our driving for the analyticity of those practices. So, for example, the figure-ground structure as an achievement is one such device, and the adumbrated object as an achievement is another. The *danger* I see is that we would sacrifice the recalcitrance of this world. That is, we would prefer to see the pulsar as the passively perceived chair, the thing guaranteed in hand. "Look, you want to know how the pulsar was discovered? Hewish laid it out in the Nobel speech."[22] Or, "You want to know how it was discovered? Well, where else are you going to look except in the available reports?" Obviously, you can't put it together from available reports. So we will use the available reports; we will go to the lab, and there we will see how those bozos are going about the business of getting the machinery and making the pulsar appear on the screen. And *ah ha*! Now we can imagine via the detective work what they had to have been going through in the first place.

---

21 In the seminar, Garfinkel occasionally uses the term "docile" in expressions such as "docile record," "docile account," "docile image," and "docile arrangements." As the term suggests, he is indicating a quality of malleability, or free play, in the recording, depiction, or reading of a textual or verbal account.

22 Woolgar (1976) provides an analysis of discovery narratives, focusing on the radio pulsar case. Numerous pulsars had been identified with radio telescopes by 1969, but it had yet to be demonstrated that any of them would have sufficient energy to appear in the optical region of the spectrum. Anthony Hewish (1924–2021) received the Nobel Prize for Physics in 1974, for the discovery of the first radio pulsar, and for theoretical research on how an astrophysical phenomenon could possibly create rapid-frequency radio waves. Jocelyn Bell (now Dame Jocelyn Bell Burnell), who was a graduate research student at the time, was credited with making the initial noticing of an anomalous bit of "scruff" on a sky survey, and participated in further analysis of it, but was not given the big prize. In the decades that followed, and increasing number of historians, science journalists, and scientists have taken issue with the fact that Bell was not also given the Nobel.

And the thing that's really tough is to turn *away* from those resources, or to say: Well, look, we'll treat those resources as furnishing us with interesting conjectures, but not settling for us what we need most to come to terms with, which is what is it to be engaged in the discovering work? That is to say, what is it first-time-through? And what are the structures of analysis that we need in order to remain faithful to the properties that a first-time-through requires?

That's why I think, maybe what we need to do is to use our gestalt themes to examine, let's say, the pulsar tape. There would be something that we would learn both ways. Maybe we can use the pulsar themes to imagine, better than we've been able to do so far, what the contingencies could have been; and what this thing that we came on as the possible *wildness* of the world might be – that is, the wildness of lab practices. . . . It may be that we have here a beginning of, and a guide to, our inquiries, an arranged way of breaking free of the depression that's found by setting up the process-product distinction; and then by respecting that understanding, well, "see, as soon as you get into the radicalizing of the process, then no record will do." The fact is, that's not even true anymore. . . . *If* we're going to be getting a look at the conversation in its course, then we need the apparatus to examine it in its course.[23] The apparatus may have to be apparatus that's adequate to the phenomenon that we are convinced of. Which is to say, it's the in-courseness of the discovering of the pulsar that we want to keep our eye on.

The seductions are on every side to abandon that enterprise in favor of the very strong and available analytic enterprises. Start in fact with the product; there is every good reason to do that. Well, if you do, it will be like my opportunities to go into the retail fur business. I had a chance to go into the mental health business. And so on. I think that, no matter how appealing they look, you will only wind up in the mental health business. I mean, who needs it? Something like that.[24]

---

23 When Garfinkel speaks of "the apparatus" here, he may be alluding to the telescopic and photon accumulator that the astronomers were using to record their data on a track of the same tape that recorded their voices on another track. In phone conversations with Don Taylor, Garfinkel explored the possibility of displaying the data in a way that would be temporally coordinated with the voice recording. This possibility did not pan out, because the original apparatus had long since been disassembled and the expense of reconstructing it would be prohibitive.

24 The remaining few minutes of the seminar session were devoted to making arrangements for the next meeting and identifying materials for students to examine in advance of the meeting. These materials included the recording and a transcript of the astronomers' voices during their observations at Steward Observatory in 1969, and a recording of a media broadcast about the discovery.

SEMINAR 4

Discovering work of the sciences (June 19, 1980)

Harold Garfinkel

Rendering Discovering Work as the Properties of a Galilean Science; an Escherian Model of Practical Actions; Contingencies of Practice

GARFINKEL: Well, what I want to try to do tonight is to get away with murder! The thing I'm talking about is that I want to offer for us what the study of the optical pulsar is all about. I want to talk about the existence of the Big Prize; I want to characterize what the Big Prize is, and in getting at it, I'm afraid I'm going to go through the very thickest part of the bore. So when it gets really thick (you can hear the grinding all right, but you can't see what the grinding is good for), then you need to say, "Stop, go back, say it again, say it this way. Is that what you're talking about?" and so on. So don't let me just go on.

Very early in our meetings, I proposed that ethnomethodological studies of work, for example the studies of the production of the ordinary society, the studies of the analyzability of ordinary action in the ordinary society, in the preoccupation to find what I spoke of as these identifying issue of the problem of order, had put aside (for reasons that we're not going to discuss) the use of constructive methods,[1] and that the methods that were to be used instead were to include such things as an indifference to the use of constructive methods, and the use of Sacks' example and Sacks' advice to find for *every* topic of order, to discover with respect to every topic of order (every topic of order now being eligible), what that topic looked like according to practitioners'

---

1 "Constructive methods" are methods of what Garfinkel and Sacks (1970) call "constructive analysis": social science and administrative interventions designed to organize, systematize, and otherwise render routine practical activities into data that afford the use of analytical procedures of aggregating, counting, comparing, and ordering equivalent cases.

knowledge of it, their interest in it, and their practices that would compose those topics as the *in situ* effectiveness of a day's work – i.e., the topics of order were to be rediscovered as practices, as practical activities.[2]

Now, then, I proposed that there was already a collection of – That is, in following Sacks' advice, I proposed that you already had in hand for some topics the appropriate, ethnomethodologically speaking, interesting settings in which those topics were to be pursued. And in several lectures I made a big deal about ethnomethodological models of horizontal phenomena of order.

Now I'll just give you a list of examples of that. For example, with respect to the topic of "analysis," there were the uses of occasion maps. And so, it was proposed that the logical properties of occasion maps would serve as an ethnomethodological model of the horizontal phenomenon of analysis – or the topic of analysis as a horizontal phenomenon of order. That was one example.

I proposed that the stuff that we had collected with Eric [Livingston] and Doug Macbeth playing chess with inverting lenses on gave us an ethnomethodological model of reasoning as a topic of order. Though we didn't ever talk about something that I spoke of as the "Mooersian catalogue," the topic of practical reasoning has as its ethnomethodological model the Mooersian catalogue for storing and retrieving small libraries of relevant facts.

With Stacy Burns, the horizontal phenomenon of topical coherence in talking sociology in lecture format had as its ethnomethodological model the occasions of talking sociology; that is, of lecturing's work of talking sociology.

Now, there are others. But that's to give you the feel now of what I'm after. To give you an example of a case that failed, there was the repeated attempt to get access to the Heideggerian thing by thinking that formatting in queues would lend itself as an ethnomethodological model of that ordered topic and others, like the so-called "existence copula" ("there exists," *et cetera*). Okay, so that's one that was tried, and so on.

Here is what I figure the study of the discovering work of the optical pulsar is all about. Here in my claiming I'm relying on the work of Mike Lynch and Eric [Livingston], and looking to the collaborative work with them as well as the collaboration that is added to by reason of the work that developed here in the seminar. So there's that invitational character to it.

Now what I want to propose as the point is that I'm thinking that what we call "lab physics" (and I'm going to put tick brackets on it)[3] is what we're

---

2 Sacks' example is discussed in the first seminar (May 22, 1980) in this series (p. 118, note 23, this volume).
3 Garfinkel used a unique form of bracket that consisted of a round bracket with an equal sign superimposed on it. The form of bracket, which he called "tick" or "ticked" brackets, cannot be reproduced on my keyboard, but {[   ]} provides an approximation. Garfinkel (2002: 139) says that this notation provides "a convenient abbreviation for case materials." He used is as part of what he called a "rendering theorem": {[   ]} —>(   ). The arrow signifies that formal analysis *renders* naturally organized ordinary activities (ethnomethodological case materials) into analyzable data. This can be

looking for as an ethnomethodological model of the horizontal phenomenon of physics' topics of order – that is to say, of physics' phenomena.

Now, there's a very short, and plainer and easier, way, and much less technical and maybe even more interesting way to speak about it. That is, I want to propose that our interest in studying the discovering practices that make up the optical pulsar is directed to treating the discovering sciences as sciences of practical action. And the set of *claims* that we're claiming ahead of what we know, and therefore the problem that I'm confronted with, is to explain the claim that the discovering sciences are sciences of practical action; that each of the discovering sciences in its technical contents is a distinctive science of practical action; that to each science– and now I'm x excusing the social sciences (and not because I'm snotty, but because I'm embarrassed; I don't know what to say about them, whereas, with the discovering sciences there are already established grounds for being preoccupied with them). In any case, the idea is that for each science, what we want to do is to think this way [audibly writing at the blackboard]; think of it as in these long brackets, meaning that whenever we put here "science," we can replace it with a discovering science, and that would then be what we were talking about. So, for example, we'll need to be speaking about astrophysics; we'll need to be speaking about lab chemistry; we'll need to be speaking about geology; we'll need to be speaking about whatsoever any one of us who has hold of a science would then need to be making a proper substitution.

SPEAKER: Engineering?

GARFINKEL: No, we're excusing engineering for the time being. At least, I ask that you excuse engineering, because I think that there are special problems that are posed in so-called engineering sciences. However, it's not the kind of excusing that we're doing where engineering is concerned as compared with, say, sociology. The thing that I'm embarrassed with sociology is that I don't know how to include as worldly stuff the fact that it's so heavily or so identifyingly a talking science. All right? Somehow or other, enzyme chemistry can't be done without the talking, but it can't be done with the talking. There seems to be practices that are such that you can be betrayed no matter how well you talk or in what company, or for how long you've been talking, or with what praise or blame, and so on. So there's a peculiar obstinacy with which the phenomena and practices of a science must deal. However, I think the big thing that's being excused is that we are deliberately turning away from any policy that requires for carrying it through that we would remain respectful of the claim that the unity of the sciences is found in their methods. We are deliberately turning away from that slogan. We are going to remain indifferent to any of the consequences that presumably can be dealt out by remaining respectful of that as a policy of the claims, as a valued state of affairs, as something you think is true, and so on.

---

simply characterized as an analytical reduction procedure through which professional analysts "render" worldly actions into analyzable data. For an elaboration, see Garfinkel (2002: 135–144).

So the big claim, then, is that for *each* of these sciences, or for *a* discovering science, that it consists of practices that are distinctive of it – distinctive of it as its own identified domain. The idea would be that these practices that are distinctive of it *as* its domain are indeed its phenomena. So that means that the entire technical content of a discovering science will be encountered, will be addressed, will be come upon as that science's distinctively unique domain, that is, its status as an ensemble of human practices. However, don't make a lot of the human practices. We just have them done by humans, not by dogs, that's the point. I mean, we have to have persons that do it. But I'm not talking in Virgil's place.

So I take that to be the thing we want to come to. The idea in our studies is to come to that as the Big Animal that we're chasing.

[A student asks Garfinkel if "we are defining a science in terms of its characteristics."]

GARFINKEL: No. We are going to find the science as distinctive practices of practical actions. It is going to be a science of practical action. The problem will be to say how the technical content of physics – the entire content, the content without anything being excused – will be recovered as the work of physicists. It's not even the work of physicists. It's in the work – It's not that we start with a preconception of what physics would have to be. However, we can't encounter the work of physics without, in fact, starting with someone who knows physics. Eric [Livingston] was asked in his [qualifying] examination, since he was going to be talking about the work of mathematicians, how he would define "a mathematician." He proposed that he didn't need to begin by defining "mathematician," but he did need to begin by going to the place where mathematics is witnessably being done. It doesn't mean, then, that it depends upon a communal *definition* of "physics," because it doesn't reside in an *agreement* that in fact there are these consensual– it's not that there are consensually available properties of triangles in general, that these are discoverables, but that they are to be come upon as worldly matters, not as matters that are assured according to the W.I. Thomas shibboleth that the social definitions are the *sine qua non* of the reality of these matters.[4]

So what I'm thinking then is that in searching for the work of physicists, we encounter it very, very simply. That is, in each particular case there is a matter of: I can say for myself that I don't know it when I see it, and I couldn't do it to save my life. And anyone who asks me for help is bound to be disappointed in specifiable ways. So then, in effect, I begin in the midst of things again. Say I don't begin with the reduced worldliness of this phenomenon: I don't begin with the philosopher's problem. I begin with the practical task at hand. In order to bring a page of physics under examination, I'll fail you in no time. "Now, here, I'll show you how." And I take that very seriously, and I take it

---

4 Thomas' "theorem" (as it is sometimes called) is: "If men define situations as real, they are real in their consequences" (Thomas and Thomas 1928: 571–72). Garfinkel, like countless others, credits this dictum (or shibboleth, as he calls it) to W.I. Thomas, omitting his co-author and spouse Dorothy Thomas. Elsewhere, he referred to the Thomas dictum as an "apothegm" (Garfinkel 1956: 185n).

very seriously that we begin our inquiries, not as the transcendental analyst, but as persons with an actual problem at hand, which is, wherever you're bringing physics under examination, then, there is the practical problem of finding the physics to study. For that we don't go to the philosophers; we need to go somewhere in the world where we will encounter some things like, for example, it being taught, or it being taught poorly, or it being claimed to be taught and it not being taught at all, and so on. But that may be a very frail reed; it may not bear much weight.

At any rate, let me begin by recapping the whole argument. We have taken on as the task: What is the work of a discovering science? And we are not talking generally speaking about a discovering science: but the seminar has taken on specifically the task, given the materials that are available out of the Cocke and Disney tape and related materials, in collaboration with Mike [Lynch] and Eric [Livingston], of finding out what was the work of discovering the optical pulsar.

Now, I've already pointed out about that, that we are going to be working with the distinction between the discovering sciences and anything else that could be called a science – most particularly, let's say, the social sciences. And the claimed distinction is that the discovering sciences are those sciences, to begin with, where you can lose the phenomenon or you can waste your time, where there are the so-called unmotivated observables of inquiry's practices (those unmotivated observables like the relevance of the *bricolage* expert, for example), where you have the relevance as well of so-called moving the machinery, and the difficulties then of teaching novices the effectiveness of working in particular places with particular equipment, given the availability of local histories and the local vernacular of the shop and the local vernacular of shop talk. We spoke about these as providing to these curious sciences standing contingencies of inquiry and, roughly for the time being, split those contingencies to provide for what we spoke of as accountable contingencies, on the one hand, and compared these with wild contingencies on the other. And we said with respect to both of those ways of speaking about the contingencies of inquiry that they spoke to, they remarked on, or they gave us a way of remarking on or making remarkable the work of theorizing and providing for the work of theorizing what its conditions would be. I'm talking about the work of theorizing, let's say, in a discovering science – chemistry, for example, or physics.

So, if you could lose the phenomenon, then it wasn't that it could be lost in any which way. Accountably, there were ways in which, losing a phenomenon, you could find yourself not knowing with respect to the historicity of a course of inquiry, with respect to the essential situatedness of a series of steps that were available to a crowd in the lab as a project that they were engaged in; and losing the phenomenon, thereby losing sight collectively of *where you were* with a problem. And that business then of losing your way could be the condition under which the theorizing would happen.

Now, given that we have as the *theme* of our inquiries the overall– that is, the Big Prize is to be able to make specific the claim that the discovering sciences are sciences of practical action. In short, our claim could be restated, say, by using kind of an analogy to conversational analysis. If we say that the conversational analysts have as their standing preoccupation the concern to learn the work of conversational interaction (which is to say that the work of conversational interaction is constitutive of the events of conversation), then the phenomena of conversation consist *in situ* of the in-course work of conversation's own produced, recognized, understood [events], where the production and understanding and recognition is itself a part of the same course of practices, so that it's not extensive.[5] Then what I'm proposing is: Look, the analogy is that the work of physicists is to the ordered topics of physics what the work of conversational interaction is to the events of conversation. That's the informing analogy. Well, while that's an informing analogy, it won't do for us. So let me proceed by speaking more specifically about that program.

I want to lay out a set of claims that some of you have already gone over. So these may be in some way already familiar. To begin with, what our policy leads us to is that the optical pulsar is not available; what we're claiming is that in looking for the discovery of the optical pulsar, we're proposing that the optical pulsar is not available to a disembodied subjectivity. That is to say, the going versions of what makes physics *physics*, and indeed what makes a discovering science a discovering science, the going version depicts the work of physics and depicts the work that makes up the discovery of the optical pulsar as the properties of a science in what Gurwitsch (1974: 34) spoke of as the "Galilean mode." Now let us say that it proposes that the work of that science exhibits the properties of a Galilean science. And that means prominently, invariably and without fail, at least *this* much: that the work is *always* accompanied by the research reports, the research papers, the published accounts, and the *publishable* talk of that work – that is, the *publicly* available and the publicly responsible talk of that work – whereby the work is spoken of and is hearable according to what I'm going to speak of as the voice (or it's heard in the voice) of a transcendental analyst. Okay?

Now, the way to see what I'm talking about is to understand that there's a comparable voice that could be spoken of when we speak more familiarly about the voice of the narrator in fiction. The narrator's voice in fiction is readable out of the words with which the story is readably there. The story being told, it is told always in the narrator's voice.

The report, the public account of the work of the science, is hearably there and readably there, again always in the voice of the transcendental analyst, by which I mean the following. First, that the work is rendered as the practices

---

5 The original transcript had the word "expensive" here, marked with a question mark in brackets. The word is not clear on the recording, but "extensive" seems a possibility.

of a disembodied subjectivity. That's a fancy way to talk. Here's what I'm saying. In speaking about the "how" a discovery was made, and thereby wherein the technical content of the discovery is claimable, provision is made for matters like the purposes of the inquiry, the grounds of the inquiry, the present problematic factual situation that was taken and for which the inquiry was undertaken as a remedy for that troubled factual situation. So the grounds for that inquiry, the good reasons for it, the adequate grounds (meaning the established facticity that one could predicate the design of the equipment or the carrying through of the particular inquiry) — we will call these now such things as the origins, the aims, the directions, the intentions, the purposes, the consequences. . . . The subjectivity of that inquiry is now provided for in such a way that with respect to all issues of adequate knowledge of origins, grounds, purposes, outcomes, consequences, and with respect to all issues that would assure or furnish the grounds for demonstration of origins, aims and the rest; that throughout, the function of that subjectivity is going to be such, that all references to embodied action of investigators and investigations are specifically irrelevant. So, to speak of the transcendental analyst is to say in the first place that the voice of the analyst is such that one can be assured that *any* references to embodied action can be properly excused, where *all* issues of adequacy are found — fancy distinctions of fact and fancy, hypotheticals, adequate grounds, et cetera, et cetera, are up for review.

Well, to say then that the public account of the work of the discovery of the optical pulsar makes use of the voice of the transcendental analyst would mean that it's already an essential distraction for our inquiries, because what we're proposing is that we can't excuse and will not excuse the relevance of embodied action. So, the resources of the transcendental analyst that would put in our hands that version of discovering the optical pulsar, where we would have to make embodied action irrelevant, is already being put aside.

Now, a second feature of the transcendental analyst is the familiar correspondence that we've spoken of previously — the correspondence of judgment and the object, where issues of truth and verifiability are concerned. The correspondence of judgment and object is provided in this way, that a proposition and its predicates, a subject and its predicates, stand in correspondence to an object and its attributes. So the issues of truth and verifiability are brought under examination by examining the adequacy with which the correspondence is depicted and encountered, or come upon, or demonstrated, or is demonstrable.

A third feature is the feature that is in the philosophy of ambiguous action or the philosophy of embodied action that Merleau-Ponty [1958: 6–7] puts on hand. He speaks about the "prejudice" of the world and means by this that objects of the world are taken to be the *sole authoritative source and cause* of everything that can be said, and found, and seen about them. It's to be spoken of too as another version of the *naturally theoretic version* of the existence of the world. When one wants a formula with which to speak summarily of the problem of the existence of the world, or what it is as a problematic to claim the existence of the world, that would be a way of specifying that as a problem.

Since I've already indicated that we have as "insteads" to the practices of disembodied subjectivity, then for the further features of the transcendental analyst – of that correspondence of judgment and object, say with respect to truth and verifiability – we have in its place much more like a *Heideggerian* version of truth and verifiability which provides for a judgment standing to its object as *revelatory* of the object, as revealing of the object, and then not of its *attributes* but disclosing of the just-what the object is identifiably that.

[A student initiates a lengthy discussion with a comment about the possible relevance of emotion in "punctuating" the events in the pulsar tape. Garfinkel and others in the seminar engage in dialogue with the student's interest in feelings and emotion, tying them into the "despair" of losing the phenomenon, before resuming the topic of the Galilean version.]

Well, that was for the point, then, that the optical pulsar is not available to a disembodied subjectivity, and that the pulsar is also not available to a Galilean *version* of the phenomenon. Nor is it available to a Galilean version of how it was discovered.

What we're doing is to make the leap. We're saying that, *instead*, the discovered pulsar consists of the *in situ* practices, the work of finding and exhibiting the analyzability of the pulsar again, that that's the achievement: that its discovery is not the work of finding and exhibiting the analyzability of the pulsar again, but its discovery is the *accountable* work. That is to say, it's the *observable* work; it's the work that can be made available to observation and report as *this* work, namely, the work of exhibiting the intelligibility, the workings of, the just how it appears in the places and in the instrumentation as it does again. And the *hunch*, or the proposal, or the claim, is that that accountable work is a very certain sort of accountable work. I'm hunching about it that it's *naturally* accountable work; that it's not, ethnomethodologically speaking, the work (we don't speak in the accents of ethnomethodology in speaking of *that* work; we speak instead in the accents of classic theorizing). So we reconstrue the practices. We construe the practices as the work of a Galilean science. We *render* the practices according to the property, or as an orderliness of, a Galilean science. That would mean, then, that the Galilean science is not anything else than a *practical* device, a *practical* terminology, a way of talking science and it's in no case to be trusted. I mean, you trust it, not because you are part of a community, or not because you will be punished for talking differently than that, but because your life *depends* on it. I mean, if you're not going to talk like that, how else will you talk? I mean, if you're not going to say of the work that, well, if the pulsar isn't exhibitable, according to the way in which that apparatus collects and aggregates these incoming photons, you have now a way of understanding how that apparatus collects those photons for you. It could be none of your business that it works in the way it does. So if, then, we adequately specified for reasons of publication that CAT apparatus,[6] then it's not that it *does* for practical purposes; that's what practical purposes consist of. Speaking of the CAT means: on that occasion the invocation of its adequacy for practical purposes is displayed in the fact that it's cited there; and therein then the adequacy of the work is rendered in that same display. You mention CAT? That's what your work might as well have consisted of, that you used that machinery. And how? What do you mean "how"? Don't you know how to use it? It's available to the competent practitioner or the competent reader, and so on. So, in every case it's not that the competence of the practitioner is presupposed. We're not talking about presuppositions. We're talking about the availability of a practical lingo, of a very very *practical* device with which the actual practices are rendered in their full intelligibility, but only in that one knows *in situ* what it is to speak like that.

So, therefore, it should come to us *never* as an ironic difference that between the writing – or the public speaking or the published report – and the practices there are invariably discrepancies. Because to the practitioner, nothing could be less interesting than that you would tell him, "See how you don't include in the report how you actually worked," because he couldn't possibly be interested in that *irony*. He couldn't be *more* interested, however, in the fact that if you put the irony aside, he has in the lab practices to know therein what a reading would have to look and sound like.

So it seems to me, then, that what we're faced with is: Well, what is it as a lab practice to include in this, having come upon the naturally theoretic or naturally accountable work, to then turn the naturally accountable work to the matter of its public version, to now speak about it in just so many words?

[An exchange with two seminar participants about writing scientific methods reports.]

. . . I think there are other issues, however: . . . questions like, in the writing of the methods section, how current the writer is with respect to – if he's in any way obligated to showing the phenomenon available to an error-free procedure, or say a criticism-free procedure, then he's already oriented to, and displays the orientation to, a *corpus* of methods, meaning that it's not only that these methods have been cited in the literature; they've been cited and criticized so that they're available for all claims about the adequacy of their use as grounds for the inquiries that are being reported. So it has to be, then, I keep wanting to say a "textured structure" of practices. That's goofy. It's a *texture* of

---

6 CAT is an acronym for computer of average transients. It was an electronic apparatus that accumulated input from the optical telescope at Kitt Peak National Observatory and was designed to detect and display on a screen a spatial rendering of variations in the intensity of incoming photons over time at a set frequency corresponding to the already documented frequency (more than 30 times a second) of a radio pulsar. The resolution of an optical telescope is much more precise than that of a radio telescope, and so the idea was to check a specific visible star (which in this case was believed to be a supernova remnant) to see if the visible light from that star manifested the pulsation that had been measured in non-visible portions of the electromagnetic spectrum.

relevancies that are being invoked, pointed to, claimed, underwritten. I mean, the work of citing must be one hell of a big responsibility. Now, that may be that I'm full of hot air. The thing that could easily make it full of hot air is that compared with the problems that Cocke and Disney were faced with in simply seeing that pulsar display, and now already being oriented to "My god, it's too good to be true," which is to say, calling up and now facing ahead projectively what kind of problems they are going to have to face if they claim that everybody else has been looking for it and not finding it there, but they found it.[7] We'll call that providing for the relevance of methods in the case of a dramatic discovery, as compared with the day-to-day, nondescript documentation of findings, for example, that are frequently cited as the legwork of the science that the day-to-day work of most scientists doesn't make for spectacular studies and doesn't make for deep breathing about the spectacular risks, or gains, or losses, and so on and so on . . . .

GARFINKEL: . . . Well, what I'm thinking of is, for example, when [James] Olds was exploiting his discovery [of the pleasure center in the rat's brain], the discovery itself was one thing, but *exploiting* the discovery was a matter of *great stamina, immense drudgery*, and *mobilizing* the efforts of persons sustaining them through the sheer difficulties of getting the damned electrodes implanted properly, getting them done to satisfy the previous criteria that had been worked out, seeing again that they were adequate to the next case, and the next case, having to wait until the actual jolt got sent through; and then you see the reading that it's in order, and you are not encountering any trouble. So the thing, then, about exploiting the discovery and having found the pleasure they were giving the rat – in fact, they were pleasuring the rat – is that they then were in the business of just turning out the next variation, the next variation and the next variation, and having to pay attention in the day's work to getting it done, getting it written and into the press. Get it done, get it written and [sent] off. So, in fact, he and his wife said that they had a high-production, low-cost mine. They knew how to implant the electrodes. They knew where they were going to implant them next. That is, wherever they needed to implant them again, they could get them there. Then the question is: Well, how do you run the variations on it, given that we can do that? So if someone came in and said, "Well, let's heat the hypothalamus." "Okay, let's heat it." Then, say, "I have a technique for cooling the hypothalamus." "Let's cool it." "Why don't we inject this drug because . . ., that drug because . . ., this drug because . . ., that one

---

7 Though incidental to the point Garfinkel is making, it seems that it was not the case that "everybody else has been looking for it and not finding it there" (training an optical telescope and CAT on a supernova remnant star). According to Cocke (interview with Michael Lynch in 1980), he and Disney were indeed surprised to see evidence that they had detected a pulsar, since they had spent the previous evenings on Kitt Peak trying to do so but failing, but it is not clear that other astronomers had been searching for an optical pulsar at that locale, and there were theoretical rationales for supposing that emissions from previously identified radio pulsars would not be detectable in the optical range of the electromagnetic spectrum.

will do," and so on. So for the first several years following the discovery, there was this enormous factory. It was an enterprise, not a factory, but a highly organized collection of persons, some of them in the lab, some of them from all over the medical center and the psychology department, because they were all told about it and they were invited. "You have an idea? Come around. We have the rats, we have the money. You want to do it? We'll show you how to do it. Here's a place in the lab. Go to it." Now, that has to be a different kind of concern with methods and the adequacy of grounds.

GARFINKEL: I'm trying to lay out what I can say at this point with any confidence about the claim that the discovering sciences are sciences of practical action. The big emphasis that we're into – tonight's emphasis – is that the discovering work is such as to be rendered as the properties of a Galilean science. And the availability of that rendering is this thing I'm speaking of as the naturally accountable work.

Now, the big topic that remains and that I just can't treat tonight because I'm not prepared for it is, well, specifically: What does it mean to say that the technical content of chemistry, for example, is to be recovered in its entirety as a science of practical action?

I would like tonight to lay out the remainder of the arguments; on the first half of our argument. That is to say, we have ways of sketching the existence of the work that naturally theoretic accounts of science have overlooked. In proposing that the pulsar is not available to a Galilean version of the phenomenon, and not available to how it was discovered, we have the big Instead. It's the *in situ*, practical work of exhibiting the analyzability of the pulsar again. That practical work, I proposed in our last meeting, is that we can perhaps get access to it by considering that the embodied practices of the night's work are such that Cocke and Disney are faced with *extracting* from the circumstantiality of the practices the animal, so to speak, in the foliage. The foliage is the circumstantiality of their own competence to what they're doing. So they must *come* upon the naturally theoretic *account* of those practices, which would then be the figurative version; that is, the figure on the ground, but visible *only* on that ground. That ground, however, is not a *bland* ground in the way in which the homogeneous blackboard shows the drawing that we scribble on it, but is instead literally discoverable as the "there" and findable "there" in the fashion of one's competent presence to the phenomenon (i.e., one's competent finding and exhibiting of it as an "it" again).

So the proposal then was that instead of treating the figure-ground structure as an analytic treatment or an analytic feature of the structure, instead of the figure-ground structure being a way of our speaking generally of what perception must consist of, we would speak instead of their achievement being elucidated in that the figure-ground structure was indeed a practical *achievement*. Then we proposed that other gestalt themes would then lend themselves similarly to that treatment as practical achievements, rather than, as for example, the theme of the adumbrated object, and the theme

FIGURE IIS4.1   M.C. Escher's 1938 woodcut, *Day and Night*. This was one of his many tessellated figures. The black and white geese flying in opposite directions in the upper portion of the figure are inscribed in the manner of complementary tiles.

Source: © 2021 The M.C. Escher Company – The Netherlands. All rights reserved. www.mcescher.com

of the object constancy, and the theme of the gestalt switch, and the theme of the relationships of alternativity, and so on. It was with respect to those themes as practical achievements that we then got into the elaboration of the distinction between accountable contingencies and the wild contingencies, and said of the wild contingencies that they're to be thought of (permit me to speak like that for the time being), and that we might as well treat them as, *lunatic components* of the accountable contingencies. It's like a *clown* that mocks the seriousness of the tragic figure. It's the *craziness* that inhabits the utterly serious, responsible version of just what the conditions of the phenomena are. Okay?[8]

Now that we're at it, it seems to me that feelings would surely have a place in that since Olds' dread when he saw his assistant moving the equipment and his rage was sure enough dread and rage.[9] And it could be that he was afraid, he literally was fearful, that his own *care* was courting betrayal, that he would

---

8   Garfinkel returns to the theme of "demonic" contingencies toward the end of the fifth seminar (July 1, 1980; pp. 196ff., this volume). An example of "wild contingencies" mentioned in connection with radio pulsar research are possible sources of apparent pulsed signals arising from such matters as pigeons roosting on the observatory apparatus, rats chewing the wires, electrical discharges from automobile ignition switches, or even signals sent by inhabitants of a distant planet.

9   Garfinkel described this incident in the second seminar in this series (May 27, 1980 p. 134, this volume), and also in Part I, section 5, of this volume (p. 34).

be betrayed in the very midst of the places where his best work was to be done. So that's what I mean by the lunatic accompaniment.

Now then, to pick up that theme, and finish it off with further talk on that topic, or that side of the accountability of discovering practice: I'm *impressed* with the way in which, given the possible attractiveness of the gestalt themes as practical accomplishments, there is the fact of [M.C.] Escher's drawings, which put in our hands many, many gestalt themes, not as practical accomplishments but as renderings of the practical accomplishments. By that I mean, in Escher's drawings you have, for example, those tessellated figures. Do you know what I mean by "tessellated figures"? Birds, for example. Black birds in one direction, white birds in another (Figure IIS4.1).

The fish. And the thing about those figures is that, to take for an example one kind of gestalt theme that he plays with, you have then a surface that is completely covered by these figures that intermesh. Now the big feature about those tessellated figures is that he's playing with the theme of the equivocal character of a common boundary. So that, *if* you're examining the functional character, the characteristics, the features of a fish facing to the right, then you see the line as the fish's belly for the one on top, but as the fish's back for the one see-ably headed in the other direction. So you have this as the theme of the possible equivocality of a boundary for tessellated figures.[10] The analogy is usable immediately because instead of seeing them as tessellated, you can now imagine that there would be for Cocke and Disney a place of establishing a bounded event for the incoming photon display of the pulsar [see Figure 2 of the Cocke et al. (1969: 525) report reprinted in Appendix One of Garfinkel et al. (1981: 143)]. But the point is, you have Escher, who now puts in our hands these drawings that play with all kinds of gestalt themes.

[A member of the class mentions reading an article about how Escher was influenced by gestalt theory, and Garfinkel identifies an article in *Scientific American* by Teuber (1974).]

GARFINKEL: However, what I want to point out about the resources that Escher puts in our hands is that these are deceptive. I mean by "deceptive" not anything different than that these are renderings of the practical achievement of these gestalt themes. And what happens is that the work, say, of a figure-ground arrangement, the achievement of a figure-ground arrangement, is rendered as the *properties* of an Escherian *display* of a figure on its ground. Among other things, what Cocke and Disney can't do is what Escher *can* do, which is to give us time enough to enjoy, and to see further, and to see to endless depths into the detail of this drawing that then presents the docile figure of an equivocal boundary.

Now, that reminds us, then, of the fact that Abner Dean [see third seminar in the series, June 3, 1980] can give us a rendering of a conversation.

---

10 Garfinkel may be referring to Escher's "Fishes Mural" (1958). What he says about tessellated fishes can be applied to the black and white birds in "Day and Night" (Figure IIS4.1).

He collects some properties, displays them figuratively as the hopeless zombie before the converter bangs him on the head, after which the flower of enlightenment is there as the aftermath. And he collects all these and presents it in a coherent, figurative account of conversation. Escher puts in our hands, similarly, the properties of – we will call them now the figuratively displayed properties of the gestalt themes.

Now then, here's the proposal. Given that we can have one hell of a good time digging out these themes from Escher's drawings – and I'll bring in some Escher drawings. I'm a great fan. I'll bring them in and put them on the table so you can all have one hell of a good time finding the themes for yourselves. Now, giving you the candy, we're going to take it away. A little poison. Here's the poison. It's by reason of Escher's artfulness, or it's by reason of the fact that he has paper and pencil and because of paper-and-pencil's ways, that he's able now to furnish in drawings the docile arrangement, and the cogent, interesting, joyful and joy-giving display, of gestalt themes. In that very rendering – that is, in that he can do it with paper and pencil – then, in *that* respect, in the very availability of paper and pencil, the arts of what paper and pencil will do, is assured that the gestalt properties of practical achievements are anything but that. If they're going to be *rendered* in those ways, then they must to that extent stand as inspectable and standing on behalf of the original. Not necessarily *representing* the original, but they're seen already to *speak* on behalf of the original, and we see in them that the original is not that.

SPEAKER: Original, what do you mean?

GARFINKEL: Well, the original is the work itself.

SPEAKER: Of Escher.

GARFINKEL: No, not Escher's work. Of the gestalt theme. See, we're reading Escher to find what the features are of Cocke and Disney's work.

SPEAKER: Oh, okay.

GARFINKEL: Well, if he has an equivocal boundary, then we can go looking for the equivocal boundary and we can be sure of one thing: it's not going to look like that. In fact, even for what we say that Escher would have provided as the property of the equivocal boundary, it's not going to be that, since we haven't [observed] to begin with that it's going to have features like that generally speaking.[11] It's not general structures that we're dealing with because if Cocke and Disney find the figure on the ground, you already see, "Well, it can't be the figure that looks like *this*." You can't, first of all, find a homogeneous ground, at least not in principle. And if there's a homogeneity to it, then it's going to have to be in the way in which it is encountered.

SPEAKER: So that would be the way in which they achieve that.

GARFINKEL: Right. So it has in every case to be tied to the work at hand. Otherwise, we might as well be frankly back to the business of model construction and use Escher to lead the way. Okay?

---

11 Garfinkel was speaking very rapidly at this point, and the transcript involved some guesswork here.

I'm finding that that's the cogency of the argument. But it may be that I'm goofy. So you need to say, "Well, it sounds good. But it's nevertheless bullshit." You know.

[A seminar participant expresses some difficulty with reading the Gestalt themes into the transcript of Cocke and Disney's recorded exchanges.]

GARFINKEL: I think you're being much more careful and thoughtful about it, because when I was doing something like that (for example, in reading this stuff on the adumbrated object), . . . I found myself immediately bored, thinking: "Oh Jeez. It's too easy that way." Which is to say, the adumbrated object is the object that is exhibited from the various points of view and various perspectives as the varying conditions under which the object appears in the way it does.[12] Now, that's a gorgeous theme. Where philosophy is concerned, it's an old standby, the object that's seen always from the point of view of repose; seen always as the appearance of, and now given as the structure of appearances. And the structure is furnished in that which remains self-same under the varying appearances. That means, then, that you're obligated to find the conditions under which the object will appear in the fashion that it does.

You could then say, okay, what Cocke and Disney are out to do is to discover what are the conditions under which the pulsar will show in the display the determinations of a certain sort. That's the problem of their inquiry. However, to my way of thinking, that sells the whole enterprise short. In one formula you can say: well look, what their job was to do was to formulate the conditions under which the pulsar could be claimed to have been shown. So, therefore, they asked the question, "Are those bastards in the valley sending up some kind of fugitive signal that we're picking up and that's giving us what looks like the pulsar?" And so on.

[Two participants in the seminar discuss with Garfinkel their difficulties with the applicability of the theme of adumbrated object to Cocke and Disney's effort to come to terms with a possible optical pulsar.]

GARFINKEL: . . . I think of the hopeless circumstantiality with which a boundary is come upon as a course of historicizing one's own inquiries *in situ*. If the two of them are into a little bit of Mutt and Jeff ("Oh, there it is." "Now, now."),[13] that it's not enough to say of seeing the animal that they will have come to an agreement, since it's only in and as a course of talk that everything coming to an

---

[12] The "stuff" Garfinkel says he was reading was likely Gurwitsch's (1964: 202–204) explication, through the lens of Gestalt theory, of Husserl's original notion of adumbration. Also see the first seminar in this series (May 22, 1980). A house-seen-from-the-front is the prototypical adumbrated object; though partial and perspectival when considered as a perceptual image, the viewer sees the house – the whole house – as the object, and not the partial house. (A film set or Potemkin village might exploit such apprehension.)

[13] See Appendix 4 in Garfinkel et al. (1981: 150–153) for the transcript of Observation #19, particularly the following exchange (p. 151):

   051   Disney: *By God! We got it!*
   052   Cocke: Naow, naow.

agreement could have come to look like. It would have been put there by *their* doings. And it's not that they're insensible to the way in which the seriality of their doings is available to them as a part of the thing that is going on.

[Lynch elaborates on notes he took about the transcript of the astronomers' talk recorded on the pulsar tape, followed by comments by Garfinkel and a student in the seminar.]

GARFINKEL: Well, I'm going to make two very brief points, and then I think we'll call it off for the evening. I would like to just invoke the existence of, I will call them, *Escherian* models of practical action. An Escherian model of practical action would be an account of practical action that would provide for what's interesting, visible, describable, and seeable, but where all of these gains are furnished by reason of the way that an Escherian model has as a docile account of that action. Which is to say, it's by reason of paper-and-pencil's way that the properties of action would then have the properties that they can be demonstrably seen to have. Similarly, . . . a conversational typescript might then provide us with an Escherian model of conversational interaction. That is to say, if we now pay close attention to the linearity of the typewriter's way, of lettering's ways (that they must come one after the other, for example . . ., that they may fall down the page in seeable one-after-the-other fashion), in that case one might have quite directly a linear version of, not what's otherwise a holistic version, but which is Escherian and, in that very way, we know not linear.

So our proposal is always – we can be talking about Escherian models of those discovering practices, and what I want to propose by way of closing the discussion – there are two proposals that offer for our consideration at some time. The first proposal is that a research paper or a published account renders the discovering work of the optical pulsar as the properties of a Galilean science. The second proposal is that the research paper, in the ways that it *renders* the discovering work as the properties of a Galilean science, is an Escherian model of that work. Now, that doesn't mean that the research paper is a *beast*. I'm not speaking ironically of the shortcomings of the research paper. Rather I am saying that it's the *work* of Cocke and Disney somewhere along the line then to be engaged, as part of a continuation of their work, to in fact Escherianize that work . . . as a distinct part of their practice.

Therefore, we ought to put aside now *any* further surprise about how an account in fact is a lying version and how it falls short, and see instead what its competence is.[14] Its competence then has to be tied finally, via the Kuhnian solution to the problem of what accounts for how it is that the experiment is demonstrably the demonstration of the objectivity of what it is – the solution to that is found in the kind of thing that the paradigm is. That's Kuhn talking

---

14 With his mention of "a lying version," Garfinkel may have been alluding to a BBC broadcast, also published as a short magazine piece by Peter Medawar (1964), in which raised the provocative question of whether the scientific paper is "fraudulent" because of the way it misrepresents actual research practice.

of what the paradigm consists of.[15] The paradigm would then consist of the essential [tie][16] of the lab practice *to* the account that it's then, witnessably (to those who are competent to the practice), the adequate account of.

That would mean that there's a whole tradition in sociology – and I have bought into it for years – that has as its dissatisfactions that it's dissatisfied with all ideal versions of practice.[17] That can't be the problem any more. I mean, that can't be the phenomenon that one could encounter as a dissatisfaction. Instead, what one would have to ask for . . . is: Well, look, if Cocke and Disney are dissatisfied with the account that they've written up, then how are we to see (from the point of view of the relevancies of the writing they must in any case do) that they have grounds for dissatisfaction and what those grounds could be? And what is it that, in fact, falls short? Because in any case, it's not that it falls short. It is, in any case, always and without relief adequate for all practical purposes. So that's so much for the renderings.

Now the next big issue is, without respect for that part of it being done, what is it then that it is composed of? If we're going to say theoretical astrophysics is a science of practical action – and what Cocke and Disney's account puts in our hands is an opportunity to say how theoretical astrophysics is a science of practical action – then the question is, what would that look like as a set of researchable issues? I guess the next thing would be to take that up, assuming that I have the combination of stamina, art, brains, and chutzpah to bring it off. I don't know if I'm up to that. You know, theoretical physics absolutely snows me. I just don't know anything about *that lab*.

---

15 See the second seminar in this series (May 27, 1980), where Garfinkel works through the postscript to the second edition (1970a) of Kuhn's *Structure of Scientific Revolutions*.
16 A cough by one of the participants in the seminar completely obscured a word in the recording. I would guess that a word like "tie" would convey the sense of how a paradigm is inseparable from the methodic practices of demonstrating its relevancy to distinctive material complexes.
17 The 1980 meeting in Toronto at which Garfinkel was scheduled to deliver the pulsar paper in a plenary session was in large part a forum for presenting and debating the "new" social studies of science. Michael Mulkay, David Bloor, H.M. Collins, and many others who presented at the meeting took aim at the idealized version of science attributed to old-school sociology and philosophy of science, and undertook to examine historical and contemporary scientific research without exemption from the way sociologists treat other modes of belief and practice. Garfinkel here is suggesting that the contrast between ideal and actual practice is not the issue for him; instead, it is the issue is how practical adequacy is achieved in situ.

SEMINAR 5

Discovering work of the sciences
(July 1, 1980)

Harold Garfinkel

Discovering Sciences as Sciences of Practical Actions; The Galilean Object; Analogy with Conversational Greetings; Gestalt Themes and the Embodied Work of a Science; The Demonic Order

[This was a summary session on the topic of "Work in a discovering science" and was held at Garfinkel's house, with refreshments served. Garfinkel handwrote a list of 13 attendees on the cover of the cassette tape that recorded the seminar, though some of the names were indecipherable. The recognizable names included visitors who attended the session, including UCLA faculty members Robert Westman of the History Department, and Gerald Platt and Rod Harrison of the Sociology Department. Others who were listed included Eric Livingston and E. Burke Rochford, who were advanced PhD students in Sociology at UCLA; Ken Liberman of UC, San Diego, who was completing his PhD dissertation at the time; Friedrich Schrecker, a visiting MA student from the University of Frankfurt; and Michael Lynch, a postdoctoral fellow at UCLA. Before the start of the seminar, an unidentified participant refers to two recently published books that he recommends as relevant to the topic.[1] After further friendly exchanges, Garfinkel begins to review what the seminar has covered in previous meetings and proposes that future meetings will involve discussions with guests invited to talk about their sciences.]

GARFINKEL: For those of you who don't know Bob Westman, he's on my right. He's the only one in the crowd who knows what he's talking about when he talks about science. He comes as a distinguished historian of science.

---

1   One of the books mentioned was a volume edited by Barnes and Shapin (1979), which included a series of contributions related to the Edinburgh Science Studies Unit's "Strong Programme" in the Sociology of Knowledge; the other was an English translation of Ludwick Fleck's (1979) social history of the Wasserman Test, originally published in German in 1935. Kuhn wrote the foreword to the translation and acknowledged that Fleck's writings were a significant source of insight for him on incommensurability.

[Garfinkel continues by saying that he had spoken earlier to Westman to propose that further meetings after this one could be turned into "an ethnographic seminar" by inviting in practicing scientists to discuss themes covered in the seminar.]

GARFINKEL: Now, the thing that I would like to do is review, for myself and for us, what I understand our interests in the work of a discovering science might look like. I want to try for a package of sorts. That doesn't mean I want to start talking and then I don't want you to interrupt. But the thing that I'm trying to do is to see through it as if it had a beginning and a course; and I want to try to bang my way through the hard part. The hard part is the claim that I take to be the aim (if it comes off, it will be our achievement; if it comes off as an achievement, it will be too good to be true), and that is that each discovering science is in its distinctive way a science of practical action. I take that to be a messy place, really messy. But perhaps in anticipation of what's on the other side of our laying out some version of what that proposal might look like initially, I will try getting it laid out. When I get to that messy part, that's when questions, yeah-buts, criticisms, "Bullshit," and all the rest of it has to start. Otherwise, it won't do you any good.

I take it that the seminar's problem – the reason that we're meeting and . . . the stuff now that's being laid out – is: What is the work of a discovering science? The problem further for us is that wherever possible we would want not to have to be talking about a discovering science generally speaking, since we're already anticipating that we have a way of locating a discovering science and contrasting discovering sciences with those that are not discovering sciences, the social sciences.

The distinction we have gone over several times, the distinction between the discovering science and – I don't want to say a non-discovering science because I'm not sure whether that direction does much for us, but let's say a discovering science contrasted, at least for the time being, with the social sciences. As you remember, I pointed out that they're curiously named when they're spoken of as sciences; and we got into some initial characterizations of the grounds for that distinction. The characterizations are the matters that we talked of as these unmotivated observables of lab practice, these unmotivated, *observable* features of lab *work* that those who must make experiments work, we think, are prepared to recognize: like the possibility that you can *lose* a phenomenon; the possibility that the time spent in the pursuit of a problem can encounter the recalcitrance of the phenomenon that's being sought out via that lab work, with the result that as a standing contingency it is possible in some sciences to have *wasted your time*, literally for there being *nothing to do* with the results in hand; that any thought of publication or any thought of carrying them further has on the face of it the character that it's a waste of one's life, it's a waste of one's money, it's a waste of collegial time, it's an imposition of various sorts, and so on.

There is a list of other contingencies that were spoken about. And the idea, then, is that these conditions are such as to furnish to the work of inquiry and theorizing the conditions under which those inquiries and that theorizing must get done. Now, it's *in* that you can lose the phenomenon, it's in that you can be wasting your time, it's in that you're going to have to be expert with bodily practice so as to make the experiment work. It's that there are not only the so-called motivated, or accountable, or formulatable contingencies of the *in situ* effectiveness of actual practices, but there are as well what we spoke of as the *wild* contingencies, the contingencies that in fact *inhabit* the effectiveness of the work and that are given in the very way in which the embodied character of the work – the fact that the practices are the practices of bodily places and bodily directions, of embodied grasps, of embodied placements, of embodied arrangements. Now, we will talk about that further. In any case, the idea is that the theorizing can be thought of not only, say, as what Eric [Livingston] several weeks ago talked about as an experiment that's *shot through* with "reasoning,"[2] but it's also the fact that the work is accompanied, as the kind of thing the course of practices is, by the way in which a *rendering* of that work is available as the *point* of that work, and is available as well as the article that one is prepared to write, if and as the course of practices turns out in its effectiveness to lend itself to a reformulation or a rendering as the just-how the phenomenon is to be obtained and is demonstrable again with the real-worldly practices that make up the work of the lab in just this place with actual materials, and so on.

So we have as our central *claim* that the discovering sciences are sciences of practical action. Now, that's a claim that's looking for its argument. So then the question follows immediately, and that is: What is it we're going to mean, or might as well mean, if we speak of discovering sciences as sciences of practical action? I'll understand that what we might as well take as our aim – I take it that what we want to do is to set up the claim that a discovering science in its technical contents is a distinctive science of practical action, and that *each* discovering science in its technical contents is a distinctive science of practical action. Briefly, I want to say *why* I think we might be *fussy, that* fussy, in this point by insisting, for example, that *each* science is a distinctive science, and that if we don't provide for it in its technical contents that the claim may lose its force and in fact become – at least in my way of seeing it – kind of trivial.

Here is what I understand to be the reason for that fussiness. Use the analogy that the work of physicists is to the topics of order of physics what the work of conversationalists is to the topics of order *of* a conversation. Now, the topic of order of a conversation – in the ethno *mishegas*, in the ethno bias, in the ethno preoccupation with the topic of order – the topic of order is an *event* of conversation.[3] So what we're proposing then, at least as the informing

---

2 This is a reference to Livingston's presentation in the first seminar in this series (May 22, 1980), which is not included the abridged transcript of the seminar in the present volume. For a discussion of his conception of how reasoning is domain-specific and distinctively embedded in the practices of performing experiments and mathematical exercises, as well as in games, puzzles, and other organized practices, see Livingston (2007, 2008).
3 Readers familiar with Conversation Analysis (CA) should recognize that Garfinkel's analogy is with a fundamental understanding exemplified by CA, which is that "analysis" is reflexively embedded in

analogy: as it is with conversational work, we are thinking it would be with physics. The work of physicists then *is to* the topics of order of physics what that work of conversation is [to the topics of order of conversation]. Well, the ordered topics of physics would have to be physics phenomena, but available via the way in which the practice is *in situ* the *apt and familiar efficacy* of physicists' work, physicists' practices being the practices of detecting and demonstrating for each other in organizational detail the existence of a phenomenon that is, via the embodied practices, made by the practitioners to look and sound as it does *in situ* for their exhibition; that is, for their witness. That their phenomena, therefore, though they may be *treated* as having a transcendental character (i.e., that they would be treated by the practitioners as existing *prior to* and *independently* of the embodied way of coming upon a demonstration, to each other via the practice, of what they are) – what we're proposing is that the organization of that lab practice is such as to *mask*, that is, to preserve an *amnesia* for the structure of practices, and in that amnesia to then offer the phenomenon as being transcendental to and independent of, indifferent to, existing prior to, and being itself the cause of everything that's to be seen about it. Which is to say, it's a straight deep interpretation of Merleau-Ponty's [1958] theory of embodied action. Okay? That's the informing analogy.

You can see, then, why we're obligated to take the *technical contents* into account. Without the technical contents, we can't find the physicist's practice. We don't want to talk about his practices generally; that loses that *how* the practices are exhibiting of the physicist's own distinctive topics of interest. So we're obligated to the technical contents. Being obligated to the technical contents means that the practices might as well, for us, be addressed, or we might as well dignify those practices by saying of them, or offering about them, that their availability as apt and familiarly efficacious *in situ* practices having that technical content would have to be such as to be *distinctive* to that science. "Have to be such." Well, for the time being what I'm figuring is we might as well let it be "have to be such." My notion is that it at least requires that we look specifically at what they're doing as physicists; [we] would have to be looking at what they're doing. This slows us down from sociologists' very favorite way of inquiring, and that is to go in immediately with a definition of that work, so as to lose immediately what indeed is not only distinctive but also preservative of that practice as the visible, organizational detail of the just-what-it-is.

Well, then, *if* we're going to be that fussy and insist that it's a distinctive science, and if their practices are such as to furnish for each other's presence the

---

the production of conversation, and that professional CA aims to recover organizational features of that primary production. As evident in Appendix 1 of Part I of this volume, Garfinkel regarded Sacks as his authoritative source on CA. As Sacks expressed in a concise remark: "By 'organization' then, we mean 'methods for achieving features', and the study of the social organization of conversation is the study of those methods participants employ to achieve the features that conversation exhibits" (Sacks 1970, chap. 2, p. 2).

phenomenon in, through, and as the distinctiveness of those practices, then that means they are in the business of practical action, nothing else. Which is to say, the troubles that they're subject to would have to be familiar troubles, the familiar lunacies of practical activity, meaning, for example, they're *hopelessly* engaged in becoming visible in the way in which the practitioners are parties to the local production of a history. The history might be called "the problem," "today's problem," "where we are in today's problem." The temporality of what they're doing is another lunacy that is going to accompany this; that they're up to their ears in the circumstantiality of what they're doing is another lunacy. You'd say it's a lunacy if you're in the analytic sociology business. Right? But I *think* it brings you into the immediate presence of *just these* phenomena of physics in their detailed availability as the practices of those birds in that lab on that day as the effectiveness of a day's work. There is this case of the optical pulsar, for example, to see it in.

Well then, that leaves us with the proposal that physics would in its *distinctive* way be available to its practitioners as a very rigorous version of an event as its being available as a course of practical action. And the theory of the event, then, is a set of instructions about how to go about doing, seeing, saying, exhibiting and demonstrating, in and as a course of collaborative practices, and on the grounds of the collaborative practices, the *just-what* is visibly there as of those visible practices.

Well then, that would mean that if a physicist can't go into a chemist's lab and do the same with them, but *they* can be doing it for each other, then that looks like it's another science of practical action — a distinctive science of practical action. With that version of how distinctiveness would be encountered, then it looks like we can take the rule (at least for our researches and for the time being) that the collection of discovering sciences is, indeed, a collection of sciences of practical action, each being a distinctive science of practical action, but each *locatable* as that distinctive science in that it preserves the *lunacies* that the ethnomethodology of practical action has turned up, coming from our dissatisfactions with analytic sociology's versions of practical action.

LIVINGSTON:[4] . . . well, if instead, the distinctiveness of those practices could have to do with, like, the floor you were on.

GARFINKEL: With the what?

LIVINGSTON: With the *floor* you were on in the physics department. In other words, if you were in the solid-state group, then whatever the plasma group was doing would be completely foreign — or not *completely* foreign . . ., right?

GARFINKEL: Yes.

LIVINGSTON: So is anything worth to be said on that?

GARFINKEL: Umm, I should be troubled by that, right?

---

4 Livingston's intervention is overlapped by coughing in the room and other contingencies that interfere with the recording.

LIVINGSTON: I don't know.

GARFINKEL: Well, wait a second. I might as well be troubled by that, or troubled long enough to get my way out of it. And the way I'll get out of it is that, for the time being, I'd rather provide for endlessly many sciences of practical action *if* in doing so I don't lose the gorgeous availability of each, indeed, as a science, in that the *just how* those phenomena are demonstrably that, is available in these gorgeous law-sketches, to use Kuhn's version of it.[5] Okay? If the plasma group, then, has as its versions of its phenomena these *renderings* of the work of the lab that render that work as a Galilean science, but that in doing so *can't* be rendering if it's disengaged from the practitioner's grasp of the practices of the lab, that it then takes on a curious life of its own that the philosophers of science are so fond of, but that Kuhn felt obligated to furnish a theory . . . of paradigms in order to furnish a solution to the curiosity that the law-sketch remained essentially vague, *except* under the circumstance that its expressions were available for interpretation, for recognition, for just what they were the expressions of, in that the grounds for that recognition was the practitioner's competent practices in the lab – which is to say, is competent access to the work of the experiment for which the rendering was the disengage-able version of what the experiment was to demonstrate. Okay?

So I'm prepared, then, to let those sciences of practical action run. Now let me give you a little hope on that. For that hope, I want to give you the story of a tremendously important failure in the social sciences, where the attempt was made to establish as a disciplined study, and possibly even as a science, the study of effective actions where the search would be for strategies of effective action that were independent of the circumstances in which that effectiveness was demonstrable and witnessable. Which is to say, Kotarbinski attempted to establish praxeology[6] as a science of effective practical action.[7] He gave as the science to begin with, from which he drew his programmatic proposals, economics. He envisaged praxeology literally as a set of production procedures, an assembly of rules of effective practice where the scientist would be interested in learning, whether he was studying how you sailed a ship or how you introduced a product into the market, what was it that made for the effectiveness of that practice, where the issue was, could you extract form the study of effective

---

5 Garfinkel is referring to the notion of "law sketch" discussed in the postscript of Kuhn (1970), which Garfinkel worked through in the 27 May seminar (Part II, Seminar 2 in this volume).

6 Garfinkel's published and unpublished writings and transcribed lectures and seminars often spell "praxiology" with an 'i', but here he is referring to Kotarbinski's usage, "praxeology" spelled with an 'e'.

7 Garfinkel does not provide a citation, although Kotarbinski (1955) would be a relevant source. Decades earlier, in a published talk to a group of psychiatrists, Garfinkel (1956) referenced a secondary source on Kotarbinski by Henry Hiz (1954). In that talk, Garfinkel (1956: 191) mentions "the praxeological rule," which he characterized as a "search for similarities of successful methods in many different domains of activity," providing as examples the theory of games and scientific methodology. Garfinkel elaborates further that this rule involves placing a demonic "accent" on questions about social phenomena, such as: How does a population go about producing a suicide rate; an unequal distribution of resources; or even a riot? The "accent" presents these recalcitrant phenomena as though they were deliberate practical achievements, which *in a sense* they are.

action, treating it as effective action generally speaking, and find in the residue that in fact you could then give good advice to persons about how to engage in effective practice?

Now, the failure is that – well, let's say *game* theory, in the hands of von Neumann and Morgenstern [1944], was envisaged as a praxeological discipline. My claim of its failure is that it's a legislative discipline. Another way, instead of speaking of it as legislative, is to speak of it . . . as *normative*. That is perhaps too high-flown. The thing to understand about a legislative discipline is that it *stipulates* relevancies, it *stipulates* facts, it *stipulates* the efficacy of rules. This is to say that it *leaves* to the practitioner the *option* that whosoever wants to act efficaciously can take up this advice but would have to know the *occasions* in which those rules would be relevant to the things he wants of them.

Now, that's a very curious kind of science. That would mean you already have to *know* the conditions under which these rules of practice would be effectively worth your pursuit, in order that they could be taken up and turned into such effective practices. That means that the sheer circumstantiality of them, which is what you want in the first place to preserve as all serious meanings of efficacy, is the first thing indeed that you know nothing of. The very thing that you ruled out in order to buy generality is the thing that you have to then look to the practitioner to provide for you, in order that the advice that you give him would be worth his time; in order indeed that he could even hear that your advice concerned *him* particularly. So it seems to me that in that course of argument, we're back to the curious thing that we've encountered in our own ethnomethodological studies, and that is that the effort of praxeology preserved the standing feature of the analytic organizational studies, which was to turn away from the *temporality* of action, from its circumstantiality, from its historicity, in the thought that you couldn't take those features seriously and still preserve the features of the generalizability, the uniformity, the standardization, the comparability of findings. Our proposal is that *that* policy misunderstands the character of generalizability and comparability as the achievements of the local action, which is to say that these are themselves local phenomena. These are the properties that practices *in situ* have, the practices of local production, i.e., that they're occasioned, unwitting, and so on, and so on. And the curious thing that ethno has as its – we're coming to call its findings of sorts, as its program, that's claimable as its hope . . . that every topic of order is now eligible for its *discovery*. It's to be found in the streets. So it needs to be found as *somebody's* achievement as practical action.

Now, when I'm talking about it being available, the thing that we're hoping for being an achievement of a sort, I'm talking now of the existence of studies with which that claim is specifiable – of Mike [Lynch]'s studies, of Eric [Livingston]'s studies, of [Albert B.] Robillard's experience, of Friederich [Schrecker]'s experience[8] – which is to say, the existence now of studies of

---

8 References to studies by these students and former students of Garfinkel's are listed in the text, endnotes, and references throughout this volume.

work that have contributed their findings as they make it possible to use those studies as grounds for what otherwise would be totally outlandish claims.

ROBERT WESTMAN: Listening to this is just very fascinating to me. It strikes me as being a kind of anti-Galilean program.

GARFINKEL: Amen. [Followed by laughter among participants in the seminar]

WESTMAN: You have come forth as the champion of Simplicio in the *Dialogue*. In the Dialogue that Galileo publishes in 1632,[9] the Aristotelian is made to look like a total fool because he says, in response to Galileo's mouthpiece who talks about a world in which, for example, bodies move on forever, he says, "I've never seen such a world. In my world I drop a body and I see it goes down. I can repeat it over and over and over again. I've never seen something that keeps on going forever."

So, Galileo argues for a world of idealized motions, motions that would occur if there were no impediments, obstructions, hinderances, and so forth. Now, it seems to me by analogy that you are proposing for a program in the sociology of science; a fairly strict anti-Galilean program.

Now, the question that I have is: you refer to practical action as the study of what happens *in situ*, when in fact it's *insitibus*. It's not just in the singular; it's not just in this location. It's in all locations. So when Eric [Livingston] says the solid state's on one floor and the plasma's on another floor, it isn't just different floors; it's different neighborhoods, different regions, different countries, different periods of time. That is to say, the number of different locations is infinite. Therefore, if one carries out this program and says that every single location has an individuality and a uniqueness that is its own, then the proper object of your program is the study of that infinite number of sites. Therefore, *insitibus*, which is the plural, becomes the object of your study and leaves open the charge from a Galilean sociologist to ask you, "Do you ever use the adjective '*shared*' or '*communal*'?" because this, after all, is the other side of Kuhn's program, which is to say that the paradigm is what is *shared*, the shared elements, and then to specify what those elements are.

So would there be a place in this program as you have been outlining now for both what you call the "familiar lunacies" – they look like lunacies from the point of view of a Galilean sociologist, but they look like familiar, everyday events from the point of view of the ethno *mishegasist*. So why not the following proposal: that I walk down the street with my glasses on like this, and then I turn the corner and I go like this? That is to say, why can't I look at the same events through different spectacles? My everyday world is the world of Simplicio; it's a world of local events. But at times I find it useful to think of the world in idealized form, so I put on a different pair of glasses and I look at it differently.

In the end, it seems to me, your program reduces to the study of the local and the local only. That's what your claim seems to amount to. It's a very

---

9 For the English translation by Stillman Drake, see Galilei (1953).

strong claim. The only thing that we can know is what we know through practical action. End of spiel [laughs].

GARFINKEL: No, my advice is: don't be afraid. First of all, the idea that the structures of practical action are available in the work of a Galilean science is accompanied by the standing dissatisfactions in every science of practical action, not counting now in any way the discovering sciences as that science. Remember, that's a programmatic proposal, and there's nothing to be taken *that* seriously until, and as, the persons in our group – those who are coming with the study of practical action for the ethnomethodology of it as order-productive work – become competent with a science.[10]

For the time being we're saying, look, wherever in the social sciences the study of practical action has been undertaken according to a program that promises to demonstrate the structures of practical action by the use of the policies of a Galilean science, that program is *everywhere* accompanied by a curious list of absurdities. I won't recapitulate those absurdities.[11] They are subject, obviously, to treatment as unwarranted claims. I'm proposing that they are warranted claims.

For example, one such claim is that wherever the attempt is directed to saying what of an occupation its work in fact consists of, that you get the curious distinction between the studies *about* that work [an of *of*] what the work *in situ* consists of, for, in the presence of, as practices of its practitioners; what in fact it looks like, and thereby wherein issues of comparability are available to its practitioners. So, for example, if *in situ* the work as its organizational detail exhibits in that detail the anonymity of authorship, then that's a local achievement and remains to be provided for as the way in which that work in its practices occurs. If *in situ* it's available for its uniformity (meaning its comparability to work like others'), then to say that it's assured by reason of the fact that these persons share a common culture is the cheapest of cheap shots. Meaning, it *settles* by fiat; it settles by invoking a characterizing feature of the action, what otherwise is problematic. It remains, in fact, to be shown how the action in being done provides for its witnessability as: "Look, I'm doing it, but don't think that it's me." If, as Merleau-Ponty points out, the feature of the cunning of perception is that it masks the organization that it exhibits, then surely we're obligated to provide for what that work in fact could look like, just how it's done.

The fascination with queues is that the exhibited places in line are such that parties engaged in their production do them in such a fashion as to literally

---

10 Garfinkel's version of Galilean science builds off of Husserl's (1970: 23–59) phenomenological critique of the Galileo's mathematization of nature, though he characterized his reading of Husserl and other phenomenological philosophers as a *misreading* (see Garfinkel [2021] on "misreading" Gurwitsch and Merleau-Ponty), in which Husserl's imaginative historical genealogy of Galilean universality is repositioned into a technically competent, ethno-methodological examination of the detailed sequences in "the night's work" that constituted the situated observability of the pulsar.

11 See page 114 of this volume for elaboration of the "curious absurdities." Also see Garfinkel (1990).

provide for an amnesia for how it's done as this might be claimably idiosyncratically done.[12] I might stand in line and turn to you as my companion and say, "Watch the way I stand in line so as to be unnoticeably in line. And that's something I know how to do that others in this line, though they may know, only know as natural theorists. They just do it; they don't know how they do it." And you might then say to me, "What the hell kind of an art is that?" And I would say, "Well, look closely because what you'll find is that, though I'm doing it, the cogency of my claim is that the others, while it's not available to them, *this* is available to them: that it's unremarkably there for their doing." And they do it, then, to preserve its unremark-on-able character.

If that's the case, then what I've come up with in my bit of art is *exactly* that part of the program that analytic sociology doesn't know about, and has no technical way of getting access to, because the way you would get *access* to the uniformity of the produced places in line is by administering a definition of "places in line."

WESTMAN: Isn't there a more moderate position, though, that the Galilean sociologists —[13]

GARFINKEL: No!

WESTMAN: Wait, wait. I'm going to use the phrase you used earlier.

GARFINKEL: *Nein!*

WESTMAN: You used the phrase when you were talking about . . . the distinctiveness of science, and you said it would *have* to be that which is distinctive to that science. Then you put a rider on it, and you said, "*it might as well be.*" Now, that's playing with ontology there.

GARFINKEL: No, no, no. It's not playing with ontology. What I'm trying to do is to preserve it as a piece of advice for our inquiry.

WESTMAN: *Right*, right.

GARFINKEL: I don't want to be obligated to an ontology.

WESTMAN: All right, but it's exactly the same move could be [made] by the Galilean.

GARFINKEL: By the what? By the Galilean?

WESTMAN: I'm only using that as a shorthand term, for what you call analytic sociology.

GARFINKEL: Right, right.

WESTMAN: The analytic sociologist could say, "Well, look, I might as well treat what appears to be a line as a line because I might learn something by adopting that perspective."

GARFINKEL: Yes.

WESTMAN: And you retort, "Well, I might as well treat a line as a series of discrete entities —

GARFINKEL: Yes.

---

12 See Garfinkel and Livingston (2003).

13 The exchange with Westman that follows is rapid fire, with many cutoffs, overlaps, and frequent laughter that the transcript does not capture.

WESTMAN: — each entity being a person who unremarkably experiences the line."
GARFINKEL: Yes.
WESTMAN: But I have a *theory* of that unremarkability which is, in effect, a meta-theory.
GARFINKEL: Well, here's the difference in our "might as well's." His might-as-well is done in the service of an established science. He has a community, he has professional associations. They have money, they have meetings, they have students.
WESTMAN: Ah hah!
GARFINKEL: They have topical courses. They have histories.
WESTMAN: This is power politics now.
GARFINKEL: They have souls. And they own the souls down to the minutiae of the talk that those souls engage in. Of that enterprise, when he says "we might as well," I hear the police at the door. Whereas, our "might-as-well" is a discoverer's might-as-well, which is to say we might as well because we don't know any better, and we might as well because we need the consequentiality of doing it, and it being a discovering science that we're into. It being what we want a sociology, ( )[14] should be a discovering science. Okay? For a change in the world, instead of our writing our way to heaven, we should be capable of wasting our time. How do you like that?

Now, to get at that we're going to have to gain time. Above all — it's not that we only want to gain time — it's that we have to find practical resources with which to *get at* these phenomena if they're going to be phenomenal. Christ knows what they'll turn into. We know that as long as we talk about them, they can be what the talk can make of them. That means they can be conjectural, interesting, lucid, and persuasive — and *wrong*. I mean that they would amount to a continuance of a rosy trail, and they wouldn't give you *any hint*. I mean, our own practices would be such that we would have *no way* of knowing better, since the world on this score is silent. All right? Yes.

So the thing that we're trying to get with this "might-as-well," as I understand it as a bit of shop advice, is: Look, you might as well take it seriously, but don't believe it. And in the meantime, get the work done. Which means all the rest of it: you have to get out, take the risk. There's the head-breaking. There's the fact that it merely sounded good when we talked about it; now that I have to move out of the office to go to the place to find it, I can't find it. I mean all the disappointments and so on. So that's the idea to be made of the "might-as-well," plus the fact that what we're into- the commitments are to the discovery of these phenomena as *radical* phenomena. Meaning, at our best, the proposal is that we're not writing footnotes to the established sciences. Another way to say it is we are not putting together a better textbook on methods. We are not saying to the Galilean scientists of practical action, any of them, "Hey, by the way, fellas. Your modest companions are offering

---

14 I could not make out the phrase here, nor could the transcriber who produced the original typescript.

to you some possibly good advice or good ideas you might have overlooked." You needn't take it seriously, right?

WESTMAN: Yes.

GARFINKEL: I mean, "if on Monday you have a few minutes, think it over." We're going for something much more —

WESTMAN: Revolutionary . . .

GARFINKEL: Yes, and much more threatening to us as well as to them. That is, there's a possibility that there's a phenomenon that *characterizes* the practices of the Galilean sciences of action. The phenomenon is that they depend upon the existence of the orderlinesses that we're picking up for their own investigations and for their own claiming, and they depend on and make use of it for their claiming, and they ignore it. That is to say, as a condition under which they can carry out their activities, their inquiries, they ignore it. That means, then, that if we're calling to their attention the existence of these *ignorances*, they are going to be very happy with us whenever we propose that there are practices that have these characteristics, that their own practice is such as not to *willfully* ignore, but to ignore at the cost that if they don't, their own practices become anonicized;[15] that is, that they lose direction, they lose origin, they lose the aimfulness of what they do. That is to say, they can't carry it through as a coherent program of inquiry.

So, in that sense, what we're proposing is that these two modes of carrying on an inquiry about practical action are — I speak of them as being asymmetric alternates. That is, if you carry through the program of one, you can't in the same fashion satisfy the requirements of carrying on the other as a coherent project. Further, it is proposed that ethnomethodology will recover in its detail the coherence of the Galilean sciences of practical action, but you can't do it the other way around. In that sense, ethnomethodology is foundational; i.e., it provides what Eric [Livingston] in his studies offers as the explanation for what accounts for the rigor of mathematics and what accounts for the effectiveness, the relevance and the cogency of the Galilean sciences of practical action. And we're saying what the Galilean sciences of practical action can't provide for, we can.

[A discussion lasting approximately 20 minutes has been deleted here. It was touched off by a student's question, and involved Garfinkel, Westman, Lynch, and Livingston, and others. The abridged transcript here resumes when a seminar participant[16] refers back to an earlier discussion and raises a question about how Garfinkel's argument about the distinctive character of each science relates to studies of quotidian activities such as conversation or queues.]

---

15 This is a phonetic spelling of what possibly is a neologism Garfinkel coins on the spot to mean something on the order of an induced agnosia or anomie, but not "anonymized" in the sense of being made anonymous as to authorship.

16 The original transcript attributed the question and the interventions in the dialogue that immediately followed to Westman, but the voice on the recording clearly differed from Westman's voice, and there are other indications that it was not Westman who was speaking at this point in the transcript. The anonymous characterization "Speaker" is thus used for the person. Evidently, this was a visitor to the seminar who was familiar to Garfinkel, and perhaps was one of the faculty members in Sociology who were visiting.

SPEAKER: ... It seems to me that the social order of the work of the discovering sciences is intimately wed to the specific content of the work. That's been made a feature of the analysis and repeated again and again, and it's in the argument *here*. Okay?

But my perplexity goes in a wholly different direction. What is the analogical feature of the *content* of the work for the phenomenon of queuing or for the phenomenon of conversational analysis? So that the work of the order of conversational analysis, in what sense is it wed to the content of the work of a conversation? I'm asking that, because I don't *see* that that type of transference occurs when you talk about conversational analysis. I don't see it occur when you talk about queuing either. What is the *content* of the work of a queue? The queue itself? Okay? If I could see *that*; if I could see in the way in which you could talk about the ethnomethodological order-production explanation for work, moving in the direction of queuing, or for the phenomenon of queuing, which would then be analogous to the phenomenon of the work of the discovering sciences, the study of the order of the production of the work of the discovering sciences, I could then move away from the argument that you're having with Bob Westman, because it would be arguing about idealization versus specificity, as I put it in my mind. And I don't see the analogy. I can't come up with one in that comparison. And if I can't come up with one, how can you argue strongly in one case and not in the other? So that's about all I would really have to say on that.

GARFINKEL: Well, the material content of a greeting; think of it in that simple way. The material content of a greeting is specified as the conditionally relevant, two-part structure of a greeting done *in situ* and available thereby for recovery according to a structure that's called the conditionally relevant character of a first part relative to a second part.[17] Now, the greeting done-and-heard-really is specified with that as a structure of the done-and-witnessable relevancies, the done-and-witnessable features of a greeting. Competent practice consists then of speaking which exhibits unanalyzedly the greeting, but does it in such a fashion that those features are the features that are unanalyzedly present.

Now, the conversational analysts are insistent that they're dealing with the structure of conversational events really. That's something they don't tell very much, because were they to make that claim, they would then have to come out *straight* with that, indeed, they're into a game where they're passing and hiding out with respect to what their serious claims are. They are *not* explicating the definition of a greeting. They are not modeling greetings. They're *finding*; they're discovering the structured work of greetings done and understood. That is, they speak of it as the greeting that is produced, recognized and understood.

---

17 See Schegloff (1968: 1083ff.) for a discussion of conditional relevance in the context of conversational openings. In his remarks shortly afterwards, Garfinkel provides a distinctive phenomenological formulation of conditional relevance.

Now, what I'm proposing as the analogy is that just as the work of the greeting is directed to providing for what the greeting is really, it turns out then to be the practices of speaking. I'm providing then that a discovering science is, for its practitioners, practices exhibited in the properties of local production; that is, practices which as an ensemble compose the local phenomenon of, what shall we say, the optical pulsar. Or the optical pulsar as a thing that we can get hold of – there is a text[18] – and they are into, not the discovered optical pulsar because we can't yet say what that consists of, but we can say that in that 18th to the 34th observation that there is now a whole series of *vernacular* provisions for, "My god, it's what the rest have been looking for. It's our good or bad luck to have come on the demonstrable just-that that the rest are looking for. And are we going to make or not as an adequate claim?"[19]

LIBERMAN: I think the comparison line is the *embodied* character of the work, and that means the unanalyzed way the people engaged in the activity are addressed to a vast array of meaningful activities that they couldn't begin to account for, and nevertheless do. If, for example, you wanted to learn how to gold mine, you could read all the books on gold mining you could find in the library, but you have to be present to some old timer who knows how to gold mine to really do it properly, to capture the phenomenon, which would be gold in the pan. And it's the infinite and unanalyzed work that's the phenomenon, as I see it anyway. . . .

SPEAKER: . . . I think I grasp that. I think it's not an ignorance on my part. I realize that it's the . . .

GARFINKEL: You're interested in the programmatic character.

SPEAKER: No. I'm looking for the legitimacy of the assertion of the weddedness to the particularity to the content of the work. So that you [Livingston] made the distinction between the physics on one floor versus the physics on another floor. Now *that* I can *understand*. And I can understand the vignette or scenario you [Liberman] generated for me about gold mining. But . . . you didn't hand me a *satisfying* solution about conversational analysis, because . . .

GARFINKEL: I didn't?

SPEAKER: *No.* I don't think so . . . because you left me with a feeling that a greeting is a greeting is a greeting. . . .

GARFINKEL: . . . I'm talking about a greeting being produced, recognized and understood as not anything else, except *this*. It's the greeting. And it's not that you could analyze something called "the greeting" to find what the work is, but it's the other way, that the ensemble of relevancies is finally formulated as a *structure* of relevancies. That *structure* of relevancies is called the "conditional relevance." That means that the

---

18 By "text" Garfinkel appears to be referring to the audio record of astronomers' voices that he was able to obtain.

19 Garfinkel is glossing a series of remarks and exchanges made during the sequence of numbered observations recorded on the optical pulsar tape and notebooks (see Garfinkel et al. 1981: 149ff.).

parts are to be understood as a practice wherein a first part, being done, is hearably a first part. It is hearably a first part independently of whether a second part occurs; on the occasion of a done and heard second part it is hear-ably a second *to* a first and therein turns the second and the first into a completed first and second part with that suitable interval. So that is to say that the answer is hear-ably the answer. You get then all the consequences of it having this as its technical content.[20]

Now, what it is that you want of that, by way of the missing *content*, I find a little mystifying, shall I say. And it can be "Hi," "Hi."? Because it doesn't have to be "Hi." "Hi." Right?

SPEAKER: Yes, uhm . . .

GARFINKEL: But it can't be anything but, "Hi," "Hi." I mean, you get this curious feature of the greeting really, that you can't say it unless someone says, "Hi," and someone else says "Hi" – unless someone says, "Hello," to which the other would say, "Hello"; unless someone would say as the first part, "Whatcha doin'?" and the other would say, "I'm glad to see you." So there's *that*. So, as they say it's not in the words, but it can't be except that it's in the words. But that's kind of mystifying to talk like that. However, it's not mystifying if you understand that you can't do it except as a course of witnessable practices of speaking. If we really want to get fancy, we'll say "speaking-showing." I mean, we're now caught up in the lameness of a practiced way of talking about the structure of greetings. Well then okay, you understand that it's merely the vernacular provisions for talking like that. We can then free ourselves of that dependency and then address directly what the force of the claim is to say that the conversational analysts aren't interested *except* in the technical content; that the technical practice, the just-how of it, is not different than the technical content; the insistence that there is the *material content* to talk's events; and that the *formalization* of it, which is what you're fond of, is that you want to administer fondly a version of the way it's done that would be indifferent to the circumstantiality of it. But conversational analysts can't be indifferent; they've taken *over* that circumstantiality and [are] turning it into a certain version of the historicity of that work. It turns out that we could be unhappy with the kind of analytic emphasis that they preserve. But still, for all that analytic emphasis, they are nowhere in sight of the Galilean version of that phenomenon. It's still a structure of practices.

SPEAKER: One last comment then, okay? I think what I'm looking for is to find a way to–

GARFINKEL: What you want me to do – you want a repeat of an old-saw criticism of yours, which is: Why don't you start with phenomena instead of starting with principles? And I'm saying to you: Listen, I've had enough with you!

[General laughter, as 'Speaker' protests]

---

20 Garfinkel's version of adjacency pairs here is reminiscent of his discussion of Gurwitsch's (1964: 102) demonstration of gestalt contexture using a pair of dots (see Garfinkel 2021: 24–25).

SPEAKER: No, no, no. That's not what I'm saying. . . . I would like you to convince me . . . that the order of work has to be wedded to the content of the phenomena that are being discovered. I was trying to seek a way to find a legitimation of that, other than saying, "Well, you've got to get into it and do it."

GARFINKEL: Oh, no. That's perfectly wrong. We really haven't come to that.

SPEAKER: What?

GARFINKEL: We hadn't come to that. I had hoped in the second part of my talk to take up, to put aside this as the programmatic provision, and to say: Look, we have as our best case in hand (as the seminar has a best case in hand) the materials on the discovery of the optical pulsar. Then I wanted to go through what I see as in hand that makes possible such a recommendation here: namely, the recommendation that the discovering sciences are sciences of practical action, to say: What is it that looks like it's in hand at present as far as the work of discovering the optical pulsar is concerned?

Now, no matter how deeply we would get into that, I doubt that any part of it finally would make you euphoric. But it would at least cure you of your obstinacy. [Laughter by several members of the seminar.] But maybe that's following the coffee [break].

In any case, I just want to follow up and at least kind of finish off the proposal by following up with the suggestion that Mike [Lynch] introduced that was set off by Bob [Westman]'s dissatisfaction: it was Mike's suggestion, when I was talking with him once about the discovering sciences being sciences of practical action, that he spoke of a discovering science as consisting of practices that are distinctive of it *as* its domain; and that the practices would be distinctive of it as its own domain would then also be so for each of the sciences. That provoked, in turn, the further suggestion that the practices that are distinctive of it as its domain are that science's phenomena.[21]

Now, that would mean then that we're obligated, as soon as we get into the stuff on the optical pulsar, to find in the practices that made up that night's work that those practices were *never* irrelevant to, disengaged from, unmindful of, or unspecifying of the optical pulsar. The question then is, in what sense is that so? In what way, given the little bit that we know of that record, is that so? I think that will be the next part of my proposal.

It seems to me that the following make up a set of recommendations thus far in hand. . . . I'm proposing that we have this kind of thing to start with. We have to begin with the overall recommendation that we have a curious disrespect to start with. The disrespect is that we're going to examine that Cocke and Disney's work, while according to a precept – a policy in which, whatever else we'll say the discovered optical pulsar consisted of, it was not in any way a disengaged pulsar that was talked about. That is to say, it was the *embodied* presence of the pulsar. It was the pulsar available *in and as* the local,

---

21 Garfinkel attributes the suggestion to me but what he elaborates is clearly the argument *he* has been making all along, not that I disagreed with the suggestion then, or now.

situated, embodied practices of finding it again; seeing it again; seeing, via the way in which the talk and the looking were chained to the looks, to what the apparatus indeed was visibly displaying of, that their own knowledgeable practices of looking made findable as the kind of thing that the pulsar consisted of for what it looked like. That would mean, then, that what they were concerned with was the *pulsar*, available for its analyzability, that the discovery was a preoccupation with the analyzability of the pulsar again. That preoccupation – it wasn't that we need to be concerned with *how* it was discovered according to the Galilean version of the phenomenon as being independent of and indifferent to that structure of practice. But it is instead that we need to be concerned with what I'll speak of now as the *in situ*, practical work of *finding* the analyzability of the pulsar again and of exhibiting that analyzability. And that their practices were practices of finding and exhibiting that analyzability. The analyzability was available to them in their knowledgeable access of the machinery and how that machinery could be showing what it was showing. So it was *in* that problematic analyzability that anything that the machine showed was itself motivating of how the machine could be leading them up a rosy trail. The very fact that they had a display already posed, projected the work ahead; and that work ahead was not different than the work of *adumbrating* the object, which in this case was adumbrating the demonstrable analyzability of that pulsar.

Now, in that sense, I think I'm talking as best I know not to the technical content but to a *sense* of that technical content. That is to say, the best I can do is with a *sense* of that technical content, because to relieve it of that sense I would then have to, in effect, be able to spend my time going through a recapitulation, so to speak. That is to say, someone at UCLA might take the crew of us and show us: "Here is what these birds were looking at when they were talking in the way they were talking." And it wouldn't be that it's merely a perceptual display. It isn't that it registers on the retina as a this-kind-of-diagram – say, that the oscilloscopic configuration of the thing we're concerned with – because they weren't concerned with the oscilloscopic configuration. They were concerned with: If the oscilloscopic configuration looks like that, where the hell is it coming from? Meaning, the machinery has to work in such a fashion that the thing that it shows has this explanatory structure to it.

So I take it that to begin with we are, even though we are lame in our competence, committed to finding on their behalf of what that analyzability consisted of, and that it is not different than the embodied practices of looking, recognizing, producing, elucidating, finding, questioning, and so on, but all these as a local, historicized project. It's in *those* embodied details that everything that they could then have come upon has the reproducible – It's the, "Jesus, it's just this. It's a bloody pulsar. It's the thing here we're looking at, just this. That's what everyone has been looking for and is available for whomsoever." It's not that it's confined, then, under this rug. It's not that I look under this rug and, if I look away, I am looking at another place. And they don't work then with a general, categorical version of indefinitely many sites. But that it's in the definiteness of *this* site, that everything that could be generalizedly available is exhibited. It's the sheer definiteness of the *just-this* that the comparability and generalizability of the phenomenon is assured.

So it has to do, then, with the curious thing that *looking* – the work of looking and recognizing – consists of. That's wherein the comparability is found; and it's with respect to that recognition in organizational detail – that is to say, the recognition via the practices of the just-what – that the discontent with the Galilean version is found. Nowhere along the line do we need to make a general definition of what they're doing in order to find the phenomenon. We find it always in their competent presence to the thing.

Remember, the thing that you need to get hold of, I guess, as the strangeness of the recommendation is that we're trying to find the existence of a science – a discovering science (of physics, for example, or astrophysics) – not by remaining disrespectful of a Galilean science because, in a way, we couldn't care less. That would be an additional benefit if it happens that, say, we could be disrespectful to the Galilean version.

WESTMAN: Well, this is pre-Galilean anyway.

GARFINKEL: Well, who knows. You could call it pre-Heideggerian or post-Heideggerian. You could say, "Well, look, we're Heidegger's heirs." [General laughter.] He recommended that there would be consequences of his philosophy for the natural sciences. So you could say, "Well, okay, we're taking up a suggestion." But, in any case, it's neither here nor there.

Again, what I'm proposing is that it's the local work that furnishes the grounds for any claims that the phenomenon exists and is demonstrable as a technically demonstrable matter, in its technical contents, in indefinitely elaborating detail. Now, unless in fact it's of *that* that our concern with the practice is a concern for, then for sure it's all hot air. To begin with, we're not even competent practitioners right now. Then on top of everything else we're making an outlandish claim. I mean, how foolish can you be!

Now, what I want to propose, given the *in situ* work of finding and exhibiting the analyzability of that pulsar again, is that the work of the *discovery* of the optical pulsar, the *practices* that are identifying of the discovered pulsar – that the work of the discovery has as its achievement the naturally formulated sensibility of that discovery. . . . The crux of that achievement is that they come to the naturally formulated *sensibility* of that work. That means, then, that the *report* (*talk of the work*), the *article* on it that is the report, that is the announcement of the discovered pulsar, is present from the beginning as a relevant task in presence to what's going on in the lab.[22] It's not that they're engrossed in the accumulation of data, pending the accumulation of which they will contemplate the possibility of a publication. They are from the beginning engaged in

---

[22] The "report" or "article" is the announcement of the discovery published in *Nature* (Cocke et al. 1969), which was reprinted in an appendix in Garfinkel et al. (1981: 143–145).

a hopelessly publicizable effort. And that effort is not something hidden away, in skulls, but is present in that room as the visible sameness of the display that the machinery is presenting to them in such a fashion that their talk is *chained* to the looks of things, and chained to it in such a way as to find the reasoning of the thing they're looking at, not only in their oscilloscopic display but in the availability that each has in seeing of the other what the other, in looking at, is saying via the thing that's being looked at as the thing being, thereby, there and being talked about. So, in that sense they are hopelessly engaged in the circumstantiality of the embodied, technical practice that makes up the way in which the sensibility of the pulsar can have been brought to an accounting. And not only an accounting generally speaking, as a certain accounting, it is a *rendition* of that work; it is a *rendering* of that work – and now we'll find the reconciliation – it's a rendering of that work as a Galilean science. It is only in the published thing that it has the character for them of a Galilean science, and in no other place. But in *that* place, it takes on the character of a Galilean science to a fare-thee-well; it's Caesar's wife. They're out to establish the virtue of that discovery in such a fashion that no one will take exception. That has to be a *mishigas*. Louis Narens and [William] Batchelder speak of how investigators, being obligated to come up – that the discovery consists finally of their coming to see the thing that they find out as available again according to an error-free procedure.[23] Now, I think that's a little loose. I think it's too easy. But it's only too easy in the sense that we don't know yet how we could be dissatisfied with that. It helps a good bit, I think it would be a mistake to say: well, look, it comes only to that.

LIBERMAN: But that property wouldn't identify or distinguish discovering sciences from non-discovering sciences, because . . .

GARFINKEL: The error-free procedure?

LIBERMAN: No, the process of having in mind the published article as you're going into the day's work and using that idea to organize the day's work. It seems to me that social scientists do that as well. So it wouldn't be distinguishing. I'm sure it goes on. . . .

GARFINKEL: Well . . . it's not as though they come in with the article in mind that they're going to be writing. The thing that sets it up as the *trouble* that they're confronted with, and the thing that I think makes up for *us* what's so hellishly hard to elucidate as the kind of thing discovery could be, is this thing that I talked about several weeks ago when I said: Look, Cocke and Disney are *without* relief . . . without the possibility of remedy or alternative . . . up against the problem that night of finding the animal in the foliage. Now, by

---

23 Louis Narens was a former PhD student from UCLA who knew Garfinkel and had been a teaching assistant for him. In 1980 he was a professor in the School of Social Sciences at the University of California, Irvine. Narens specialized in mathematical psychology, but remained in contact with Garfinkel. William (Bill) Batchelder was a professor of mathematical psychology, and a colleague of Narens' in the School of Social Sciences at Irvine. Garfinkel may be referring to Batchelder and Narens (1977).

"the animal in the foliage" I don't mean at the outset what I had talked about earlier as finding the figure against that ground.

[Deleted summary of a study of a sociology lecturer's work.]

[T]he idea was that there are the practices in the lab; that these embodied practices have curious production properties; and that the *foliage* consists in this:[24]

(1) that being at work in that place, their practices are, to begin with, occasioned;

(2) that they also are done, but they are unwittingly done;

(3) that they are hidden to them in the familiar and apt efficacy of what they're doing;

(4) that that familiar efficacy is the efficacy of the practices of *embodied* production, and embodied recognition and embodied witness;

(5) that their practices are available to them for their doing according to a *vulgar* competence.[25] That means a competence that they're in no way answerable for; . . .

(6) that their practices are not available and can't be obtained by reasoned reflection, and they are not obtainable by their stopping to tell themselves stories about what they've been doing. Even when they recapitulate what they've been doing as a history for the telling, and then examine, "Let's see, what were we doing?" and now examine that to see wherein the efficacy of the practice is found, that it's not available to that;

(7) further, that the practices, in that they are real-worldly, are available to them as detail (meaning they are available not only as detail but as everything that detail could be).[26] So neither can they import, then, into the version of the practice an in-principle version of what they're doing according to rule. So that means, then that their practices have to be otherwise available to them as the locally visual, technical, material content of what they're up to. And in that way, what is it that the detail could consist of is available for what the detail *looks* like (that is, what the *practice* looks like, and therein what the detail could be). So even though they would like to import an in-principle *version* of the worldly detail, they are *chained* to the inexorable development of the thing that they want to be in the presence of;

(8) further, that their practices are, for them, naturally available. That's already a distraction. Meaning, what they're doing has a naturally accountable sensibility, which is to say, we all know that they're prepared to say what they're doing there that night. But it's also the case that no exploitation of the *purposive character* of what they're doing, or of the strategic or rational

---

24 Garfinkel can be heard at the blackboard. In the original typescript, the list was not enumerated; numbers have been added here.

25 Garfinkel et al. (1981: 140, n. 26) say that by "vulgar competence we understand embodied practices whose efficacy has achieved an ordinariness and 'equipmental transparency' that allows no call for credentials."

26 On Garfinkel's conception of "detail," see Part I, Appendix 3 in this volume.

character of what they're doing, can be counted on to elucidate for them or to give them access to the discovery in its availability as the apt, efficacious practice that the recognition consists of, and so on;

(9) and, finally, that their practices can't be *imagined*. We only think that they can be imagined, because we're convinced that all that stuff goes on in their heads. But it doesn't. And it can't be imagined; it can only be discovered.

Now then, if you ask, "Well, *what is the foliage* from which they have now to find and extract an animal?" It would be the practices for which the phenomenon is *unprecedented* with respect to properties that their practices would have of that sort. So the *search* for the animal, then, is the search to *find* the naturally accountable rendition of the work that they've done; to find, then, of the practices that they are displaying of the analyzability of that pulsar, that naturally accountable version of the what it is; to *turn* their work into a talk-about-ably sensible course. So that means that the discovery is available in being *displayed* via a course of talk, a course of discourse; and they must find a discourse. Okay? It's not only that it's a course of talk. It's not that they can talk any which way. They will do that in any case; we might as well say they will do that. But it's that the talk doesn't correspond to the properties of the phenomenon. The talk is revealing of the phenomenon as something appropriately talked of like that.

Now, that's what makes us Heidegger's heirs,[27] because if the talk, indeed, stood in its appropriateness to the phenomenon, available now propositionally in such a fashion that the proposition in its subject and its predicates corresponded to the phenomenon in its presence as the object and its properties, then in that case we would remain respectful of the version of the discovery as a Galilean science would put in our hands. But it's not that. And in that the talk is *revealing* of the phenomenon that is talked of, it means the talk is *chained* to the phenomenon via the practices that looking consists of. So the looking is *hopelessly* reasoned. It's, in the character of what looking could be, reasoned looking, not other than reasoned. But then to simply say that it's reasoned means that as Eric [Livingston] pointed out in his talk,[28] unless you're capable of working with the sketched version of the experiment as a sketched version, such that you would know how, via the sketched version, how it is an appropriate way to speak, and therefore what it's technical content would consist of when you say "and at this point you have a magnet to deflect the beam," as to be something other than a mention of the demonstrability of the existence of the electron, then it's going to have to be something hopelessly different than that, and in way recoverable, no matter how bright and

---

27 Although it is unclear if Garfinkel is referring to a specific source from Heidegger, at the time he was reading Heidegger's (1967) *What is a Thing?* and reading it in connection with the research on the optical pulsar materials.

28 Garfinkel is referring to a presentation Eric Livingston made about J.J. Thompson's experiments on elementary particles during an earlier seminar (May 22; the first seminar in this series, but not included in the abridged transcript of Part II, Seminar 1 in this volume).

interesting and lucid and coherent the mention is. That is, you are going to have to be capable of the displayed material course of a technical argument in its material details . . . . As Kuhn says, you have to have it in your fingers.[29]

So that's what I think you're up against for the animal in the foliage. And the problem is that what you can do is *extract* the animal from the foliage, and that means to render the work of the tick-bracketed optical pulsar accountable as the properties of a science in the Galilean mode, and to do so in established terms. So, I want to then propose that the research paper, the published account, *renders* discovering work as the properties of a Galilean science; and it does it in such a fashion that the analyst's voice is the familiar voice – it's for us the familiar voice of the transcendental analyst. We discussed at our last meeting what some of the properties of the voice of the transcendental analyst would be, as, for example, the practices in the anticipated rendering of the so-called practice of the disembodied subjectivity of the analyst – meaning that the notions of motive, origin, aim, purpose and good-reasons-for are done in such a fashion that all references to the embodiment of the analyst are for good reasons excused and need not be taken into account.

LYNCH: I came across a superficial version of this while working with a small telescope last week.[30]

GARFINKEL: Oh, fabulous! Say!

LYNCH: It was cold out, and the fact that it was cold out had all sorts of things to do with how long we looked at things. And I think it was mentioned in the [pulsar] tape that it was . . . cold. But you never see that in the published account, that they were cold.

WESTMAN: I once had the opportunity to look through the Palomar telescope with an astronomer who took me up there at night, and it was really cold.[31] The controls on that telescope are so extraordinary. They will control, for example, for vibrations of the earth. The thing rides on a disk which is in a bed of oil so that the vibrations are knocked down, and there are various other controls. The only thing they haven't been able to control for is the heat generated by the eye of the astronomer who puts his eye near the lens. Believe me, it is cold up there. And there is a lot of sensory deprivation from sitting in this cage that moves around. So, yes, that's a problem for observing astronomers. I think they must be very hardy; and this business of the hot and cold is very important.

[A speaker (barely audible on the recording) makes a comment about the "animal in the foliage" theme, and Garfinkel continues on the topic.]

GARFINKEL: Well, having to the begin with put this "foliage" aside, the idea of a figure-ground structure, the gestalt theme of figure and ground – I now want to

---

29 For Garfinkel's explication of Kuhn's (1970a) postscript, see the second (May 27, 1980) seminar in this series.

30 Here I am referring to overnight outings at around that time in the mountains with a friend who possessed an 8-inch telescope.

31 Professor Westman (email to Michael Lynch, June 12, 2020) identified the astrophysicist as Leonard Searle (1930–2010), who was director of the Carnegie Observatories in Pasadena, California.

introduce it again, but this time from the point of view of our interest in what that gestalt theme ought to be looking like. It's not that we inherit the gestalt theme in the way in which the gestaltists and experimental psychologists have provided for it. But rather, coming on the fact that there is an animal in the foliage, we now find that the gestalt theme of the figure and ground is an illuminating thematic characterization of the problem that they must in fact come to a solution of. With *that*, then, I want to offer that other gestalt themata[32] might as well be treated by us as suggestions for which we now go in search by starting with Cocke and Disney's work with *what* there was of their work for which the gestalt theme might as well be a thematic characterization. Okay?

So instead of *starting* with the gestalt theme and saying, "See, it's not a perceptual function that they're concerned with, it's a practical achievement," which is the way I treated it previously, we need to start again, by starting with Cocke and Disney's work and then asking what there could have been of that local practice for which the gestalt theme might be a thematic characterization, in the way in which finding, for example, for the production properties of their practices what we might as well call the foliage, could we then find what there was of their practices that would pose as the embodied practice that we'll speak of as the problematic theme of the adumbrated object, or the object constancy, for example. Similarly then for the gestalt switch. It may be, then, that Kuhn was on to something very, very *big* in the notion of the gestalt switch, but didn't know the half of how big that could be, given that he was formulating and solving a problem as *hailing* a technical theory of practice, and didn't have an adequate theory of embodied practice. So his sensibility was such . . . that Kuhn is an appropriate predecessor of our work. And according to Eric [Livingston's] reading of it, he had already established a problem and offered, in the notion of the paradigm, a solution to the problem. The problem was: what was there of experimental procedure that provided for the demonstrability of matters that the experimental procedures were witnessably demonstrable of? And the paradigm, then, was a solution to that, *in that* it spoke *directly* of the relevance of a knowledge of and a competence with lab practice. But he *didn't* have a theory of *practice* beyond, let's say, what the exquisite scholarship of the man put in his hands.

Question: can ethnomethodology be of service? Can it do better? Can it be informed now by his own difficulties in the matter? It can do *one* thing, and that is it can refuse to be taken in by Kuhn's critics, and on good grounds refuse.

Question: Can it find its alliances with Kuhn and Kuhn's program or Kuhn's students?

WESTMAN: But unlike Kuhn, who was taken in by his critics.

---

32 Garfinkel's mention of "themata" here may be playing off a somewhat different treatment of "themata" by Holton (1975). For an edited transcript of a later seminar (from 1993) in which Garfinkel focuses on "misreading" the gestaltists, see Garfinkel (2021).

GARFINKEL: Well, that poor guy. I never heard it from him. But I heard it from Holton in 1975 that he was practically put into a depression. That is, he gave up working, among other things, being required, I *guess* under the dynamics of academic debate, of having to answer, or else.

WESTMAN: I'm not sure it was that. I think in some ways the people who first took seriously his work, the academic philosophers from a certain tradition of philosophy, I think were a group that Kuhn had *already* taken seriously, even before they approached him in the role of critics. I mean, I think they were part of his idealizations about science that he must be working through. So when they came at him with the knives sharpened, he retreated excessively. I mean, he has come out publicly and said, "I don't use paradigm anymore. I talk about disciplinary matrix."

GARFINKEL: Yes.

WESTMAN: Which is – it's very watered-down paradigm. See, but on the other hand, sociologists and the sons and daughters of Kuhn in the field went and said, "What are you worrying about, man? We can develop all kinds of theories and accounts in the spirit of the first version of structure," which now Kuhn has publicly disowned; he's very afraid of it, almost like he's afraid of his own creation.[33] His most recent book about Planck is a retreat into a very internalist history of science.[34] Planck *himself* is an example of somebody who was afraid of his own creation. It's almost like the subject itself is – you know, Planck was absolutely frightened by what he discovered. He took a very conservative position on it; this led some later people to say, "What are you frightened about?" So something similar may be happening to Kuhn.

[An exchange between Garfinkel and Westman follows on the possibility of getting Kuhn to visit UCLA. A student then follows with some remarks about the connection of discovery and creativity. The student expresses unease with the "animal in the foliage" metaphor, and suggest that, rather than picking out an object from a background, a discovery could be more like "trying to get two things to fit."]

GARFINKEL: Yes. Like when you're preparing a lock, you don't know what key will fit it. But when you see the key, you'll know."

[The student then adds that such an analogy is preferable to that of "doing a lot of rummaging around in the foliage," Garfinkel then resumes on the topic of the animal in the foliage.]

GARFINKEL: Is it of any use to us, to pick up as a benefit later, to start with the animal in the foliage without acknowledging at the outset that what we have in mind is finally to come to the use of the gestalt theme of figure-ground structure, and to

---

33 Westman's remarks here foreshadow what Kuhn later publicly expressed in a 1990 presidential address to the Philosophy of Science Association on "The Road Since *Structure*." In an aside, he disavowed enthusiasts in social and cultural studies of science who promoted various relativist versions of his famous argument about paradigm shifts. In the published version of the address, he expressed a need "to defend notions like truth and knowledge from, for example, the excesses of post-modernist movements like the strong program" (Kuhn 2000a: 91) – misleadingly identifying the Strong Programme in the Sociology of Knowledge (e.g., Bloor 1976) as a "postmodernist movement."

34 Westman is referring to Kuhn (1978).

kind of *smuggle* it along as a kind of hidden intent until finally we know enough about what the foliage could be and know enough about what they're doing practice-wise such that they've come to the natural accountability of the work they have been doing, that being the stuff that the discovery consists of? That is, the *discovery* is what we're concerned with. So we make use of the gestalt theme. And what I'm asking is do you have reason to be uneasy with that?

[The student responds, "Yes I do," and elaborates on a concern with creativity and imagination. Livingston makes a suggestion about the gestalt switch.]

LIVINGSTON: My hearing was that the gestalt switch wasn't to be used generally, but was to be used for particular examples. So that, in the case of black-body radiation, that problem created a history. It would have a historical problem that the available methods of theorizing about the particular event did not account for the actual experimental findings. But then at some point you could speak about the transformation from the previous ways of viewing black-body radiation to the quantum mechanical way. That could then be spoken of as a gestalt switch. I'm hearing what you're saying as not speaking of all discovering work, but of that *possibly* being one example of the appropriateness of using the gestalt switch.

[Following some further exchanges, Garfinkel resumes on the topic of "animal in the foliage" and the gestalt switch.]

GARFINKEL: Well, there's no question that the idea of the animal in the foliage, at least as it was previously presented, was a very tame version of the work of discovery, and that something more dialectical, for example, would have been much more faithful to the insistence on just the *looks* of things in that way. And also your idea, as I originally understood it, was that there's this goofy business of preparing a lock and not understanding what key will fit it, but when you see it, you know. So, it's not that you prepare a lock and it becomes so evident in the pattern that it exhibits that you can design the key in the way the lock looks. And I think that insistence is very suggestive and keeps things *kosher*, keeps us in sight of the human practice that we're talking about. It keeps us from becoming ethnomethodological schmucks. It's absolutely a possibility. But, I mean, why shouldn't we be prepared, let's say, in the face of the opposition of the defenders of the Galilean version of scientific practice, to take the academic response and put together a coherent denunciation which would lose the enterprise. . . ."

I think one further comment on the gestalt switch – I called it up before – which is that I understand about the gestalt switch that it's in the very way in which one has in hand a convincing version of the phenomenon that presents to the practitioner the very grounds for *distrusting* the version he has. So it's *not* that he's caught in the fascinations of a coherent position that he can't break free of. It's that the very coherence of it is the thing he's *afraid* of. He knows: well, if it's all that, it can't be that. Now, that has to be a very curious kind of practice indeed, that the very availability of the phenomenon is the thing that provides you the grounds for your uneasiness. "It's all that good? It's not good enough." Or, "It's all that good? It's too good." Or, "It's all that good? Then, we're damned for sure. We're doing something just awful." Now, what would it be as the day's work to have to turn away, because the very coherence of it is the promised victory, right? I mean, it's like you'd have such a love of God that nothing would do except that the faintest whisper in His ear would have to be such as to tell Him everything. You have everything except that you can't get His ear. And that's the thing that you're uneasy with. So fake it. So . . . don't let go.

Well, I'm going to summarize this thing. Assuming that, for Cocke and Disney having *found* the animal in the foliage, that they can then *afterwards* claim and teach, "See how it's there." In fact, in the renderings, in the American Institute of Physics version of the discovery, the thing that's so interesting about it is its ingenuousness. That is, it in fact drops from consideration what we're proposing is exactly the precariousness of the discovery, and makes it inevitable, makes it available and doable and done, in accordance with the romanticism of that work (for example, that Koestler is such a busybody with).[35] What I want to remind you of is the thing that we had such a good time with it during this meeting, as a final point, and that is that the *claims, even when* the discovery is in hand – the *claims* of the pedagogy (which is to say, they still have the teaching of colleagues, and the teaching of colleagues is itself the occasion on which the *demonic* order of the demonstration is there to remind them again that it's discovering work that they have to be practiced with, careful of, mindful of, adequate to, and so on).

I just want to finish by proposing that I think that our discussions of the difference between accountable contingencies of work and the demonic contingencies of work, the *wild* contingencies – my hunch is that these contingencies, particularly the demonic contingencies, are intimately tied to the so-called motivated observables,[36] to the kind of things we talk about when we talk about *losing* the phenomenon. However, that is *strictly* a tie that, in talking about, I'm making. And it has *only* a programmatic character. However, it's accompanied by a big hunch that the demonic order is a gold mine that's waiting for us, and that the goldenness of it will be found in the way in which it's tied to these contingencies, these unmotivated contingencies of, like, losing the phenomenon, being felt(?) as a bricolage;[37] and the cunning treachery that equipment, for example poses – the kind of thing that's in the story of, let's say, Olds and his theory of the limbic system, and so on.[38]

---

35 This appears to be an allusion to Arthur Koestler's (1964) *The Act of Creation*, and other writings on discovery and creativity.
36 Garfinkel uses the expression "unmotivated observables" in Part I, pp. 42-3, (and especially endnote 44, p. 92) of this volume as unquestioned features of laboratory work. He does not discuss "motivated observables," elsewhere, and just below speaks of losing the phenomenon as one of the "unmotivated contingencies". From the recording he clearly seems to say "motivated", though he might have meant to say "unmotivated".
37 The transcriber marked the word "felt" as questionable, and it certainly is. One of the "contingencies" of scientific work that Garfinkel lists in Part I is the "local availability to 'our shop' of improvisational and bricolage expertise," and this would be a good substitute for whatever it was that he is saying here.
38 James Olds, who also is discussed in Part I, Section [5], was best known for experiments on the pleasure center of the brain, but in other phases of his career he developed psycho-neurological theories of learning and motivation, using among other resources a version of Gestalt theory involving "cell assemblies" and "sign-gestalts" (Olds 1954), which was far removed from Garfinkel's account of Gurwitsch's phenomenological treatment of gestalt themes.

By the way, if anybody has any references on demonic order, I surely would be indebted for all the citations.

SPEAKER: The demonic order? What's that?

GARFINKEL: Well, the demonic order in the sense that there's the orderliness of practice, which has an above-ground, just-that, available to us folks and *free* of treachery. All good folks, let's say, who are compliant to the requirements of the legitimate order of practice will, in fact, come into the orderly ways of the world. They're coming to them, present to them; they see them; their lives will consist of those orderly ways. The *demonic* order proposes that there accompanies in every occasion of the above-ground order of things the *wildness* of any order.

SPEAKER: Like hidden . . . orders of contingency?

GARFINKEL: Yes, the hidden orders of contingency: contingencies, in their orderliness, that the devils have charge of.

[A participant raises a question that is largely unintelligible in the recording, which mentions something about "natural symbols," Mary Douglas, dress codes, and hippies.]

GARFINKEL: Yes. Well, we already know, let's say, from the conventional sociology that the legitimate order has an accompanying ideology which can be expected to find what an underground could look like. Now, let's take that seriously, and say yes, they're probably preoccupied with what the underground could look like because there is a real underground. Which is to say, the reason we could be so concerned with the presence of God in the world is that the devils are actually in the world. And the sooner we go looking for them, the sooner we will know what we're talking about by "the demonic order." Well, since we're so preoccupied with good work, then we might as well take seriously that the good work is visible and elucidated by reason of the accompanying presence of sloppiness, failure, forgetfulness, and so on.

So, then, if these two go together, then why would we want to elucidate – that is, why would we insist that the rules of action are those that were composed by middle class sociologists who knew a good thing when they saw it, knew how to feel good about good things, knew how to feel bad about bad things? Versions of norms and rules, then, are motivated by their competence in that respect.

SPEAKER: It sounds like you could inspect the religious literature.

GARFINKEL: That's what I'm thinking. I mean, I was brought up a New York Jew. So I wouldn't know of that stuff. But I really think that if I had training in, let's say, theology –

SPEAKER: Dante.

GARFINKEL: Dante? Is that right? Good!

SPEAKER: I've read about it. I was thinking . . . Middle Ages Protestant theologians. . . .

SPEAKER: What's orderly about the demonic order?

GARFINKEL: Well? Here's what's orderly about it. There is something that has been called the "cunning of objects." Have you ever heard of it?

You are on your way to a very serious appointment. It's really consequential and you have been brooding about it. Now it's coming close to the time you are going to have to get the car out of the garage and be on your way. You start looking for the keys. It's not that you've lost the keys; it's that the keys are hiding. Because as soon as it's clear that you don't have to be there, the keys will come forth. [Laughter in background.] Right?

I don't know how it is with you, but with me if I drop anything on the floor, it disappears. And if it's important that I pick it up immediately, that is what assures that that lousy thing will find a way to *escape*. [More laughter.] I get down on the floor and look; it's not there.

LIBERMAN: I've got a great illustration. I just finished an outline about two weeks ago that was about 40 pages. No sooner did I finish it, go out for a walk and come back than it was nowhere to be found. I looked in every drawer, I looked on every table. I asked my neighbor *suspiciously*.

GARFINKEL: Well now, the thing that you need to do is to take the properties that objects have on those occasions and put them together as a coherent version of the properties of such objects; and that will give you some notion of what a demonic order would look like.

LIBERMAN: But that's order just in an ironic sense.

GARFINKEL: *Oh really*? Sounds to me like it has a very curious kind of existence to it. If I say to you, "Goddamn it, it's just when I need a reference the most...." Think of it this way. You didn't have the slightest reservation when I was talking about the errors of occasion maps.[39] I said about errors of occasion maps that they have this curious feature that just when you need to consult the map the most and when it's the most consequential that it yield the information you most want from it, that's when you can't have it and it is that information in particular that you don't have. The fault of maps for a Vietnam patrol was that they couldn't tell whether that rise was such [that] it provided on the other side enough of a dip for an ambush to be there. It was on the occasion that they needed to know by looking at the map that the map failed them.

Well, you were perfectly willing to buy into the faults of maps, right? Then why wouldn't you be willing to consider the cunning of objects? Think of it this way. Think of the cunning of objects as a *practical* account of the way in which objects prepare a consequential frustration for persons that must make use of these things. So you're not anthropomorphizing the object. You are instead providing for a coherent way of treating for their availability to the requirements of effective, familiar practice.

[Exchanges among members in the seminar. One mentions "curses."]

Cocke and Disney are doing lots of it. There is something more to it than they're simply cursing in the face of a good thing that might yet fail them. "Son of a bitch, it's the pulsar."

[Long pause]

GARFINKEL: Can we have coffee?

---

[39] Occasion maps are discussed in the second seminar of this series (May 27). Ken Liberman, whose remark Garfinkel is addressing here, later published a chapter, "Following sketched maps" (Liberman 2013: 45–82), in which he describes a student exercise of following occasion maps.

REFERENCES TO PART II

Editor's note: The references listed below are to all five of Garfinkel's seminars, plus the editor's footnotes. Garfinkel gave few complete references to sources he mentioned during the seminars, but some of them were listed in assigned readings. The editor's footnotes also list works by authors mentioned during the seminars, as well as some later publications that are relevant to the discussions.

Batchelder, William H. and Louis Narens (1977) "A Critical Examination of the Analysis of Dichotomous Data," *Philosophy of Science* 44(1): 113–135.
Bloor, David (1976) *Knowledge and Social Imagery*. London: Routledge and Kegan Paul.
Brannigan, Augustine (1981) *The Social Basis of Scientific Discoveries*. Cambridge: Cambridge University Press.
Brown, Barry, and Eric Laurier (2005) "Maps and Journeys: An Ethno-Methodological Investigation," *Cartographica* 4(3): 17–33.
Carr, David (1974) *Phenomenology and the Problem of History*. Evanston, IL: Northwestern University Press.
Ceruzzi, Paul E. (2019) "Calvin Mooers, Zatocoding, and Early Research on Information Retrieval," in T. Haigh (ed.) *Exploring the Early Digital History of Computing*. Springer International Publishing, 69–86. https://resolver.ebscohost.com/Redirect/PRL?
Cocke, W.J., M.J. Disney, and D.J. Taylor (1969) "Discovery of Optical Signals from Pulsar NP 0532," *Nature* 221 (8 February): 526–527.
Davidson, Judy A. (1984) "Subsequent Versions of Invitations, Offers, Requests, and Proposals Dealing with Potential or Actual Rejection," in J.M. Atkinson and J. Heritage (eds.), *Structures of Social Action*. Cambridge: Cambridge University Press, 102–128.
Dobbs, B.J.T. (1975) *The Foundations of Newton's Alchemy, or 'The Hunting of the Greene Lyon'*. Cambridge: Cambridge University Press.
Dreyfus, Hubert and Patricia Allen Dreyfus (1964) "Translators' Introduction," to Maurice Merleau-Ponty, *Sense and Non-Sense*. Evanston, IL: Northwestern University Press: ix–xxvii.
Eglin, Trent (1986) "Introduction to a Hermeneutics of the Occult: Alchemy," in H. Garfinkel (ed.), *Ethnomethodological Studies of Work*. London: Routledge and Kegan Paul, 123–159.
Fleck, Ludwik (1979) *Genesis and Development of a Scientific Fact*, trans. F. Bradley and T.J. Trenn. Chicago, IL: University of Chicago Press.

Galilei, Galileo (1953) *Dialogue Concerning Two Chief World Systems*, trans. S. Drake. Berkeley, CA: University of California Press.
Garfinkel, Harold (1956) "Some Sociological Concepts and Methods for Psychiatrists," *Psychiatric Research Reports* 6: 181–198.
Garfinkel, Harold (ed.) (1986) *Ethnomethodological Studies of Work*. London: Routledge and Kegan Paul.
Garfinkel, Harold (1990) "The Curious Seriousness of Professional Sociology," in B. Conein, M. de Fornel, and L. Quéré (eds.) *Les formes de la conversation*, vol. 1. CNET, 69–78. Available at: www.persee.fr/doc/reso_0984-5372_1990_hos_8_1_3531 (accessed 20 October 2021).
Garfinkel, Harold (2002) *Ethnomethodology's Program: Working Out Durkheim's Aphorism*, edited with introduction by Anne Rawls. Lanham, MD: Rowman & Littlefield.
Garfinkel, Harold (2021) "Ethnomethodological Misreading of Aron Gurwitsch on the Phenomenal Field." Edited seminar transcript, Sociology 271, 26 April 1993. C. Eisenmann & M. Lynch (eds.), *Human Studies* 44(1): 19–42.
Garfinkel, Harold, and Eric Livingston (2003) "Phenomenal Field Properties of Order in Formatted Queues and Their Neglected Standing in the Current Situation of Inquiry," *Visual Studies* 18(1): 21–28.
Garfinkel, Harold, Michael Lynch, and Eric Livingston (1981) "The Work of a Discovering Science Construed with Materials from the Optically Discovered Pulsar," *Philosophy of the Social Sciences* 11(2): 131–158.
Garfinkel, Harold, and Harvey Sacks (1970) "On Formal Structures of Practical Actions," in J.C. McKinney and E.A. Tiryakian (eds.), *Theoretical Sociology: Perspectives and Development*. New York: Appleton-Century-Crofts, 337–366.
Gurwitsch, Aron (1956) "The Last Work of Edmund Husserl," *Philosophy and Phenomenological Research* 16(3): 380–399.
Gurwitsch, Aron (1964) *The Field of Consciousness*. Pittsburgh, PA: Duquesne University Press.
Gurwitsch, Aron (1974) *Phenomenology and the Theory of Science*, Lester Embree (ed.). Evanston, IL: Northwestern University Press.
Gurwitsch, Aron (2010) "Appendix: Outlines of a Theory of 'Essentially Occasional Expressions'," in R. Zaner (ed.), *The Collected Works of Aron Gurwitsch (1901–1973) Volume III: The Field of Consciousness*. Dordrecht: Springer, 519–537.
Hanson, Norwood Russel (1965) *Patterns of Discovery: An Inquiry into the Conceptual Foundations of Science*. Cambridge: Cambridge University Press.
Heidegger, Martin (1967) *What Is a Thing?* Chicago, IL: Henry Regnery.
Hiz, Henry (1954) "Kotarbinski's Praxeology," *Philosophy and Phenomenological Research* (December): 238–243.
Holton, Gerald (1975) "On the Role of Themata in Scientific Thought," *Science* 188(4186): 328–334.
Holton, Gerald (1978) "Subelectrons, Presuppositions, and the Millikan-Ehrenhaft Dispute," *Historical Studies in the Physical Sciences* 9: 161–224.
Husserl, Edmund (1970) *The Crisis of European Sciences and Transcendental Phenomenology: An Introduction to Phenomenological Philosophy*, trans. David Carr. Evanston, IL: Northwestern University Press.
Knorr-Cetina, Karin (1981) *The Manufacture of Knowledge: An Essay in the Constructivist and Contextual Nature of Knowledge*. Oxford: Pergamon.
Koestler, Arthur (1964) *The Act of Creation*. New York: Macmillan.
Kotarbinski, Tadeusz (1955) *Praxeology: An Introduction to the Sciences of Efficient Action*. Oxford and New York: Pergamon Press.
Kuhn, Thomas S. (1962) *The Structure of Scientific Revolutions*. Chicago, IL: University of Chicago Press.

Kuhn, Thomas S. (1970a) "Postscript – 1969," in T.S. Kuhn, *The Structure of Scientific Revolutions*, Second Edition. Chicago, IL: University of Chicago Press, 174–210.

Kuhn, Thomas S. (1970b) "Reflections on My Critics," in I. Lakatos and A. Musgrave (eds.), *Criticism and the Growth of Knowledge*. Cambridge: Cambridge University Press, 231–238.

Kuhn, Thomas S. (1978) *Black-Body Theory and the Quantum Discontinuity, 1894–1912*. Chicago, IL: University of Chicago Press

Kuhn, Thomas S. (2000a) "The Road Since Structure," in T.S. Kuhn, *The Road Since Structure*. Chicago, IL: University of Chicago Press, 90–104. Originally published in A. Fine, M. Forbes, and L. Wessels (eds.), *PSA 1990, Proceedings of the 1990 Biennial Meeting of the Philosophy of Science Association, Volume II*.E. Lansing, MI: Philosophy of Science Association, 1991.

Kuhn, Thomas S. (2000b) "The Natural and the Human Sciences," in T.S. Kuhn, *The Road Since Structure*. Chicago, IL: University of Chicago Press, 216–223.

Langmuir, Irving (1989) "Pathological Science," *Physics Today* 42(10): 36–48.

Latour, Bruno, and Steve Woolgar (1979) *Laboratory Life: The Social Construction of Scientific Facts*. London: Sage.

Levi-Strauss, Claude (1966) *The Savage Mind*. Chicago, IL: University of Chicago Press.

Liberman, Kenneth (2013) *More Studies in Ethnomethodology*. Albany, NY: SUNY Press.

Livingston, Eric (1986) *The Ethnomethodological Foundations of Mathematics*. London and New York: Routledge and Kegan Paul.

Livingston, Eric (2007) "Circumstantial Reasoning in the Natural Sciences," in S. Hester and D. Francis (eds.), *Orders of Ordinary Action: Respecifying Sociological Knowledge*. Aldershot: Ashgate/Routledge, 121–133.

Livingston, Eric (2008) *Ethnographies of Reason*. Aldershot: Ashgate/Routledge.

Lynch, Michael (2019) "Garfinkel, Sacks and Formal Structures: Collaborative Origins, Divergences and the Vexed Unity of Ethnomethodology and Conversation Analysis," *Human Studies* 42(2): 183–198.

Lynch, Michael, Eric Livingston, and Harold Garfinkel (1983) "Temporal Order in Laboratory Work," in K. Knorr-Cetina and M. Mulkay (eds.), *Science Observed: Perspectives on the Social Study of Science*. London: Sage, 205–238.

Medawar, Peter (1964) "Is the Scientific Paper Fraudulent?" *The Saturday Review* (1 August): 42–43.

Merleau-Ponty, Maurice (1958) *Phenomenology of Perception*. London: Routledge and Kegan Paul.

Merton, Robert K. (1965) *On the Shoulders of Giants: A Shandean Postscript*. Chicago, IL: University of Chicago Press.

Merton, Robert K. (1968) *Social Theory and Social Structure*. New York: Free Press.

Mialet, Hélène (2012) *Hawking Incorporated: Stephen Hawking and the Anthropology of He Knowing Subject*. Chicago, IL: University of Chicago Press.

Olds, James (1954) "A Neural Model for Sign-Gestalt Theory," *Psychological Review* 61(1): 59–72.

Price, Derek de Solla (1984) "Of Sealing Wax and String," *Natural History* 93: 49–53.

Psathas, George (1979) "Organizational Features of Direction Maps," in G. Psathas (ed.), *Everyday Language: Studies in Ethnomethodology*. New York: Irvington, 203–226.

Sacks, Harvey (1970) "Aspects of the Sequential Organization of Conversation." Unpublished manuscript, School of Social Sciences, University of California, Irvine.

Schegloff, Emanuel (1968) "Sequencing in Conversational Openings," *American Anthropologist* 70(6): 1075–1095.

Schrecker, Friedrich (1980) "Doing a Chemical Experiment: The Practices of Chemistry Students in a Student Laboratory in Quantitative Analysis." Unpublished paper, Department of Sociology, University of California, Los Angeles.

Schutz, Alfred (1964) *Collected Papers, Volume II: Studies in Social Theory*. The Hague: Martinus Nijhoff.

Simon, Herbert and Alan Newell (1958) "Heuristic Problem Solving: The Next Advance in Operations Research," *Operations Research* 6: 1–10.

Sudnow, David (1978/2001) *Ways of the Hand*. Cambridge, MA: Harvard University Press; Revised & Rewritten, MIT Press.

Teuber, Marianne L. (1974) "Sources of Ambiguity in the Prints of Maurits C. Escher," *Scientific American* 231(1): 90–105.

Thomas, W.I., and D.S. Thomas (1928) *The Child in American Behavior Problems and Programs*. New York: Knopf.

Todes, Samuel (2001) *Body and World*. Cambridge, MA: MIT Press.

Von Neumann, John, and Oskar Morgenstern (1944) *The Theory of Games and Economic Behavior*. Princeton, NJ: Princeton University Press.

Watson, James D. (1968) *The Double Helix: A Personal Account of the Discovery of the Structure of DNA*. New York: Simon & Schuster.

Wittgenstein, Ludwig (1958) *Philosophical Investigations*. Oxford: Blackwell.

Woolgar, S.W. (1976) "Writing an Intellectual History of Scientific Development: The Use of Discovery Accounts," *Social Studies of Science* 6(3–4): 395–422.

Zuckerman, Harriet (1977) *Scientific Elite: Nobel Laureates in the United States*. New York: Free Press.

Zuckerman, Harriet, and Joshua Lederberg (1986) "Postmature Scientific Discovery," *Nature* 324: 629–631.

INDEX

absurdities: in social sciences 21, 114, 116, 179
accountability 51; natural 51, 87–89n15, 166; reflexive 10, 51, 56
action: embodied 110, 160; in-its-course 63; practical 72–74; *see also* discovering sciences; instructed actions; practical action
activities, naturally organized ordinary 4, 53n1, 57
adequacy, in ethnomethodological studies 11–12, 73, 75; *see also* unique adequacy
adumbrated object 120–121, 149–150, 168
Agre, Phil 24, 39, 44–45, 55
agreement 157
alchemy 103, 104–107; and modern chemistry 105–106; Newton and 104; *see also* Eglin, Trent; Newton, Sir Isaac
alternating-figures *see* gestalt themes
analytic ethnography 23, 26; dissatisfactions with 41–42, 47, 50–51; *see also* ethnography
animal in the foliage 25n4, 117–120, 147–148, 189–192, 194–195; *see also* gestalt themes
astronomy *see* astrophysics
astrophysics 117–118
asymmetric alternates 53n1, 182

basketball: detail of play in 60–61; example for ethnomethodology 58–59; lived-play of 72; *see also* detail★
biochemistry 135–136; *see also* Garfinkel, Arlene

Bittner, Egon 57
Bjelic, Dusan 60n1
Bloor, David 8
Boden, Deirdre 11, 53n1
bricolage expertise 31n7, 136
Burns, Stacy 54–55

chemistry 30, 38, 110, 140n4, 147; and alchemy (*see* alchemy)
classic studies 55–56, 75
coat hangers elicitation 7, 33, 39, 42–44; *see also* contingencies, schedule of
Cocke, John 102, 111n9, 114, 120n27, 163n7, 166
Collins, H.M. 9–10
competence 30, 50–51, 60, 72–74, 169, 190; *see also* incompetence
conditional relevance 112–113, 184–185
constructionism 8–9
constructive analysis 73, 75, 154
contextures, gestalt 121–122n32; *see also* gestalt themes; Gurwitsch, Aron
contingencies 33–35, 38–40, 43–44, 49; accountable 135, 165; demonically wild 33–35, 83n10, 134–137, 196–198; schedule of 23–24, 33, 39–40, 43
conversational greetings 116, 183–184
conversation analysis (CA) 12, 53–54, 72n2, 112–113, 116, 159, 183–186
conversion 140–142, 144

Davidson, Judy 132–133
demonic order *see* contingencies, demonically wild; devil

204 Index

detail* 32, 71–76; tendentious use of 71; see also tendentious uses
devil 197
discovering sciences 10–11, 22–23, 42–43; contrast with social sciences and humanistic sciences 115; as sciences of practical action 22, 25–26, 48–51, 115–117, 174–177
discovering work 10, 21, 155–156; first time through 151–153; rendered as properties of Galilean science (see Galilean science)
discovery 10–11; of optical pulsar (see pulsars); see also discovering sciences; discovering work
Disney, Michael see Cocke, John
docile figure 166
docile record 152
Dreyfus, Hubert 34, 137

Eglin, Trent: on alchemy and modern chemistry 104–107, 139
Ehrenhaft, Felix see Millikan, Robert
embodied practices see action, embodied
empirical cases: for ethnomethodology 11, 25, 74, 82n7
empiricism 82n7
engineering 156
error-free procedure 189
errors: in maps and transcripts 134
Escher, M.C. 140, 146n14; tessellated figures 165–167
Escherian models of practical action 146, 161
ethnography: analytic 27; dissatisfactions with 41–42, 47, 50–51
ethnomethodological indifference 22, 74, 154
ethnomethodological phenomena 5, 25–26, 54–56, 73–76, 118, 132, 181; strange phrases for 55–56
ethnomethodological studies of work: origins of 115–116; summary on 154–155
ethnomethodology: and 'agreement between Athenians and Mancunians' 57; and constructionist sociology of science 9; and conversation analysis 53–54; definitions of 1, 3; hybrids with sciences and mathematics 28, 55, 89n17; scientific status of 117
evidence 56
evidential proof 29, 83–87n12, 87–89n15
e-wise 44, 92–93n47

Fermi, Enrico 30–31, 136
figure-ground structure 147–148; see also animal in the foliage; gestalt themes, as practical achievements
first time through 49; see also discovering work
formal analysis 58–60
formal structures 92–93n47
formulating 119, 148

Galilean object 12
Galilean science 51, 78–79, 159–161; discovering work rendered as properties of 169, 176, 192
Galileo; inclined plane experiment 24; law of free fall 103
games 76; see also basketball
game theory 177
Garfinkel, Arlene 2, 135–136, 140–141
Garfinkel, Harold: archive of 7; authorship of respecifying manuscript 6, 19; on conversation analysis 53n1, 112n14, 116n19; and phenomenology 12; and pulsar study 101–102; and science studies 8–9, 109n8, 170n17; writings and plans in later years 13, 77–80
gestalt switch 121, 132–134, 140, 193, 195
gestalt themes: as practical achievements 11–12, 120–122; see also animal in the foliage; contexture; Escher, M.C.; figure-ground structure; gestalt switch; Gurwitsch, Aron
Gödel's theorem 28–29, 83–87n12; schedule of theorems and their proofs 28; see also Livingston, Eric
golden hands 38
grace, in action 62
Gurwitsch, Aron 11, 55–56, 141, 152; on Galilean mode 159; on gestalt figures 150; on notes as part of melody 141–142; on wasting time 30

Heidegger, Martin 155; see also phenomenology
Heidegger's heirs 188, 191
Hewish, Anthony 102, 152n22
history of science 194; compared with local historicity 36n12
Holton, Gerald 31, 35, 101, 107–110; on 'anti-science' 9; on Kuhn's reaction to critics 194; on Millikan's oil drop experiment 36–37, 123–124, 137; on optical pulsar discovery 112; on pathological science 138

Husserl, Edmund 76; on adumbrated object 149–151; on Galilean object 179n10; on polythetic objects 143
hybrid studies *see* ethnomethodology

incompetence: of analyst 41–42, 46; *see also* competence
indexical expressions 129, 131; laws of physics as 103
inductive inference 75
instructable reproducibility 11, 34–36, 45, 48–49
instructed actions 32, 35; praxiological validity of 24, 45; *see also* occasion maps
inverting lens experiments 12, 76, 121

Knorr Cetina, Karin 8
Kotarbinski, Tadeusz 13; failure of program in praxeology 176–177
Kuhn, Thomas S.; comparing natural and social sciences 32, 125–126; conception of paradigm 127–129, 139–140, 169–170, 178; interviews with Heisenberg 110; response to critics 193–194

laboratory practice *see* practice(s)/practical actions
Latour, Bruno 8–9
Lebenswelt 76
Lebenswelt Pair 28, 51, 83–87n12
Lederberg, Joshua 108–109
Liberman, Kenneth 13, 55, 184, 189, 198
lived work 83; of discovering the pulsar 119; of following instructions 86; of mathematical proving 28–29; of neuroscience 27
Livingston, Eric 54, 76, 107, 115, 155, 193; comparison with Lynch's analytic ethnography 7, 28–29, 83n10; on gestalt switch 195; on Godel's proof 82n5, 83n11, 83–87n12; on mathematicians' work 28–29, 157, 182; on physics 173, 175; on pulsar study 155
local affairs 62
local historicity 36n12, 38, 136, 177
looking: on basketball court 63, 66–67; for evidence of pulsar 134, 184; for scientific phenomenon 140; the work of 199; *see also* animal in the foliage
losing the phenomenon *see* phenomenon
Lynch, Michael 36, 42, 76, 90, 101; on adumbrated object 149–151; analytic ethnography 27; on neurological diagnosis 54; on pulsar study 163n7; *see also* Livingston, Eric

Macbeth, Douglas 58, 71–72, 155
making experiments work 30–31
mathematicians' work *see* Livingston, Eric
melody: as gestalt phenomenon 141–142; *see also* gestalt themes
Mendlovitz, Saul 42
Merleau-Ponty, Maurice 12, 110, 160; chiasm 49; cunning of perception 179
Merton, Robert K. 119n26; on discovery 110–111; on Newton 106
methods: of constructive analysis (*see* constructive analysis); endogenous to activities 2; exportability between laboratories of 35; *see also* scientific methods; unique adequacy
Millikan, Robert: oil-drop experiment 31–32, 36–37, 123–124, 137
misreading phenomenology *see* phenomenology
Mooers, Calvin 76
Mooersian catalog 131, 155
Mooersian descriptors 89n23
Mulkay, Michael 8
Murray, Pauli 3n1

natural accountability *see* accountability
naturally organized ordinary activities 4
natural sciences: ability to settle issues in 31–32; as discovering sciences of practical action 25–26; *see also* discovering sciences; social sciences
Newton, Sir Isaac 104; and alchemy 105, 107

object: cunning of 197; recalcitrant 32; signed 74; *see also* Galilean object
objectivity: Kuhnian solution to 179; of practical action and reasoning 54
occasional expressions *see* indexical expressions
occasion maps 129–131, 198
Olds, James 33, 134, 163–165; discovery of pleasure center in brain 33–34; dread of demonic contingencies 34–35
optical pulsar 102; discovery of 110–113; recording of discovery of 112; *see also* Cocke, John; discovering work
order, topics of 154–155, 173–174; respecification of 75

206 Index

paranoia 35
pathological science 138
perspicuous settings 75–76, 118n23
phenomenal field properties 51, 121–122n32
phenomenology 13; Garfinkel's deliberate misreading of 76, 179n10
phenomenon 76; getting out of the data 36–37; local production of 55, 177, 185; losing the 29, 158, 196; recalcitrance of 32, 48, 146; *see also* ethnomethodological phenomena
philosophy 76, 160, 168
physics 115; Galilean 25–26, 78–79; history of 105; laboratory 35; as science of practical action 117
Planck, Max 194
Polanyi, Michael 36n11, 76, 108
Pollner, Melvin 4
polythetic phenomenon 143
Popper, Karl 11
practice(s)/practical actions: laboratory 106, 126; of mathematical proving 29, 83–87n12; studies of scientific 8–11, 21–23, 35, 41; *see also* action
praxeological validity 24, 32
praxeology *see* Kotarbinski, Tadeusz
pulsars 102, 119–120; *see also* Hewish, Anthony; optical pulsar

queues 76, 131–132, 155, 179–180
quiddity 114

Rawls, Anne 2
recalcitrance of phenomena *see* phenomenon
relevance: of contingencies of scientific work 45; of detail in the course of activity 60–61, 72–73, 90–91n34; *see also* conditional relevance
religious conversion *see* conversion
rendering theorem 55, 155n3
representations of details 43, 74–75; of discovering work 21
respecification: manuscript about 2, 10, 13, 19–20; of natural sciences as discovering sciences of practical actions 77–79; of topics of order as phenomena (*see* order, topics of)
Robillard, Albert B. 54
rules 76, 197; failure of to account for practice 66, 176–177

Sacks, Harvey 11, 173–174n3; adequate scientific accounts 11; on formulations 148n18; joke about footnotes 145–146; perspicuous phenomena 118n23, 154–155
Schegloff, Emanuel 74n2, 183n17
Schrecker, Friedrich 38, 90n33, 140n4
Schutz, Alfred: Garfinkel and 12–13; on music 145; on rational action 62; on science 9
science *see* discovering sciences; natural sciences; pathological science; social sciences
science studies 8–9
scientific methods 35, 162–163
Senior, James K. 36n11, 90n28
Shapin, Steven 8, 171n1
shop floor problem 23n1
shop floor contingencies *see* contingencies
signed object *see* object
sketch map *see* occasion maps
skills 24; in lab work 30, 38; *see also* bricolage expertise; competence
social sciences 11, 58, 73–74; compared to discovering sciences 156, 158, 172; Kuhn's dismissal of 125–126; *see also* discovering sciences; natural sciences
sociology 117–118: in Galilean mode 126–127, 178–179, 180, 187–188; of knowledge 18; as talking science 156
Suchman, Lucy 12, 24n2
Sudnow, David 116

tacit knowledge 18, 21, 36n11; *see also* Polanyi, Michael
talk, studies of 53–55; *see also* conversation analysis (CA)
talking science *see* sociology
temporality 61, 63, 66, 122–123, 152
tendentious uses 4, 71–72
Todes, Samuel 122–123
topics of order *see* order, topics of
transcendental analyst 160, 192; voice of 146, 159–160
transcendentality: of phenomenon: 26, 35; of results 90–91n34
truth: contingencies as constraints on 45; revelation of 57; and verifiability 160; *see also* Agre, Phil

unforgivably strict sequences 38
unique adequacy: requirement of methods 28, 117–118

unmotivated observables 42–43, 92n44, 136

voice: alchemy's 106; narrator's 159; of transcendental analyst 146, 159–160

wasting time 29–30
Westman, Robert 101, 171–172, 178–182, 192–194

Wieder, D. Lawrence 55
Wittgenstein, Ludwig 2, 69, 121n32
Woolgar, Steve 8–9, 109n8; on pulsar discovery narratives 152n22
work, studies of *see* ethnomethodological studies of work

Zimmerman, Don 11, 53n1
Zuckerman, Harriet 108–109

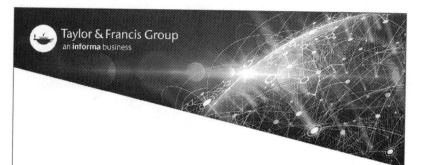

Printed in the United States
by Baker & Taylor Publisher Services